Tracing the Relational

TRACING THE RELATIONAL

THE ARCHAEOLOGY OF WORLDS, SPIRITS, AND TEMPORALITIES

Edited by
Meghan E. Buchanan and B. Jacob Skousen

THE UNIVERSITY OF UTAH PRESS
Salt Lake City

Foundations of Archaeological Inquiry
James M. Skibo, series editor

Copyright © 2015 by The University of Utah Press. All rights reserved.

 The Defiance House Man colophon is a registered trademark of the University of Utah Press. It is based on a four-foot-tall Ancient Puebloan pictograph (late PIII) near Glen Canyon, Utah.

19 18 17 16 15   1 2 3 4 5

Library of Congress Cataloging-in-Publication Data

Tracing the relational : the archaeology of worlds, spirits, and temporalities / edited by Meghan E. Buchanan, B. Jacob Skousen.
     pages ; cm. — (Foundations of archaeological inquiry)
     ISBN 978-1-60781-435-1 (paperback) — ISBN 978-1-60781-436-8 (e-book)
1. Indians—Antiquities.   2. Material culture—America.
3. Human ecology—America.   4. Land settlement patterns, Prehistoric—America.   5. Social archaeology—America.   6. Sacred space—America.   7. Indian mythology—America.   I. Buchanan, Meghan E., 1981– author editor of compilation.   II. Skousen, B. Jacob, 1981– author editor of compilation.
  E61.T83 2015
  973.04'97—dc23
                                                                   2015015501

Printed and bound by Sheridan Books, Inc., Ann Arbor, Michigan.

Contents

List of Figures   vii

Introduction: Advancing an Archaeology of Movements and Relationships   1
B. Jacob Skousen and Meghan E. Buchanan

Part I: Worlds

1. Settlement Survey, Landscape Transformations, and the Meaning of Unoccupied Land in Postclassic Nejapa, Oaxaca, Mexico   21
Stacie M. King

2. Moonbeams, Water, and Smoke: Tracing Otherworldly Relationships at the Emerald Site   38
B. Jacob Skousen

3. Adena-Hopewell Earthworks and the Milky Way Path of Souls   54
William F. Romain

Part II: Spirits and Forces

4. War-Scapes, Lingering Spirits, and the Mississippian Vacant Quarter   85
Meghan E. Buchanan

5. Weaving Together Evil Airs, Sacred Mountaintops, and War   100
Margaret Brown Vega

6. Maya Religion and Gods: Relevance and Relatedness in the Animic Cosmos   113
Eleanor Harrison-Buck

Part III: Temporalities

7. Entanglements of the Blackfoot: Relationships with the Spiritual and Material Worlds   131
Gerald A. Oetelaar

8. Unraveling Entanglements: Reverberations of Cahokia's Big Bang   146
Melissa R. Baltus

List of Contributors   161
Index   163

Figures

0.1.	Geographic regions discussed in this book	viii
1.1.	Vegetation in Nejapa region	26
1.2.	Painted hands, Mano de Gente, San Juan Lajarcia	29
1.3.	Rock art panel from Piedra de los Monos	30
1.4.	Carved stone monument from the site of Nejapa Viejo	31
1.5.	Ceramic incense burner left as an offering, Piedra la Boluda, Santa Ana Tavela	31
1.6.	Updated place-name map, Santa Ana Tavela and San Juan Lajarcia	34
2.1.	Cahokia, Emerald, and other sites in the American Bottom	43
2.2.	Overview of the Emerald site	44
2.3.	Plan view of structures excavated at the Emerald site	45
2.4.	Plan map of the Emerald site	46
2.5.	Plan map of excavations on Emerald's primary mound	48
3.1.	Annotated Salisbury 1862 map of the Newark Earthworks	56
3.2.	LiDAR images of Newark Earthworks Complex	58
3.3.	Details of the Salisbury map	59
3.4.	LiDAR and lunar alignments at Newark earthworks	60
3.5.	LiDAR view of the Great Circle–Observatory Mound solstice alignment	62
3.6.	LiDAR and the Great Hopewell Road	63
3.7.	Milky Way alignments	65
3.8.	Hypothetical spirit paths associated with the Newark Earthworks	66
3.9.	Sugarloaf Mountain and the Great Hopewell Road	67
3.10.	Chillicothe-area mounds and earthworks	68
3.11.	Serpent Mound, Sugarloaf Mountain, and celestial alignments	72
3.12.	Serpent Mound and Scorpius	74
4.1.	Vacant Quarter.	86
4.2.	Aerial photograph of the Common Field site	90
5.1.	Map of the Huara Valley	101
5.2.	Cerros San Cristóbal	104
5.3.	Detail of Cerros San Cristóbal fortifications	104
5.4.	Excavation of pit features from the summit structure	106
5.5.	Textile bundle	107
6.1.	Droplet glyphs	117
6.2.	A personified Itzamnaaj	118
6.3.	Late Classic period examples of Itzamnaaj	119
6.4.	Breath glyphs	120
6.5.	Itzamnaaj as "Principal Bird Deity"	122
7.1.	The Blackfoot homeland, winter camps, and sun dance grounds	133
7.2.	The Blackfoot homeland, sheltered winter camps, and trade centers	135
8.1.	Midwestern social-political entanglements during the twelfth to fourteenth centuries	148
8.2.	American Bottom and upland sites of Olin, Copper, and Emerald	154
8.3.	Jars from the Copper site	155

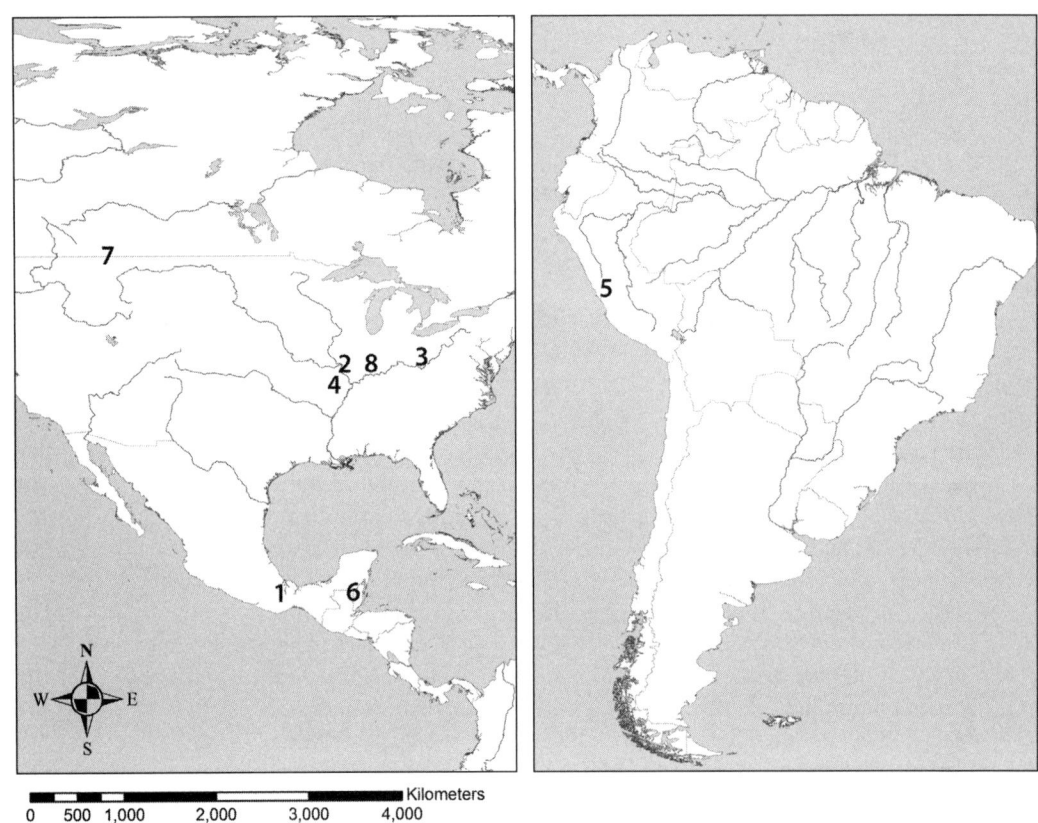

FIGURE 0.1. Geographic regions discussed in this book. 1. (King) Nejapa, Oaxaca, Mexico; 2. (Skousen) Midwest, United States; 3. (Romain) Ohio River Valley, United States; 4. (Buchanan) Midwest, United States; 5. (Vega) Huara Valley, Peru; 6. (Harrison-Buck) Mesoamerica; 7. (Oetelaar) Northern Great Plains, United States and Canada; 8. (Baltus) Midwest, United States.

Introduction

Advancing an Archaeology of Movements and Relationships

B. Jacob Skousen and Meghan E. Buchanan

In the last decade there has been increased recognition that conventional archaeological constructions of the past are problematic. These analyses, which have evolutionary, functional, or structural underpinnings, are inherently representational, meaning that the material world is seen as representative of human thoughts and behavior. In essence, artifacts, features, and landscapes are viewed as products of the mind or the result of actions (see Barrett 1994, 2000). Such perspectives, it is now recognized, are opposed to many non-Western ontologies, which consider the material world to be generative, not representative, of events, practices, time, and life in general (Bird-David 1999; Conneller 2011; Harvey 2006; Ingold 2011:67–75; Viveiros de Castro 1998, 2004). Even those analyses that incorporate ethnohistories or ethnographies of indigenous groups to better understand past realities tend to make overly simplistic analogies between past and present groups that minimize or ignore diversity and change (see Binford 1967, 1978; see critiques in Gosden 1999; Gould and Yellen 1987; Stahl 1993). These formulations should instead be acknowledged as products of Western ontologies that contrast with the ancient worlds that archaeologists attempt to understand. Moreover, archaeological evidence increasingly points to a diverse, messy, and complex past where people and practices were continually altered, traditions were performed and negotiated, and humans, nonhumans, things, and places were interconnected and together constructed the world (Alberti et al. 2013; Harris and Robb 2012; Hodder 2012; Jones 2012; Olsen 2010; Olsen et al. 2012; Watts, ed. 2013).

In light of these developments, many archaeologists are adopting what are called "relational perspectives" (Alberti and Bray 2009; Hutson 2010; Watts, ed. 2013). According to Christopher Watts (2013:1), relationality in archaeology embodies "a suite of approaches aimed at conflating the abstract and immutable dualities of modernist ontologies" (see also Alberti et al. 2011; Jones and Alberti 2013). Relational perspectives, therefore, rectify the problems of representational approaches by positing that there was no inherent dichotomy between human and object, nature and culture, or mind and body as Western ontologies suggest, and that human and nonhuman entities, places, things, and knowledge were situated in a world of relationships and were hence continuously constructed, negotiated, and in a state of becoming (Alberti and Bray 2009; Alberti et al. 2013; Hutson 2010; Ingold 2000, 2007, 2011; Jones 2012; Pauketat 2013a). Moreover, relational perspectives parallel indigenous ontologies and better account for the complexities of the countless realities of the past by acknowledging the agency of materials, the effects of nonhuman entities, and continual flux and transformation (see Alberti and Bray 2009; Harris and Robb 2012; Walker 2013).

Building on these trends, the authors in this book explore relationality in past ontologies. More specifically, the focus is on relationships between people, places, and things and seemingly intangible realms, bodies, forces, and temporalities. This emphasis, in part, is to remedy the practice of separating these "ephemeral" phenomena from everyday life and experience, another common but unwarranted dichotomy applied to past contexts. The overarching theme that unites the chapters, however, is movement. Movement is the foundational principle of many non-Western ontologies, is what constitutes experiences, identities, meanings, and becomings, and is the cause of disruptions, intersections, and convergences in the relational webs that constitute the world (see Baires et al. 2013; Ingold 2000:219–242, 2011:67–75; Pauketat 2013a:36–40). In short, movement is the means through which the world is thrown into a constant state of flux, complexity, and ever-emerging relations (Kirby 2009). The chapters in this book demonstrate that movement must be a key component of any study that seeks to understand past realities. Significantly, contributors consider the movements not only of humans but of nonhuman entities as well (e.g., nonhuman persons, materials, things, substances, ideas, forces, powers) (see also Baires et al. 2013; Baltus and Baires 2012; Pauketat 2013a). This, we suggest, addresses the modernist trend of separating humans and nonhuman entities by allowing for a wider field of relational potentialities that constitute non-Western ontologies.

In the rest of this chapter, we offer a historical overview of relationality in archaeology, followed by a more comprehensive discussion of movement and why we believe it is an essential aspect of relational perspectives. We also introduce the individual chapters in the book. In the end, we argue that archaeologists (and anyone attempting to understand the past) must consider movements of all kinds and how they afforded and altered relationships between various entities in the world. Such a perspective allows us to investigate the more salient questions of ontology, alterity, and continuity in the past (see Alberti et al. 2011; Harris and Robb 2012; Henare et al. 2007; Jones and Alberti 2013). Situated on these premises, this book endeavors to provide a richer account of how such alternative realities were lived, experienced, and negotiated in the ancient world.

Relationships in Archaeology

Relationships have long been vital to the disciplines of anthropology and archaeology. Early twentieth-century functionalists focused on the relationships between different cultural institutions (e.g., religious, political, and economic structures) and how they functioned together to ensure the well-being and stability of the entire society (Trigger 2006:319–322). Later, American anthropologists in particular began to focus on the relationship between cultures and their environments. The goal of cultural ecology, founded by Julian Steward (1955), was to examine how each group adapted to its local environment; thus the relationship between the environment and cultural group was mediated by an adaptive mechanism. Proponents of the New Archaeology of the 1960s drew heavily from these two camps, claiming that all aspects of culture had functions that were related and worked together to enable human survival and adaptation to the environment (Binford 1962; Caldwell 1959; Taylor 1948; see also O'Brien and Holland 1992). They often saw culture as a system, or "an intercommunicating network of attributes or entities forming a complex whole" (Clarke 1978:495; see also Binford 1965; Flannery 1968; Plog 1975). Some theorists even argued that major developments throughout the world—such as the rise of agriculture—were caused by convergences of historically and contextually specific events and innovations (Flannery 1968, 1973).

Theories in the 1980s and 1990s moved away from adaptive mechanisms and the environment and focused instead on the interplay between structures, practices, symbols, and meanings. Pierre Bourdieu's (1977) theory of practice, for instance, investigated the dialectic relationship between the habitus, or the unconscious dispositions of a person, and his or her practices. Specifically, he argued that the habitus dictated practices while the practices simultaneously restructured the habitus. Critiques of the New Archaeology, broadly labeled postprocessual archaeology, focused on relationships between artifacts, symbols, and meaning. Context was also critical—the meaning of ancient materials could be decoded only through an in-depth investigation of their distributions and contexts (Hodder 1991, 1999; see also McFadyen 2013). Furthermore, many of these scholars saw archaeological interpretation as a hermeneutic process (Hodder 1991, 1999; Shanks and Tilley 1987). Hermeneutics is a method of interpretation that brings together contextual data, theories, and the analyst's own biases, perspectives, and experiences. For archaeologists at this time, the hermeneutic process involved immersing themselves in contextual data, asking questions about the data, and, by drawing on personal experiences and historical imagination, providing answers to these questions. The answers were validated by determining whether they made sense according to the interpreter's background and the material evidence (Hodder and Hutson 2003:195–199; see also Hodder 1991).

This brief survey shows that relationships have long been a fundamental part of major archaeological theories and practices. However, these perspectives were still premised on the idea that there was a singular function or preexisting structure or meaning that could be discovered through the materials—in short, they were representational. In the early 2000s, however, relationality was regarded in a different light—archaeologists began to see it as a central ontological tenet of the past. This shift occurred alongside studies of personhood, studies of materiality and memory, critiques of representational approaches, and the avocation of "alternative" ontologies (see contributions in Alberti and Bray 2009; see also Alberti et al. 2013; Barrett 1994, 2000; Fowler 2004; Harvey 2006; Ingold 2011:67–75; Meskell 2004; Mills and Walker, eds. 2008; Pauketat 2013a).

Early archaeological studies on personhood were among the first to recognize the importance of relational principles in the past (Bruck 2001, 2006; Chapman 2000; Fowler 2001, 2002, 2004; Gillespie 2001; Hutson 2010; Kirk 2006). These studies, influenced by Marilyn Strathern's (1988) idea of "dividual" persons, contended that social persons were "composite and multiply-authored," meaning they were constituted by their relations with other people, objects, bodies, and so on (Fowler 2004:7–8). These insights contrasted with Western views of personhood, which gave primacy to the human body and individuality. Thus, it became clear that applying modern perspectives of personhood to past societies was problematic; ancient notions of personhood instead seemed fractal, dispersed, or extended outside the individual. In short, personhood had more to do with other human and nonhuman entities that a person dealt with on an everyday basis.

Theories of materiality, broadly defined as the study of relationships between humans and things (Meskell 2004:2), posited that such human-object relationships are an inherent part of social life. While it has long been known that humans modify the material world, studies of materiality have shown that materials simultaneously shape human experience as well (Meskell 2004, 2005; Latour 2005; see also Barrett 1994, 2000). In a similar vein, scholars of social memory have argued that materials and landscapes are integral to how memories are constructed, transmitted, modified, remembered, and forgotten (Mills and Walker 2008:4). Memory work, as these processes are often called, does not just incorporate the past into the present and future but comes from a milieu of temporalities, materials, spaces, bodies, practices, and persons (Jones 2007; Meskell 2004; Mills and Walker, eds. 2008; Van Dyke and Alcock 2003).

Four themes dominated critiques of representational approaches. The first and most important was that representational perspectives, largely premised on Western epistemologies, contrasted with indigenous practices, experiences, and ontologies described in past and present native accounts. Second, representational approaches established and perpetuated modernist dichotomies (e.g., nature vs. culture, mind vs. body, human vs. object), which ignored the gaps, inconsistencies, and "fuzziness" between these seemingly rigid categories. Third, the relational qualities between people, places, and things were downplayed or discounted. Finally, agency, or the ability to have effects, was essentialized as a solely human quality (see Alberti and Bray 2009; Ingold 2000, 2011; Jones 2012; Latour 1993, 2005; Watts 2013; Witmore 2007). In short, these critiques argued that representational approaches were reductive and simplistic, and misrepresented indigenous realities.

The use of "alternative" ontologies in archaeology, driven in part by a resurgence of studies on animism, closely accompanied these critiques (see contributions in Alberti and Bray 2009; also Bird-David 1999; Brown and Emery 2008; Harrison-Buck 2012; Harvey 2006; Hill 2011; Herva 2009, 2010; VanPool and Newsome 2012). In contrast with Edward Tylor's (1993 [1871]) early contention that animism was a belief in souls and spiritual beings in primitive societies, animism is now seen as "a way of engaging with the world that is ontologically distinct from that of 'the moderns'" (Alberti and Bray 2009:338). Indeed, this new brand of animism acknowledges that "the world is full of persons, only some of whom are human, and that life is always lived in relationship with others" (Harvey 2006:xi). Overall, the new animism forces us to consider relationships with nonhuman persons and entities as well as how these things were vital in the construction of past realities.

Relational Archaeology Today

In the wake of these important developments there has been an ever-growing body of literature on relational perspectives in archaeology. In this section we briefly outline a few of the more prominent trends. This by no means represents all the theories or bodies of thought on the issue, but it should give the reader a taste of how relationality has been applied in archaeology.

Relations with Things

One of the more popular themes of relationality in archaeology is the interconnectedness of things and humans. Since the advent of the New Archaeology, humans, not things, were the focus of archaeological inquiry; the goal was always to find "the societies and cultures, women and men, *behind* the artifact" (Olsen 2010:25, emphasis original). As proponents of "symmetrical archaeology" argue, however, there is no a priori reason to separate humans and things at all (Witmore 2007; see also Latour 2005). The privileged status of humans has recently been questioned through discussions of materiality and object agency (Gell 1998; Gosden 2005; Meskell 2004, 2005; Pels 1998; see above), the new animism (see above), the development of "symmetrical archaeology" (Olsen 2007; Webmoor 2007; Witmore 2007), a renewed "concern" with things (Olsen 2010), and new studies that interrogate the biases and theoretical perspectives of archaeologists in constructions of the past (Fowler 2013; Lucas 2012). These perspectives have dismantled the subject-object duality so that now things are seen as being able to act on their own, apart from human interference, and produce effects in various ways (e.g., Baltus and Baires 2012; Conneller 2011; Gosden 2005; Hodder 2012; Jones 2012; Olsen 2010; Olsen et al. 2012).

Perhaps the most influential scholar on this subject is Bruno Latour, who argues that nonhuman entities play an immediate and essential role in the social world (Latour 1993, 1999, 2005). One of Latour's (2005) primary arguments is that "the social" is not an isolated unit separate from all other domains (e.g., economics, politics, religion), nor is it a catchall category used to explain reality when these other domains cannot. Instead, "the social" refers to a network or "trail of associations between heterogeneous elements" within the world (Latour 2005:5). Significantly, this network consists of actants, which include things, collectives, and other nonhuman entities. Actants, according to Latour, are just as concrete, affective, and capable as humans in creating and maintaining associations of all kinds (Latour 2005:54). Thus, we can think of agency as being distributed among the connections between actants, and not solely the domain of human intentions and actions.

Ian Hodder (2006, 2010, 2012) has formulated a "theory of entanglements" to emphasize the complexity and messiness of relationships between humans and things. Specifically, Hodder argues that the development of settled village life and the rise of religion at Çatalhöyük had to do with the formation of increasingly complex relations between humans and the material world over a long period of time (Hodder 2006, 2010; see also Shults 2010). These entanglements, which may have at first been inadvertent and seemingly insignificant, eventually led to a mutual dependency between things and humans. However, these entanglements were unstable and therefore stimulated constant reconfiguration and negotiation (Hodder 2012:158–178). More generally,

Hodder argues for a "dialectic of dependence and dependency between humans and things," meaning that some relationships are enabling (dependence) and others are constraining (dependency) (Hodder 2012:206). In other words, inequality and imbalance are always inherent in such relationships; in certain circumstances, some humans and things have more influence, power, or sway over other humans and things.

Meshworks

Relationships are a crucial part of Tim Ingold's idea of meshwork (2007:80; 2011:67–75). According to him, life is a web of relationships that is constantly in the process of becoming. This perspective reverses "the logic of inversion," or a way of seeing entities and organisms as lone, bounded, and closed off from the world; in Ingold's words, they are "reconfigured as the outward expression of an inner design" (Ingold 2011:68). Rather than dwelling in or inhabiting the world, organisms are the occupants of a prefurnished world. Further, Ingold (2007, 2011:69) believes that entities and organisms are actually lines of "movement or growth" with no beginning or end. These trails of movement weave themselves into the world, thus making them inseparable from the surrounding environment (Ingold 2011:69). Furthermore, as lines issue forth, they are always redirected, renegotiated, and reintegrated into the meshwork of life, and the result is the continual reweaving of the meshwork, or the continual rebirth of the world (Ingold 2011:74). Significantly, Ingold emphasizes that the relationships that make up the meshwork are not direct, linear connections between discrete, static points—instead, they are trails that flow and meander, creating tenuous connections that are never the same from one moment to the next (see Ingold 2011:85).

Ingold's (2013) more recent idea of correspondence builds on the theme of meshwork. Correspondence, according to him, is a reciprocal negotiation between humans and other entities in the world and is an integral part of knowing, learning, and making. Correspondence comes about from practical engagement with these other entities—the goal of correspondence is not to describe or represent the world but "to open up our perception to what is going on there so that we, in turn, can respond to it" (Ingold 2013:7). Our engagements, practices, and works are experiments or acts of creation and discovery in which we navigate and come to grips with the meshwork. This, according to Ingold (2013:11), is "knowing from the inside."

Assemblages

Assemblage is a term that has developed alongside the concept of meshwork, and is used most notably by Oliver Harris and Chris Fowler (Fowler 2013; Harris 2012, 2013; see also Conneller 2011; Lucas 2012:193–198). This term, originally coined by Gilles Deleuze and Felix Guattari (2004), refers to heterogeneous groups of bodies, including humans, nonhumans, and animals, which have histories of their own, have the ability to affect other bodies and assemblages, and are generative of entirely new entities and assemblages (Harris 2013:177; see also Jones 2012). Indeed, all persons, things, and places are themselves assemblages or part of assemblages, each of which is different due to its creation in unique historical contexts. According to Harris (2013:177), assemblage is akin to Ingold's idea of "knots," and refers to accumulations or gatherings of various entities within a meshwork. And much like meshworks and knots, assemblages are always changing because they are constantly moving, gaining and losing parts, and becoming articulated with other assemblages.

Bundles

Several complementary theories of binding or bundling, analogous to knots, assemblages, and haecceities (see Ingold 2011:84), have been developed in the last decade (Keane 2005; Küchler 1999, 2002; Pauketat 2013a, 2013b; Zedeño 2008, 2009). Webb Keane (2005:188), for example, argues that bundling is a collection of associated material qualities or properties embodied in a given object. Bundling is an inherent aspect of all material things and provides icons and groups of icons through which an object is signified in both the present and future. Thus, the material nature of an object, with all its qualities and bundles of qualities, in part determines the object's meaning and how it resembles something else. Signification, in other words, is not solely the result of human intentions (Keane 2005:189).

Timothy Pauketat (2013a:25) argues that a bundle "is a set of otherwise distinct things, substances, or qualities" wrapped or entangled in unique ways. These bundles are "nodes" in larger relational fields (akin to Ingold's meshwork) that, depending on their components and positioning in the larger meshwork, mediate relationships and thus change the course of history (Pauketat 2013a: 27, 34–36; 2013b). Specifically, the configuration, density, and number of entities, qualities, and so on that comprise the bundle dictate its significance, power, and effects (Pauketat 2013a:27–28, 34–35). Bundles, much like assemblages, are the primary constituents of persons, things, places, and so forth. For Pauketat, a critical part of a bundle is that its parts are always moving and positioning themselves according to other entities and parts (Pauketat 2013a:36–40; 2013b; see below).

Another concept of bundling is articulated by María Nieves Zedeño (2008, 2009) in her descriptions of Blackfoot medicine bundles. These medicine bundles consist of various objects gathered together in a cloth or animal skin wrapping as well as songs, stories, gestures, and other practices and rituals associated with unwrapping or caring for the overall bundle. Each object contains its own qualities, powers, and biographies that, due to their being associated with other things in the bundle, together channel "cosmic power contained in the material and spiritual worlds" for a specific purpose (Zedeño 2008:366). Indeed, Zedeño argues that three concepts—animacy, transfer, and transmutation—underlie the bundle system; in other words, things within bundles, depending on their origin and position in the bundle, could animate, transform, or transfer power to other things, persons, and assemblages. Special objects, called "index objects" (e.g., red paint, fossils, crystals), are able to do this because of their natural, "god-given" powers (Zedeño 2008:374–375). These principles, embodied in the bundling process, are an inherent aspect of indigenous taxonomies and thus fundamental to Native American ontology and epistemology (Zedeño 2009). Using these ontological principles allows archaeologists to construct relational taxonomies and better address questions regarding past notions of personhood, agency, and relationships between humans and objects (Zedeño 2009:415).

Moving through Relationships

Movement is one of the overarching themes in this book. It is an integral part of a relational perspective, and in this section we elaborate on why this is so. To begin, we accept that movement is meaningful and certainly is more than a physical response to external stimuli or a set of mechanical sensorimotor characteristics shared by all humans (see Farnell 1994, 2003; Mills 2005:96). We also agree that movement is the primary component of engagement, experience, and being-in-the-world. As Maxine Sheets-Johnstone (2011:117) states, "it is in and through movement that the life of every creature…'acquires reality'" (see also Ingold 2000; Mills 2005). Most importantly, we argue that movement is how associations, entanglements, and relationships (i.e., the stuff history is made of; see Pauketat 2013a:27–28) continually converge and become. What sets our perspective apart is that we see movement as not only a human quality—all sorts of persons, bodies, entities, ideas, forces, and powers can and do move alongside humans, and these movements matter in the ongoing formation of life and experience (cf. Baires et al. 2013; Baltus and Baires 2012; Ingold 2000, 2007, 2011; Pauketat 2013a). Additionally, we argue that the term "movement" itself has various uses, meanings, nuances, and implications, and these are worth investigating. For example, sensory and emotional experiences "move" us; social, political, and religious movements have occurred throughout history, often with monumental impacts; and memories transport us through time and space. Certainly a better understanding of associations, entanglements, and relationships requires a necessarily broad view of the various kinds of movements that are possible and a more generous consideration of what can and does move.

The physical movement of humans has been the primary focus of studies on movement in anthropology and archaeology. A number of early anthropologists focused on specific bodily movements like dance and gestures. However, Marcel Mauss (1979 [1935]) was the first to consider movement itself as a topic of study (see Farnell 1999:348–350). He recognized that "techniques of the body," or learned, culturally specific movements or actions (walking, running, swimming, digging, etc.), varied across time and space and signified group affiliation and identity. The large-scale movement of people was how early twentieth-century anthropologists explained cultural similarity. Franz Boas and others, for example, rejected the evolutionary perspectives of their predecessors (i.e., that all societies passed through the same series of increasingly complex stages) and argued that the diffusion of cultural traits through various population movements and contacts accounted for similarities across different societies; for these anthropologists, the independent invention of similar traits was unlikely because of each society's unique history and context (Boas 1896; see also Bender 2001:76–77; Trigger 2006:217–223). Later archaeologists, most notably V. Gordon Childe (1939, 1969 [1950]), likewise argued that cultural change occurred through diffusion and migrations. Though Childe believed that diffusion accounted for most changes, he claimed that only migration could explain the complete replacement of one culture (i.e., a suite of associated artifact types) by another (Childe 1969 [1950]:8–10). Although these diffusionist models were eventually rejected as normative and overly simplistic (and also because of critiques of colonialism; see Bender 2001:76), they rightly viewed the movement of people as an important factor in social change. Not surprisingly, studies on population movement are again popular, though they do not contain the normative assumptions of earlier diffusionist models (see Bender 2001:77). Examples include studies of long-distant journeys, migration, pilgrimage, and diaspora (e.g., Alt 2006; Bauer and Stanish 2001; Beekman and Christensen 2003; Bender 2001; Close 2000; Cummings and Johnston 2007; Knott and McLoughlin 2010; Pauketat 2003; Snead et al. 2009; see also Oetelaar, Romain, and Skousen, all this volume).

Human bodily movement comprises the core of most theories of perception. Descartes, for instance, argued that "the basis of perception is an awareness of states of the brain that are the remote effects of physical causes" (Harré 1986:155, cited in Farnell 2003:133). Thus, while Descartes acknowledged bodily action as a factor in perception, he believed that the body provided only external sensory information; the brain processed the information and thus constructed representations and perceptions of the world. Other scholars have likewise emphasized the role of movement in perception but have rejected Descartes's separation of the mind and body. Maurice Merleau-Ponty (1962:67–69), for example, argued that to see a "completed" object is to see it "from everywhere," meaning the object is disclosed as one experiences it continually from numerous perspectives and in context with other things; movement around and about the object is necessary for its discovery. In short, perception, according to Merleau-Ponty, does not consist of the brain's conjuring up mental perceptions of what is seen, but is an act of exploring, engaging, and communicating with entities in the world, with which the body is intimately entwined (Merleau-Ponty 1962:90–97). Similarly, James Gibson (1986:66) argues that observations of the environment are made "from a moving position." This moving position is an exploratory, intentional act of the entire body. Significantly, Gibson considers the mind to be a part of the body. Vision, he suggests, "depends on the eyes in the head on a body supported by the ground"; the brain is simply one of the organs in the "complete visual system" (Gibson 1986:1). Thus Gibson too rejects Descartes's mind/body separation.

Building on these studies of perception, Brenda Farnell (1994, 1996, 1999) argues for a theory of "dynamic embodiment," which recognizes that humans continually participate in a variety of complex bodily activities fraught with meaning and significance, and that these activities produce a person's knowledge of society, self, and the world. Thus, while Westerners generally see the mind as the source of intelligence, communication, and rationality, a theory of dynamic embodiment recognizes that bodily movements too are a source of knowledge, communication, and meaningful actions (Farnell 1999, 2003). From this perspective there is no separation of the mind and body because embodied persons engage in multiple kinds of semiotic practices (body movements, sign language, talking, etc.) simultaneously. Furthermore, Farnell (1999:348), drawing on Harré's "causal powers theory," rejects the idea that human agency is located within the mind; instead, she argues that it lies in a person's ability to engage in meaningful movements and actions (Farnell 1994, 1996).

Human movement was also a key component in archaeological studies of landscape phenomenology. Like many observers of human perception, scholars such as John Richards (1993, 1996), Julian Thomas (1993), and Christopher Tilley (1994) saw the human body as the center of experience; thus the location, orientation, and movement of one's body dictated one's experience and perspective. On the other hand, they also recognized that the way the landscape was modified could control the movement and experience of the observer. Michael Parker Pearson and others (Parker Pearson and Ramilisonina 1998; Parker Pearson et al. 2006), for example, have argued that the site of Stonehenge was a domain of the dead and the nearby site of Durrington Walls was a domain of the living, and funerary processions along constructed avenues between the sites reinforced these domains. Many scholars also assumed that the physicality of the body provided a uniform frame of reference for all human perception—in other words, one person's perspective was just like any other's because each had a physical body. Following this logic, archaeologists assumed they could experience the world like those in the past through their own bodily engagements with monuments and landscapes. Though many of these studies failed to recognize that landscapes are socially constructed and have different meanings for different people through time and space (Ashmore 2004:259; see also Bruck 2001) and that ontological perspectives of the body are complex and multifaceted (Harris and Robb 2012), they highlighted the importance of movement in experiencing and understanding the world. Perhaps more importantly, these studies recognized that the ways in which humans moved and perceived the world depended in part on entities located outside the human body (e.g., monuments, pathways, natural features) (see Olsen 2010:27; Tilley 1994, 2004). John Barrett (1994), for instance, argued that human movement and the material world is what structures human agency, not preexisting social systems or structures.

While these studies of human movement have undoubtedly been useful, they have neglected the countless other entities in the world that similarly move and alter society. This problem has been addressed in part by material culture studies and formation theory. Material culture studies investigate the movements and dynamism of things and materials, and how these in turn move and affect humans (Conneller 2011; Ingold 2011:19–32, 2013:93–94; Hodder 2012:4–5; Olsen 2010; Olsen et al. 2012; Tilley 2004). Creating things, for instance, requires the simultaneous movements of body, mind, and material (Conneller 2011:24–48; Ingold 2013). On a molecular level, materials themselves "are relentlessly on the move—flowing, scraping, mixing and mutating" due to their instantiation in mediums (Ingold 2011:28; see also Conneller 2011:19). In other words, objects are never stable or complete because they are continually undergoing subtle, if not sometimes drastic, movements and modifications, due largely to other forces and movements in the world (Ingold 2011:19–32), and these movements are often of great concern to humans. Formation theory is a body of theories that attempt to explain the processes that led to the formation of the archaeological record as uncovered by archaeologists (see Schiffer 1976; Shott 2006). For instance, while things were often discarded or deposited in specific ways by people, natural processes and other nonhuman agents (rodents, insects, bacteria, etc.) also modified things once they were deposited (though, admittedly, formation theory is much more complex than this; see Lucas 2012:74–123). Although formation theory is by and large an epistemological rather than ontological pursuit, it still recognizes that nonhuman movements and processes took place in the past, and that these had direct consequences for the material world and the humans that dwelt there.

However, the most comprehensive and fruitful view of movement, and the one we espouse here, has been developed by Tim Ingold (2000:189–208, 219–243; 2011; 2013). In his early work Ingold argued, much like Gibson, that perception takes place not at discrete points but along paths of movement, or "in the passage from place to place, and in histories of movement and changing horizons along the way" (Ingold 2000:227). In other words, knowledge of the world comes from movements within it. As mentioned earlier, he has more recently argued that all entities are lines that entangle to create the meshwork of life. However, these lines are ever-moving, meaning that the world is in perpetual motion—animals wander, birds fly, rocks tumble, wind blows, rain falls, and celestial bodies progress—and thus is never the same from one moment to the next. It follows, therefore, that human movements are interconnected with the movements of other entities, powers, and forces in the world. In the words of Ingold (2013:94), "we do not...experience ourselves and one another as 'packaged' but as moving and moved, in ongoing response—that is in correspondence—with the things around us" (see also Ingold 2000:219–242).

Other scholars have elaborated on Ingold's work, and they have been equally influential for our perspective. For instance, our view parallels the work of Timothy Pauketat (2013a) and Sarah Baires and colleagues (2013) in that we see movements as enabling entanglements within larger fields or webs of relationships. These scholars consider movement to be physical actions, perceptions, and sensory experiences that "position" beings, things, places, and powers together in ways that potentially create new entanglements (Baires et al. 2013:199). Pauketat calls these entanglements "bundles" (see above), and argues that they are made up of movements of all kinds, such as meandering bodies as well as the more direct movements or links with past entities, experiences, memories, and so on. Bundling, then, moves various things or groups of things together in unique ways (Pauketat 2013a:38–40). Furthermore, these movements, positionings, and entanglements occur in various ways, places, contexts, and realms and incorporate various beings, senses, and temporalities. The practices of pilgrimage, mound building, and pipe smoking in the ancient American Midwest, for instance, are examples of how movements of humans, earth, and smoke in larger relational fields initiated convergences between multiple realms and beings (Baires et al. 2013). Pauketat (2013a) argues that a new Cahokian religion was due to the movements and convergences of people, places, and things with cosmic powers and realms.

In sum, our view of movement considers not only human movements but also the movements of nonhuman bodies, things, places, materials, substances, forces, and powers. We also suggest that movement is a broad, variable phenomenon that can mean or refer to a number of different things: bodily motions, gestures, and practices; journeys of human and nonhuman entities, bodies, substances, and elements; emotional or spiritual experiences; sensory perceptions; thoughts, meditations, and visions; memory work; and social, religious, and political transformations. Additionally, movements occur in many different contexts, dimensions, and scales. The crucial point is that movement is a dynamic quality that, in many ways and through various means, generates ongoing interactions, positionings, convergences, and entanglements in webs of relationships (see Baires et al. 2013; Ingold 2007, 2011:67–75; Pauketat 2013a:37–38). Movement is everywhere, and it generates flux, process, and transformation—it is what throws the world into a constant state of becoming.

Organization of the Book

Most of the chapters in this book began as presentations given at a symposium at the Society of American Archaeology annual meeting in 2012 (organized by Buchanan and Skousen). The chapters deal with various geographical regions and time periods throughout the Americas (Figure 0.1), but all concentrate on how the movements of various entities altered relationships and thus engendered continual change and transformation in the meshworks of life.

More specifically, the authors are concerned with relationships between otherworldly realms and dimensions; spirits, deities, and ancestors; and temporalities. This is important, as most archaeological studies have focused exclusively on relationships between humans, nonhuman persons, and things (Gell 1998; Gosden 2005; Hodder 2012; Jones 2012; Latour 2005; Knappett and Malafouris 2008) (some notable exceptions are Baires et al. 2013; Baltus and Baires 2012; Harrison-Buck 2012; Herva 2010; Pauketat 2008, 2013a; and Walker 2008). This negligence, we believe, is due to surviving vestiges of Christopher Hawkes's (1954) "ladder of inference," which suggests that inferring religious institutions and spiritual life from archaeological materials is more difficult than inferring technological production, subsistence economics, and social and political institutions. Since otherworldly dimensions, spirits, deities, and temporalities are typically attributed to religion or spiritual matters (though the notion of "religion" itself is problematic in pre-Columbian contexts; see Fowles 2013), they are considered to be confined to the mind, intangible, epiphenomenal, or at best represented by "ritual" artifacts and features; in short, these phenomena are inaccessible to archaeologists (see Lucas 2012:137–142). More recently, however, archaeologists have argued that religion and spirituality are practiced; in other words, they come into existence as they are enacted (Bell 1992; Bradley 2005; Fogelin 2007; Insoll 2004). Severin Fowles (2013), in fact, claims that the term "doings" better describes what archaeologists have long dubbed "rituals" or "religious ceremonies," and that there was no inherent dichotomy between sacred and profane, belief and ritual, or religious and secular life in the ancient past. Building on these arguments, the chapters in this book show that worlds, spirits, and temporalities were continually encountered, experienced, and constructed through practices, performances, movements, and relationships of all kinds. In short, "religion" and "spirituality" in these past contexts do not fit modern Western categories of religion or spirituality (see Harrison-Buck, this volume).

With these points in mind, we divided this book into three sections: "Worlds," "Spirits and Forces," and "Temporalities." The chapters in the first section examine relationships between otherworldly places and dimensions. The existence of a multidimensional cosmos was prevalent among native groups throughout the Americas, though the particular conception of these worlds varied from group to group. For instance, notions of a lower world, an upper world, and a realm where spirits traveled after death were prevalent among the Maya, Aztec, and many indigenous groups throughout North America (see Christenson 2000; Freidel et al. 1993; Hall 1997; Lankford 2007; see also Skousen, this volume; Romain, this volume). Unlike the case in many Western cosmologies, however, the boundaries between these otherworldly realms were blurred or nonexistent, and entities of all kinds moved to, from, and through them. For example, Stacie King questions how archaeologists traditionally view settlement data, arguing that seemingly uninhabited landscapes in the Nejapa region of Oaxaca, Mexico, were intertwined with nonhuman beings and worlds. She suggests that when constructing settlement histories, archaeologists consider how landscapes and worlds were continually rewoven through time by the movements of both human and nonhuman persons. Jacob Skousen suggests that connections to the upper and lower worlds through moonbeams, a spring, and smoke from sacred fires drew people to the Emerald site, an important Cahokian mound center, between AD 1050 and 1200. Because these connections were always in flux, however, people made multiple journeys to Emerald through time to remember and reestablish these otherworldly associations. Similarly, William Romain argues that the Great Hopewell Road and the nearby Sugarloaf Mountain in southeastern Ohio embodied the Path of Souls and the axis mundi, respectively. Together these features connected the upper and lower worlds, and processions along the road during rare lunar occurrences allowed the living and dead to travel between these realms.

The chapters in the second section focus on relationships between spirits, ancestors, and deities. The underlying tenet of this section is that some objects, places, and nonhuman entities had their own animacy—they were sentient and alive, and notably did not need humans to render them so (see Holbraad 2009). On the other hand, some nonhuman objects or places became imbued with the spirits and essences of human and nonhuman beings (following Hallowell 1960; Harvey 2006; Pauketat 2008; Strathern 1988; Weiner 1992). In either case, these entities were important because of their movements and entanglements with humans, objects, substances, spirits, and other forces (Baltus and Baires 2012; Brown and Emery 2008; Brown and Walker 2008; Harrison-Buck 2012; Mills and Ferguson 2008; Pauketat 2008). These chapters describe situations in which nonhuman spirits, deities, and forces were involved in everyday life and experience. Meghan Buchanan, for example, argues that practices surrounding warfare and abandonment in the pre-Columbian Midwest involved animate forces. Spiritual protections were sown into physical defensive structures, and the spirits of those killed in violent encounters continued to inhabit spaces even after the living had fled. Margaret Brown Vega shows that the pre-Columbian landscape of the Andean site Cerros San Cristobal was imbued with animate beings such as winds and mountains. These malevolent entities were intertwined with the world of humans, and placating them through rituals and ceremonies at mountaintop fortifications was seen as an act of both physical and spiritual protection for surrounding communities. Eleanor Harrison-Buck considers Maya deities to be forces in a constant state of flux due to their interaction and association with the lives of humans. She specifically argues that the paramount Maya god Itzamnaaj was viewed as a life force that was contained within sacred substances, manifested in multiple forms, and embodied the cosmos, and that other named gods were manifestations of Itzamnaaj.

The final section concentrates on relationships between temporalities. This topic has received considerable attention in the archaeological literature in the last decade (see Jones 2007; Mills and Walker, ed. 2008a; Van Dyke and Alcock 2003). Studies on temporality have rejected the premise that time and history occur only as a linear series of unfolding events that people merely witness (Ingold 2000:189–208). Rather, the past, present, and future are gathered together such that they all are actively brought into being as bodies engage with spaces, places, and other actors. For instance, Gerald Oetelaar describes how Blackfoot pilgrimages assembled past, present, and future human and nonhuman beings, events, practices, and places. He also highlights how, to the Blackfoot, disruptions in the physical movements of Blackfoot pilgrims caused the spread of disease, the appropriation of their lands, and the abandonment of sacred places and rituals. In a somewhat different vein, Melissa Baltus demonstrates that religious movements and the movements and entanglements of human and nonhuman agents, practices, and objects underlay major shifts in Mississippian history, particularly at the earliest Mississippian polity of Cahokia. She argues that while a religious movement and entanglements with certain people, places, and things incited Cahokia's rise circa AD 1050, a new series of entanglements and disentanglements, forged in the early thirteenth century, proved to have lasting historical impacts throughout eastern North America.

We have separated the chapters into these three sections for heuristic purposes, but it is imperative to recognize that otherworldly dimensions, spirits and forces, and temporalities are not mutually exclusive phenomena. In every chapter they overlap, mix, or in some cases are not distinguishable at all. For instance, both Romain and Skousen demonstrate that journeys involved the convergence not only of worlds but also of nonhuman beings and temporalities. King argues that nonhuman agents, separated by both time and space, played an important role in the construction of ancient Oaxacan realities. Buchanan suggests that certain animate objects were powerful because of their location in liminal spaces between transdimensional realms. As Brown Vega and Harrison-Buck describe the forms, abilities, and movements of nonhuman beings, they simultaneously blur the boundaries between human and nonhuman worlds. Baltus argues that in addition to numerous changes in the Cahokia region over time, other-than-human beings played a critical role in making and remaking Cahokian history. Finally, Oetelaar specifically describes how failing to adhere to the timing of cyclical pilgrimages was detrimental to Blackfoot society because it displeased powerful ancestral spirits. In short, the chapters illustrate that these phenomena were at least intimately entangled, if not altogether inseparable.

Conclusion

Overall, we argue that archaeologists can better understand past realities by adopting a relational perspective and recognizing the primacy of movement. We have not laid out a specific outline or set of methods or procedures on how this can or should be done. Indeed, we believe there are many fruitful ways to approach movement and relationships, and the chapters in this book provide good examples of such analyses. They support Ingold's (2000:219–242; 2011:67–75; see also Baires et al. 2013; Pauketat 2013a) view that the world is a meshwork of relationships and that movement causes continual negotiations and transformations among these relationships. They also show that there are many ways to think about movement—clearly it is not limited to human gesticulations or the physical travels of people or animals across the landscape. It also includes the activities, flows, and dissemination of nonhuman entities, bodies, spirits, ideas, forces, and memories through time and space in various dimensions and scales. Furthermore, movement can be viewed in a number of different ways. Baltus, for example, discusses both political-religious movements and the physical movements (migrations) of groups across the ancient Midwest and how these two movements were dependent on each other (see also Hodder 2012).

In closing, we emphasize that this book and its focus on relationships and movements continue to overturn Hawkes's (1954) ladder of inference, which is still deeply entrenched in archaeological thinking. Certainly the realms and beings Hawkes referred to are not intangible or confined to the mind. On the contrary, they were practiced, experienced, and tied to, caught up in, and thoroughly mixed with other people, things, places, and beings (see Pauketat 2013a). Archaeology, then, is not simply a matter of inferring past human behavior through material residues; it is an endeavor to understand how movements and relationships of all kinds generated, constrained, or transformed past worlds consisting of human and nonhuman persons, places, things, realities, dimensions, and temporalities that were always in the process of becoming. Archaeologists can, and should, study these phenomena.

References Cited

Alberti, Benjamin, and Tamara L. Bray
2009 Animating Archaeology: Of Subjects, Objects and Alternative Ontologies. *Cambridge Archaeological Journal* 19:337–343.
Alberti, Benjamin, Severin Fowles, Martin Holbraad, Yvonne Marshall, and Christopher Witmore
2011 "Worlds Otherwise": Archaeology, Anthropology, and Ontological Difference. *Current Anthropology* 52 (6): 896–912.
Alberti, Benjamin, Andrew Meirion Jones, and Joshua Pollard (editors)
2013 *Archaeology after Interpretation: Returning Materials to Archaeological Theory*. Left Coast Press, Walnut Creek, California.
Alt, Susan M.
2006 The Power of Diversity: Roles of Migration and Hybridity in Culture Change. In *Leadership and Polity in Mississippian Society*, edited by Brian M. Butler and Paul D. Welch, pp. 289–308. Occasional Paper No. 33. Center for Archaeological Investigations, Southern Illinois University, Carbondale.
Ashmore, Wendy
2004 Social Archaeologies of Landscape. In *A Companion to Social Archaeology*, edited by L. Meskell and R. W. Preucel, pp. 255–271. Blackwell, Malden, Massachusetts.
Baires, Sarah E., Amanda J. Butler, B. Jacob Skousen, and Timothy R. Pauketat
2013 Fields of Movement in the Eastern Woodlands. In *Archaeology after Interpretation: Returning Materials to Archaeological Theory*, edited by B. Alberti, A. M. Jones, and J. Pollard, pp. 197–218. Left Coast Press, Walnut Creek, California.
Baltus, Melissa R., and Sarah E. Baires
2012 Elements of Ancient Power in the Cahokian World. *Journal of Social Archaeology* 12:167–192.

Barrett, John C.
1994 *Fragments from Antiquity: An Archaeology of Social Life in Britain, 2900–1200 BC*. Blackwell, Oxford.
2000 A Thesis on Agency. In *Agency in Archaeology*, edited by Marcia-Anne Dobres and John Robb, pp. 61–68. Routledge, London.
Bauer, Brian S., and Charles Stanish
2001 *Ritual and Pilgrimage in the Ancient Andes: The Islands of the Sun and the Moon*. University of Texas Press, Austin.
Beekman, Christopher S., and Alexander F. Christensen
2003 Controlling for Doubt and Uncertainty through Multiple Lines of Evidence: A New Look at the Mesoamerican Nahua Migrations. *Journal of Archaeological Method and Theory* 10 (2): 111–164.
Bell, Catherine
1992 *Ritual Theory, Ritual Practice*. Oxford University Press, New York.
Bender, Barbara
2001 Landscapes on-the-Move. *Journal of Social Archaeology* 1 (1): 75–89.
Binford, Lewis R.
1962 Archaeology as Anthropology. *American Antiquity* 28 (2): 217–225.
1965 Archaeological Systematics and the Study of Culture Process. *American Antiquity* 31 (2): 203–210.
1967 Smudge Pits and Hide Smoking: The Use of Analogy in Archaeological Reasoning. *American Antiquity* 32 (1): 1–12.
1978 *Nunamiut Ethnoarchaeology*. Academic Press, New York.
Bird-David, Nurit
1999 "Animism" Revisited: Personhood, Environ-

ment, and Relational Epistemology. *Current Anthropology* 40:67–91.

Boas, Franz
1896 The Limitations of the Comparative Method of Anthropology. *Science* 4 (103): 901–908.

Bourdieu, Pierre
1977 *Outline of a Theory of Practice*. Cambridge University Press, Cambridge.

Bradley, Richard
2005 *Ritual and Domestic Life in Prehistoric Europe*. Routledge, London.

Brown, Linda A., and Kitty F. Emery
2008 Negotiations with the Animate Forest: Hunting Shrines in the Guatemalan Highlands. *Journal of Archaeological Method and Theory* 15:300–337.

Brown, Linda A., and William H. Walker
2008 Prologue: Archaeology, Animism and Non-human Agents. *Journal of Archaeological Method and Theory* 15:297–299.

Bruck, Joanna
2001 Monuments, Power and Personhood in the British Neolithic. *Journal of the Royal Anthropological Institute* 7:649–667.
2006 Fragmentation, Personhood and the Social Construction of Technology in Middle and Late Bronze Age Britain. *Cambridge Archaeological Journal* 16 (3): 297–315.

Caldwell, Joseph R.
1959 The New American Archaeology. *Science* 129: 303–307.

Chapman, John
2000 *Fragmentation in Archaeology: People, Places, and Broken Objects in the Prehistory of South-Eastern Europe*. Routledge, London.

Childe, Vere G.
1939 *The Dawn of European Civilization*. 3rd ed. Kegan Paul, London.
1969 [1950] *Prehistoric Migrations in Europe*. Anthropological Publications, Oosterhout, The Netherlands.

Christenson, Allen J.
2000 *Popol Vuh: The Sacred Book of the Maya*. O Books, Winchester, U.K.

Clarke, David L.
1978 *Analytical Archaeology*. Methuen, London.

Close, Angela E.
2000 Reconstructing Movement in Prehistory. *Journal of Archaeological Method and Theory* 7 (1): 49–77.

Conneller, Chantal
2011 *An Archaeology of Materials: Substantial Transformations in Early Prehistoric Europe*. Routledge, New York.

Cummings, Vicki, and Robert Johnston (editors)
2007 *Prehistoric Journeys*. Oxbow Books, Oxford.

Deleuze, Gilles, and Felix Guattari
2004 *A Thousand Plateaus: Capitalism and Schizophrenia*. Continuum, London.

Farnell, Brenda
1994 Ethno-Graphics and the Moving Body. *Man* 29 (4): 929–974.
1996 Metaphors We Move By. *Visual Anthropology* 8:311–335.
1999 Moving Bodies, Acting Selves. *Annual Review of Anthropology* 28:341–373.
2003 Kinesthetic Sense and Dynamically Embodied Action. *Journal for the Anthropological Study of Human Movement* 12 (4): 132–144.

Flannery, Kent V.
1968 Archaeological Systems Theory and Early Mesoamerica. In *Anthropological Archaeology in the Americas*, edited by B. J. Meggers, pp. 67–87. Anthropological Society of Washington, Washington, D.C.
1973 The Origins of Agriculture. *Annual Review of Anthropology* 2:271–310.

Fogelin, Lars
2007 The Archaeology of Religious Ritual. *Annual Review of Anthropology* 36:55–71.

Fowler, Chris
2001 Personhood and Social Relations in the British Neolithic with a Study from the Isle of Man. *Journal of Material Culture* 6 (2): 137–163.
2002 Body Parts: Personhood and Materiality in the Manx Neolithic. In *Thinking through the Body: Archaeologies of Corporeality*, edited by Y. Hamilakis, M. Pluciennik, and S. Tarlow, pp. 47–69. Kluwer/Academic Press, London.
2004 *The Archaeology of Personhood: An Anthropological Approach*. Routledge, London.
2013 *The Emergent Past: A Relational Realist Archaeology of Early Bronze Age Mortuary Practices*. Oxford University Press, Oxford.

Fowles, Severin M.
2013 *An Archaeology of Doings: Secularism and the Study of Pueblo Religion*. School for Advanced Research Press, Santa Fe, New Mexico.

Freidel, David, Linda Schele, and Joy Parker
1993 *Maya Cosmos: Three Thousand Years on the Shaman's Path*. William Morrow, New York.

Gell, Alfred
1998 *Art and Agency: An Anthropological Theory*. Oxford University Press, Oxford.

Gibson, James J.
1986 *The Ecological Approach to Visual Perception*. Lawrence Erlbaum, Hillsdale, New Jersey.

Gillespie, Susan D.
2001 Personhood, Agency, and Mortuary Ritual: A Case Study from the Ancient Maya. *Journal of Anthropological Archaeology* 20:73–112.

Gosden, Chris
1999 *Anthropology and Archaeology: A Changing Relationship*. Routledge, London.
2005 What Do Objects Want? *Journal of Archaeological Method and Theory* 12:193–211.

Gould, Richard A., and John E. Yellen
1987 Man the Hunted: Determinants of Household Spacing in Desert and Tropical Foraging Societies. *Journal of Anthropological Archaeology* 6:77–103.

Hall, Robert L.
1997 *An Archaeology of the Soul: Native American Indian Belief and Ritual*. University of Illinois Press, Urbana.

Hallowell, A. Irving
1960 Ojibwa Ontology, Behavior, and World View. In *Culture in History: Essays in Honor of Paul Radin*, edited by Stanley Diamond, pp. 19–52. Columbia University Press, New York.

Harré, Rom
1986 *The Social Construction of Emotions*. Blackwell, Oxford.

Harris, Oliver J. T.
2012 (Re)assembling Communities. *Journal of Archaeological Method and Theory* 21 (1): 76–97.
2013 Relational Communities in Prehistoric Britain. In *Relational Archaeologies: Humans, Animals, Things*, edited by C. Watts, pp. 173–189. Routledge, London.

Harris, Oliver J. T., and John Robb
2012 Multiple Ontologies and the Problem of the Body in History. *American Anthropologist* 114 (4): 668–679.

Harrison-Buck, Eleanor
2012 Architecture as Animate Landscape: Circular Shrines in the Ancient Maya Lowlands. *American Anthropologist* 114:64–80.

Harvey, Graham
2006 *Animism: Respecting the Living World*. Columbia University Press, New York.

Hawkes, Christopher
1954 Archaeological Theory and Method: Some Suggestions from the Old World. *American Anthropologist* 56:155–168.

Henare, Amiria, Martin Holbraad, and Sari Wastell
2007 Introduction: Thinking through Things. In *Thinking through Things: Theorising Artefacts Ethnographically*, edited by A. Henare, M. Holbraad, and S. Wastell, pp. 1–31. Routledge, London.

Herva, Vesa-Pekka
2009 Living (with) Things: Relational Ontology and Material Culture in Early Modern Northern Finland. *Cambridge Archaeological Journal* 19:388–397.

2010 Buildings as Persons: Relationality and the Life of Buildings in a Northern Periphery of Early Modern Sweden. *Antiquity* 84:440–452.

Hill, Erica
2011 Animals as Agents: Hunting Ritual and Relational Ontologies in Prehistoric Alaska and Chukotka. *Cambridge Archaeological Journal* 21:407–426.

Hodder, Ian
1991 Interpretive Archaeology and Its Role. *American Antiquity* 56:7–8.
1999 *The Archaeological Process*. Blackwell, Oxford.
2006 *The Leopard's Tale: Revealing the Mysteries of Catalhoyuk*. Thames and Hudson, New York.
2012 *Entangled: An Archaeology of the Relationships between Humans and Things*. Wiley-Blackwell, Oxford.

Hodder, Ian (editor)
2010 *Religion in the Emergence of Civilization: Catalhoyuk as a Case Study*. Cambridge University Press, Cambridge.

Hodder, Ian, and Scott Hutson
2003 *Reading the Past: Current Approaches to Interpretation in Archaeology*. 3rd ed. Cambridge University Press, Cambridge.

Holbraad, Martin
2009 Ontology, Ethnography, Archaeology: An Afterword on the Ontography of Things. *Cambridge Archaeological Journal* 19:431–441.

Hutson, Scott R.
2010 *Dwelling, Identity, and the Maya: Relational Archaeology at Chunchucmil*. AltaMira Press, Lanham, Maryland.

Ingold, Tim
2000 *The Perception of the Environment: Essays on Livelihood, Dwelling, and Skill*. Routledge, London.
2007 *Lines: A Brief History*. Routledge, London.
2011 *Being Alive: Essays on Movement, Knowledge, and Description*. Routledge, London.
2013 *Making: Anthropology, Archaeology, Art and Architecture*. Routledge, London.

Insoll, Timothy
2004 *Archaeology, Ritual, Religion*. Routledge, London.

Jones, Andrew Meirion
2007 *Memory and Material Culture*. Cambridge University Press, Cambridge.
2012 *Prehistoric Materialities: Becoming Material in Prehistoric Britain and Ireland*. Oxford University Press, Oxford.

Jones, Andrew Meirion, and Benjamin Alberti (with contributions from Chris Fowler and Gavin Lucas)
2013 Archaeology after Interpretation. In *Archaeology after Interpretation: Returning Materials

to *Archaeological Theory*, edited by B. Albert, A. M. Jones, and J. Pollard, pp. 15–42. Left Coast Press, Walnut Creek, California.

Keane, Webb
2005 Signs Are Not the Garb of Meaning: On the Social Analysis of Material Things. In *Materiality*, edited by Daniel Miller, pp. 182–205. Duke University Press, Durham, North Carolina.

Kirby, Peter Wynn
2009 Lost in "Space": An Anthropological Approach to Movement. In *Boundless Worlds: An Anthropological Approach to Movement*, edited by P. W. Kirby, pp. 1–27. Berghahn Books, New York.

Kirk, Trevor
2006 Materiality, Personhood and Monumentality in Early Neolithic Britain. *Cambridge Archaeological Journal* 16 (3): 333–347.

Knappett, Carl, and Lambros Malafouris (editors)
2008 *Material Agency: Towards a Non-anthropocentric Approach*. Springer, New York.

Knott, Kim, and Sean McLoughlin (editors)
2010 *Diasporas: Concepts, Intersections, Identities*. Zed Books, London.

Küchler, Susanne
1999 Binding in the Pacific: Between Loops and Knots. *Oceania* 69:145–156.
2002 *Malanggan: Art, Memory and Sacrifice*. Berg, Oxford.

Lankford, George E.
2007 The "Path of Souls": Some Death Imagery in the Southeastern Ceremonial Complex. In *Ancient Objects and Sacred Realms: Interpretations of Mississippian Iconography*, edited by F. Kent Reilly III and James F. Garber, pp. 174–212. University of Texas Press, Austin.

Latour, Bruno
1993 *We Have Never Been Modern*. Harvard University Press, Cambridge, Massachusetts.
1999 *Pandora's Hope: Essays on the Reality of Science Studies*. Harvard University Press, Cambridge, Massachusetts.
2005 *Reassembling the Social: An Introduction to Actor-Network Theory*. Oxford University Press, Oxford.

Lucas, Gavin
2012 *Understanding the Archaeological Record*. Cambridge University Press, New York.

Mauss, Marcell
1979 [1935] Techniques of the Body. In *Sociology and Psychology: Essays by Marcel Mauss*, edited by K. Paul, pp. 97–123. Routledge, London.

McFadyen, Lesley
2013 Designing with Living: A Contextual Archaeology of Dependent Architecture. In *Archaeology after Interpretation: Returning Materials to Archaeological Theory*, edited by B. Alberti, A. M. Jones, and J. Pollard, pp. 135–150. Left Coast Press, Walnut Creek, California.

Merleau-Ponty, Maurice
1962 *Phenomenology of Perception*. Translated by C. Smith. Routledge, London.

Meskell, Lynn
2004 *Object Worlds in Ancient Egypt*. Berg, Oxford.

Meskell, Lynn (editor)
2005 *Archaeologies of Materiality*. Blackwell, Malden, Massachusetts.

Mills, Barbara J., and T. J. Ferguson
2008 Animate Objects: Shell Trumpets and Ritual Networks in the Greater Southwest. *Journal of Archaeological Method and Theory* 15:338–361.

Mills, Barbara J., and William H. Walker
2008 Introduction: Memory, Materiality, and Depositional Practice. In *Memory Work: Archaeologies of Material Practices*, edited by B. J. Mills and W. H. Walker, pp. 3–23. School for Advanced Research Press, Santa Fe, New Mexico.

Mills, Barbara J., and William H. Walker (editors)
2008 *Memory Work: Archaeologies of Material Practices*. School for Advanced Research Press, Santa Fe, New Mexico.

Mills, Jessica
2005 Movement as a Mentalité: Mobile Lifeways in the Neolithic and Bronze Age Great Ouse, Nene and Welland Valleys. In *Elements of Being: Mentalities, Identities and Movements*, edited by D. Hofmann, J. Mills, and A. Cochrane, pp. 96–106. British Archaeological Reports, International Series 1437, Oxford.

O'Brien, Michael J., and Thomas D. Holland
1992 The Role of Adaptation in Archaeological Explanation. *American Antiquity* 57:36–59.

Olsen, Bjornar
2007 Keeping Things at Arm's Length: A Genealogy of Asymmetry. *World Archaeology* 39 (4): 579–588.
2010 *In Defense of Things: Archaeology and the Ontology of Objects*. AltaMira Press, Lanham, Maryland.

Olsen, Bjornar, Michael Shanks, Timothy Webmoor, and Christopher Witmore
2012 *Archaeology: The Discipline of Things*. University of California Press, Berkeley.

Parker Pearson, Mike, Josh Pollard, Colin Richards, Julian Thomas, and Christopher Tilley
2006 Materializing Stonehenge: The Stonehenge Riverside Project and New Discoveries. *Journal of Material Culture* 11 (1/2): 227–261.

Parker Pearson, Mike, and Ramilisonina
1998 Stonehenge for the Ancestors: The Stones Pass on the Message. *Antiquity* 72:308–326.

Pauketat, Timothy R.
2003 Resettled Farmers and the Making of a Mississippian Polity. *American Antiquity* 68:39–66.
2008 Founders' Cults and the Archaeology of Wa-Kan-da. In *Memory Work: Archaeologies of Material Practices*, edited by B. J. Mills and W. H. Walker, pp. 61–79. School for Advanced Research Press, Santa Fe, New Mexico.
2013a *An Archaeology of the Cosmos: Rethinking Agency and Religion in Ancient America*. Routledge, London.
2013b Bundles in/of/as Time. In *Big Histories, Human Lives: Tackling Problems of Scale in Archaeology*, edited by J. Robb and T. R. Pauketat, pp. 35–56. School for Advanced Research Press, Santa Fe, New Mexico.

Pels, Peter
1998 The Spirit of Matter: On Fetish, Rarity, Fact, and Fancy. In *Border Fetishisms: Material Objects in Unstable Spaces*, edited by P. Spyer, pp. 91–121. Routledge, New York.

Plog, Fred T.
1975 Systems Theory in Archaeological Research. *Annual Review of Anthropology* 4:207–244.

Richards, Colin
1993 Monumental Choreography: Architecture and Spatial Representation in Late Neolithic Orkney. In *Interpretive Archaeology*, edited by C. Tilley, pp. 143–178. Berg, Oxford.
1996 Monuments as Landscape: Creating the Centre of the World in Late Neolithic Orkney. *World Archaeology* 28 (2): 190–208.

Schiffer, Michael B.
1976 *Behavioral Archaeology*. Academic Press, New York.

Shanks, Michael, and Chris Tilley
1987 *Re-constructing Archaeology*. Cambridge University Press, Cambridge.

Sheets-Johnstone, Maxine
2011 *The Primacy of Movement*. Expanded 2nd ed. John Benjamins, Amsterdam.

Shott, Michael J.
2006 Formation Theory's Past and Future: Introduction to the Volume. In *Formation Theory in Archaeology: Readings from American Antiquity and Latin American Antiquity*, compiled by M. Shott, pp. 1–18. SAA Press, Washington, D.C.

Shults, LeRon
2010 Spiritual Entanglement: Transforming Religious Symbols at Catalhoyuk. In *Religion in the Emergence of Civilization: Catalhoyuk as a Case Study*, edited by I. Hodder, pp. 73–98. Cambridge University Press, Cambridge.

Snead, James E., Clark L. Erickson, and J. Andrew Darling (editors)
2009 *Landscapes of Movement: Trails, Paths, and Roads in Anthropological Perspective*. University of Pennsylvania Museum of Archaeology and Anthropology, Philadelphia.

Stahl, Anne B.
1993 Concepts of Time and Approaches to Analogical Reasoning in Historical Perspective. *American Antiquity* 58:235–260.

Steward, Julian H.
1955 *Theory of Culture Change*. University of Illinois Press, Urbana.

Strathern, Marilyn
1988 *The Gender of the Gift: Problems with Women and Problems with Society in Melanesia*. University of California Press, Berkeley.

Taylor, Walter W.
1948 *A Study of Archaeology*. Memoir No. 69. American Anthropological Association, Menasha, Wisconsin.

Thomas, Julian
1993 The Hermeneutics of Megalithic Space. In *Interpretive Archaeology*, edited by C. Tilley, pp. 73–97. Berg, Oxford.

Tilley, Christopher
1994 *A Phenomenology of Landscape: Places, Paths, and Monuments*. Berg, Oxford.
2004 *The Materiality of Stone: Explorations in Landscape Phenomenology*. Berg, Oxford.

Trigger, Bruce G.
2006 *A History of Archaeological Thought*. 2nd ed. Cambridge University Press, Cambridge.

Tylor, Edward B.
1993 [1871] *Primitive Culture: Researches into the Development of Mythology, Philosophy, Religion, Art, and Custom*. John Murray, London.

Van Dyke, Ruth, and Susan Alcock (editors)
2003 *Archaeologies of Memory*. Blackwell, Oxford.

VanPool, Christine S., and Elizabeth Newsome
2012 The Spirit in the Material: A Case Study of Animism in the American Southwest. *American Antiquity* 77:243–262.

Viveiros de Castro, Eduardo
1998 Cosmological Deixis and Amerindian Perspectivism. *Journal of the Royal Anthropological Institute* 4 (3): 469–488.
2004 Exchanging Perspectives: The Transformation of Objects into Subjects in Amerindian Ontologies. *Common Knowledge* 10:463–484.

Walker, Polly
2013 Research in Relationship with Humans, the Spirit World, and the Natural World. In *Indigenous Pathways into Social Research: Voices of a New Generation*, edited by D. M. Mertens,

Walker, William H.
2008 Practice and Nonhuman Social Actors: The Afterlife Histories of Witches and Dogs in the American Southwest. In *Memory Work: Archaeologies of Material Practices*, edited by B. J. Mills and W. H. Walker, pp. 137–157. School for Advanced Research Press, Santa Fe, New Mexico.

Watts, Christopher
2013 Relational Archaeologies: Roots and Routes. In *Relational Archaeologies: Humans, Animals, Things*, edited by C. Watts, pp. 1–20. Routledge, London.

Watts, Christopher (editor)
2013 *Relational Archaeologies: Humans, Animals, Things*. Routledge, London.

Webmoor, Timothy
2007 What about "One More Turn after the Social" in Archaeological Reasoning? Taking Things Seriously. *World Archaeology* 39 (4): 547–562.

Weiner, Annette B.
1992 *Inalienable Possessions: The Paradox of Keeping-while-Giving*. University of California Press, Berkeley.

Witmore, Christopher
2007 Symmetrical Archaeology: Excerpts from a Manifesto. *World Archaeology* 39 (4): 546–562.

Zedeño, María Nieves
2008 Bundled Worlds: The Roles and Interactions of Complex Objects from the North American Plains. *Journal of Archaeological Method and Theory* 15:362–378.
2009 Animating by Association: Index Objects and Relational Taxonomies. *Cambridge Archaeological Journal* 19 (3): 407–417.

[Note: Entry above Walker begins: F. Cram, and B. Chilisa, pp. 299–315. Left Coast Press, Walnut Creek, California.]

Part I

Worlds

1

Settlement Survey, Landscape Transformations, and the Meaning of Unoccupied Land in Postclassic Nejapa, Oaxaca, Mexico

Stacie M. King

As students learn in introductory archaeology classes, full-coverage systematic survey is a standard field technique that archaeologists employ during early stages of archaeological fieldwork to examine changes through time in settlement distribution, population density, and site function. Settlement surveys generate regional-scale data that allow archaeologists to begin to think about changes through time in regional political organization and the migration of people into, out of, and through places. Interpretations of settlement survey data are typically derived from estimated population densities, site sizes, and the relationships between sites of different sizes occupied at the same time. This is how I have explained settlement survey to my Introduction to Archaeology students every year for the last decade.

Yet I have never been wholly satisfied with the incompleteness of survey data—both in terms of how I explain the method to my students and in terms of how I have incorporated archaeological survey in my own research. In spite of having collected (or rather created) two field seasons of systematic survey data in southeastern Oaxaca, Mexico, I still feel hesitant about eliciting meaningful interpretations based on these data. Part of the reason, certainly, is that our coverage remains small compared with the size of the region as a whole, and every day we seem to hear about new sites that fall outside or just beyond our survey boundaries. However, other concerns stem from my general discomfort with settlement survey's underlying definitions, categories, and methods, as well as the structural/functional framework on which it relies.

In the field (as a team) my students, colleagues, and I have struggled with the question of how best to define a site. We have debated vigorously where one site ends and another begins. Other discussions emerge when we elicit interpretations from collected field data. For example, do we draw different site boundaries for each time period represented even if such determinations are based on a few sherds? How do we account for what might lie just outside the surveyed area or in the terrain where a given landowner or community did not grant us permission to survey? How do the surface artifacts indicate change through time? All these questions do not yet even engage rather obvious problems connected to differential preservation, artifact visibility, and surface bias (the tendency to find the largest, most recent, most sturdy, and most elaborated sites on the surface). Given all these issues, how then are we to make sense of these data? What do our resulting maps really show? How in the end do these data help us to understand and interpret change through time? Is settlement survey a futile endeavor or is it meaningful practice?

When I received the invitation to contribute to this book, I was in the field—doing survey, in the process of creating and recording archaeological evidence and mapping and naming sites that had never before been documented by any archaeological team. The sites were not yet registered with the federal government of Mexico, a process that requires specific kinds of information and creates particular contingencies. The organizers of this book challenged us to rethink the frameworks we use to understand culture change by applying Tim Ingold's (2007, 2011a, 2011b) work on relational ontologies, and I took some time to decide if I had anything meaningful to contribute.

I kept thinking about the many sites that we had been recording and mapping. We see some general patterns of change through time—the earliest sites are located in the valley floors and date to 800 BC or so based on ceramic styles. We see some population movement between the valley, piedmont, and mountains between the Late Classic (AD 500–800) and Postclassic (AD 800–1521), and an absolute explosion of settlement between AD 1400 and 1600, precisely when the Zapotec, Aztec, and Spanish militia and migrants supposedly moved through on their campaigns of conquest to secure the rich coastal plains of Tehuantepec and Soconusco. Late Postclassic/Early Colonial period settlements account for nearly 94 percent (60/64) of our dated sites.[1] Before this time, the survey data are too incomplete for us to make any arguments with respect to regional political organization. During the Late Postclassic/Early Colonial period, most of the largest sites—by area and by structure counts—were located in the highest mountaintops. Although many of these sites were naturally fortified, people living in these mountain locations nonetheless added extensive defensive and terrace walls that further restricted access to these sites from the outside.

In July 2011, I reported in a Mexican conference presentation and press release that we had recorded sixty-seven new sites during our 2011 field season, bringing our total to somewhere close to one hundred newly identified sites. And once again in 2013, we recorded another fifty-nine new sites, for which site forms have been submitted. Yet I continue to struggle with thinking about what the survey data mean. Why were people making and using pottery and constructing stone building foundations in some locations and not others? Why did some people have access to obsidian while others used only chert for fashioning their stone tools? Why were some hilltops apparently left untouched (or unaltered) while others were engineered to create terraced, human living space? Particularly important, what about all that empty space outside our site boundaries? Were these spaces really untouched? How did this presumably unoccupied space figure into the world of the living?

I offer this brief personal narrative because I think it provides the background for the productive, generative moments I had in writing this chapter. What I have found is that Ingold's thinking gives us some useful tools and insightful critiques of traditional settlement survey methods and the structural/functional framework on which they are based. It shows how entities, in our case archaeological sites, become named, placed, and eventually bounded in discourse and in practice. Likewise, our reliance on overly simplified categories and visual representations in traditional settlement pattern survey methods and interpretations ultimately eliminates all possibilities for seeing complexities, interwovenness, and interrelationships across time and space. Ingold's work also challenges us to consider some thought-provoking alternate methods and interpretations. This chapter focuses on three key topics for which Ingold's work on relational ontologies makes an important contribution: (1) the mapmaking enterprise and the construction of the unoccupied, (2) living in, on, and through, and (3) inhabiting an enduring, animate world.

Regional Background

The archaeological data generated by my field research clearly demonstrate that there were a wide variety of ways that people in the mountains of southeastern Oaxaca interacted with the world around them, through time and across space. I established the Proyecto Arqueológico Nejapa y Tavela (Nejapa/Tavela Archaeological Project) in 2007 to examine an intermediary zone between the arid highlands of urban Mexico and the coastal Isthmus of Tehuantepec. Historically, this area was inhabited by Mixe, Zapotec, and Chontal language-speakers and, according to Spanish ethnohistoric records from the sixteenth and seventeenth centuries, was heavily fought over between AD 1400 and 1600, during Zapotec, Aztec, and

Spanish colonial campaigns to control the lucrative trade in lowland cotton, salt, and chocolate. In my archaeological work, I have been trying to understand the long-term history of the Nejapa region, tracing how and when the area was first occupied and how people living near this important trade and conquest corridor interacted with foreign regimes, merchants, migrants, and each other (King 2010, 2012; King et al. 2012). Relations between communities within the Nejapa region may have varied from contentious and divisive to friendly and supportive depending on a variety of factors. I am also considering the ways in which people in these different communities chose to interact with outsiders, whether in the short term or in sustained encounters. So far, my work has included both systematic survey and test-pit excavations to help develop and refine our ceramic chronology. Project team members have documented a great variety of sites, including large ceremonial centers, residential villages, heavily engineered mountaintop fortified settlements, panels of rock art, temporary encampments in rockshelters and caves, isolated offerings left in front of boulders and rock faces, abandoned colonial-era town sites, and the ruins of colonial and postcolonial sugarcane-producing haciendas. These data are complemented by extensive archival and oral history research on the political, economic, and social history of the region. In sum, the Nejapa region, over the course of more than two thousand years, was a complex and dynamic place where various groups of people, themselves of diverse origins, languages, and histories, established homes. Local residents and migrants responded to and perhaps took advantage of the many unique opportunities afforded by living alongside a well-traveled and frequently contested international trade corridor, drawing themselves into conversations and struggles with peoples of equally diverse backgrounds from other regions.

The Mapmaking Enterprise and the Construction of the Unoccupied

When we conduct archaeological survey and create site maps, we are noting where on the ground we can observe remnants of human habitation. In Mexico, these traces tend to be visible in the form of scattered ceramic debris and remnants of rectangular building foundations made of cobbled or cut stone, above which a structure would have been built using perishable materials—mud and wood (wattle and daub) or adobe, with palm thatching as roofing material. If occupied for some length of time, and depending on building traditions or intended use, sometimes remnants of these structures are recognizable by the mounded ruins they leave behind. With high accuracy (subfoot) GPS, we map all visible architecture, features, and artifact collection points; then, using a combination of topographic parameters and artifact density fall-off, we draw lines outlining the areal extent of visible human traces to indicate the limits of each site. In Ingold's terms, what we have created here is an inversion; we have turned a pathway of life into boundaries within which it is enclosed (Ingold 2011a:145). Inside the lines, we mark the spaces in which people occupy the world. But what does this mean for the space outside the lines? It is really "unoccupied"?

A study by Brown and Emery (2008) brings into focus some of these ideas about the mapmaking enterprise and the notion of the unoccupied. Brown and Emery conducted an ethnoarchaeological study of Maya hunters in the Guatemalan highlands who differentiate between community lands where *milpas* and houses are constructed, and forests, which are considered precarious and dangerous places—places that fall outside the protection of the guardian spirits of the town/milpa. Nonetheless, these forests are believed to be inhabited by animal guardian spirits who must be propitiated on a regular basis to ensure successful hunts. For this reason, any time a hunter enters the forest, the hunter, and any hunting dog with him, must "maintain engaged relations based on commensality and mutual respect" with animal guardian spirits, relations that consist of making offerings at shrine altars decorated with palm fronds and flowers (Brown and Emery 2008:304). At the shrines, hunters burn copal incense; leave small items such as candles, skulls, stone carvings, wooden crosses, and rocks in the form of earth deities or zoomorphic creatures; and perform short rituals and dances to ask permission to enter. Following the hunt, the hunter must then carefully and respectfully return all bones from the hunted animal to their place in the forest, putting the bones on the ground in front of the shrines. Brown and Emery argue that this forest is very much alive and that nonhuman agents continue to have a real impact on the human world.

Further, they explain that no land is unoccupied or unmodified: even what is considered forest still has the remains of fallow fields, reforested areas, and managed orchards, including the regularly visited shrines. In highland Mesoamerican environments, remote mountains were routinely traversed by traders and visited by people and ritual practitioners as sacred places. In Mesoamerican cosmology, mountains are considered water- and flower-filled places of sacred human origins, places where ancestors reside and where life springs forth (Hill 1992; Taube 2004). Many features associated with mountains (caves, large boulders, springs, and rockshelters) were considered conduits between the human and spirit world by Mesoamerican peoples (Brady and Ashmore 1999). Thus, it is no surprise that hunting shrines are created at these locations, the doorways between worlds, on the outside of settlements in the forest world. But what this also shows us is that there is little divide between human and animal worlds. Even though these sites might not include constructed architectural spaces and dense ceramic domestic debris, the forest is still very much part of the living world of people, one where we might be able to see material remains and present and past travel corridors. In the same way, Brown and Emery (2008) argue that forest products, including the materials used to construct houses, also required special ritual behavior and propitiation, and were viewed as nonhuman animate beings living alongside and affecting human settlements. New migrants to and long-standing residents of Nejapa alike could have had similar understandings.

Drawing site boundaries fixes sites in space, which gives the false notion that sites are bounded, contained, and enclosed. The practice also sends the equally false message that the unoccupied areas are devoid of use and lack importance and relevance to people's daily lives. Instead, the spaces outside these boundaries, the excluded areas, were spaces that were open to possibility and should not be eliminated from our interpretations of the past. As Brown and Emery (2008) show, it was in the border zones between constructed villages and forests where human and nonhuman agents came into direct communication with one another. When people moved across the land to settle in new locations and major changes occurred in already established places, this necessarily entailed a renegotiation with the nonhuman agents and guardian spirits who inhabited the world. If the human and nonhuman worlds were not sharply divided, then it implies that occupied and unoccupied human space was also never so sharply divided, across time and space.

Living On, In, and Through

Ingold (2011a:119) argues that landscape is never a solid surface that people occupy. Survey maps flatten things out into a two-dimensional picture, giving the impression that there is a singular surface and that all places were contemporary and inhabitable in the same way at all times. I quite agree with Ingold when he argues that people live *in* the land and not *on* it (Ingold 2011a:120). Placing a circle on a map presupposes that there is a solid interface, flat surface, or fixed line that marks the separation between earth and sky (Ingold 2011a:97; 2013:80). Land, he maintains, is "a vaguely defined zone of admixture and intermingling between mediums and substances" (Ingold 2011a:119), that is, a zone between solid rock below and sky above, with fluidity between.

Most archaeologists are well aware of the precariousness of the concept of a land surface. We often see the results of mud slides, seasonal changes, river action, and human modification of topography. We regularly climb and descend craggy rocks and undulate through multiple changes in elevation. We inevitably reach places where we seem to be crawling on top of branches and meters of leaf litter rather than walking on solid ground. We see the results of site destruction, places where rocks have been removed from prehispanic structures or where landscapes have been flattened by farm machinery. When I am out doing survey, I am acutely aware that the surface below my feet and in front of me is both permeable and ever-changing. Human construction and other kinds of alterations and modifications of land surfaces create new temporary surfaces, which later, through processes of renovation, abandonment, erosion, and deterioration, become buried, changed, and altered once again. What we see when we are out on survey are amalgamations of multiple events, including accumulations and erasures. We are not walking *on* a singular surface. Rather, we are within a zone of mixed slow and fast geomorphological and anthropogenic alterations.

Multiple sites drawn on two-dimensional maps appear separate and closed off from another, as if each place was a separate entity and there were no regular communication and movements between places. Stacking multiple maps on top of one another to represent change through time also freezes these places in time, collapsing beginning, middle, and end, as if there is a presupposed plan or result in mind (Ingold 2011b:188). As Ingold argues, cartography renders life "still and silent" and creates objects (2011b:242). In a relational framework, all these places entangle together, in space and time, through dense webs of relationships. Such relations can never be depicted on a site map; they are neither lines connecting sites nor dendritic networks of communication or change through time (Ingold 2011a:151). To depict them in this way creates fixed destinations (named starting and ending points) and destroys the meaning and coherence of the relationships (Ingold 2011a:151, 155). What gives meaning to these relationships is movement itself, the ways in which people integrate prior knowledge and plans of action as they move and experience the world. Ingold talks about how people live "alongly" (2011a:154); as terrain is walked and surveyed, people know as they go. This way of knowing is repeatedly evidenced in the information our guides share with us while on survey. They tell stories about which families once farmed this remote terrain, when places were abandoned and why, how long and in what ways certain plots of land were modified and used through time. As they share with us these stories, we learn different place names, the locations of old and newer footpaths, town history, and details about many of the towns' current and former residents. As Ingold argues, people rely on, recall, and modify place names, histories, and experiences as they move through life and connect to one another (Ingold 2007:97–90). Those stories our guides share say more about the relationships among and between people than the abstracted path we depict on a map (Ingold 2011a:161). So, as Ingold (2011a:222) notes, the end result of survey is that we draw circles and lines on paper, but in so doing, we completely erase content and meaning.

In contrast, life is something people live *through*—it is movement, which writ large creates dense webs of entanglements (Ingold 2011a:168). Thinking about these things in terms of archaeological survey, I could not help but remember clawing through dense masses of intertwined and entangled spiderwebs, thorny brush, or thick vines while trying to get from one place to the next. That is, the methodological model that Ingold's interpretive framework evokes in my mind brought me back to the phenomenological experience of *doing* survey, crawling through brush, fording streams, sopping through mud, and scaling boulders. To be honest, sometimes doing survey in Nejapa is just like that. I, along with graduate students and local laborers who help us in the field, struggle through dense thorns and thick brushy, mean vegetation that relentlessly snags, scratches, and rakes at our bodies and equipment from every angle (Figure 1.1). Combine this with the heat, sweat, stinging eyes, and physical exhaustion, and it is hard not to think about what these worlds must have been like when people lived here. Imagining the structures present at any given settlement at different stages of building, occupation, and abandonment; viewing the land with varying degrees and kinds of cleared agricultural fields; and disentangling the crisscrossed old and new footpaths that connected old and new communities at different times and under different circumstances is difficult, yet tantalizing.

For this reason, when I consider how to effectively adopt a model that foregrounds relational ontologies in traditional archaeological settlement pattern survey, I always seem to gravitate back toward how persons and bodies in the past were constituted by the physical experiences of living in these worlds; in other words, foregrounding phenomenological experience, history, action, and movement (Gosden 1994; Johnson 2012; Tilley 1994). The data that we traditionally create using survey methods fail to convey the raw feeling of the present and past acts of movement through the world. In this sense, it is the "doing" of survey in Nejapa that probably gives us our best way to begin to talk productively about how people in the past lived on,

FIGURE 1.1. Thick, thorny low-altitude vegetation (*above*) and moss in high-altitude pine/oak forest (*below*), both of which are common in the Nejapa region.

in, and through the world (Ingold 2011a:168). By taking the "doing" out of our reports and maps, we strip out some of our most evocative observations and limit our potential interpretations. Sites with obvious building foundations and older ceramics mean so much more when you also hear about the family that once lived, raised children, and farmed there. Often we only hear such stories when we are standing in particular places, as we move from place to place and see particular places again, and when we closely observe each location's material traces. Place names abound for every hill, seasonal stream or watering hole, lowland, or pass between mountains. Much of the time, the names themselves carry important historical information: "Arroyo de Julián" is the seasonal stream where Julián used to plant; "Mango de Genáro" is the land around the small grove of mango trees that once belonged to Genáro (and now likely belongs to one of his children or grandchildren). Footpaths in the forests wind back and forth, often connecting older, long-abandoned ranches and farmlands to newly cleared land. The evidence fits together into a set of historical relationships and local knowledge that helps us to contextualize and understand the material traces we see and study in the present. Such diversity, change, and movement are what we should expect for the distant past as well. Our interpretations can only be improved by recording all this information and considering the myriad ways that the landscape and human relationships have been modified and changed through time in both the ancient and more recent past.

Inhabiting the Enduring, Animate World

To understand changes through time in settlement choices in indigenous Mesoamerica, we need to try to understand how indigenous peoples connected themselves to one another, to nonhuman agents, and to the rest of the world around them. In Mesoamerica, we need only look to ethnographic accounts to try to get a better sense of the world of indigenous peoples. For example, in a recent ethnography of Isthmus Zapotec peoples of Oaxaca, Anya Royce argues that the long-standing success of the Isthmus Zapotec community of Juchitan is based on Juchitecos' focus on achieving balance, which values both fluidity and calculated change built around a "solid core" of tradition and persistence (Royce 2011:5–7). Success in Juchitan is measured by both accomplishment and innovation, as well as the active fulfillment of social and ritual obligations to the benefit of the community. Both change and tradition are necessary to achieve balance and a healthy state. Thus, balance or equilibrium is a core concept of Mesoamerican cosmology and body ideology (López Austin 1984).

In the same way that communities and persons are created through action, Royce (2011:5) argues, so is the world in which people live. It is widely recognized that indigenous peoples of Mesoamerica considered caves, springs, mountains, and similar places to be sacred locales (Brady and Ashmore 1999; Maldonado Alvarado 2002; Taube 1986). Since life in one domain was/is contingent on life in the other, people in indigenous Mesoamerica in the past and the present have often visited such places as part of regular cycles of pilgrimage for ritual performances, petitions, and offerings; the ethnographic and archaeological record in Mesoamerica is replete with examples in which indigenous peoples in Mesoamerica made (and in many cases continue to make) presentations of offerings at places that are likened to doorways, thresholds, and borders between worlds (e.g., Brown and Emery 2008; Carrasco 1990; Greenberg 1981; Marcus 1989; Monaghan 1998; Parsons 1936; Royce 2011). The rituals performed in these places appease human and nonhuman spirits and thereby stave off disequilibrium, danger (in the form of spirits), and bad health (López Austin 1984).

Villages and architectural spaces derive their meaning and importance in part from conceptual linkages with sacred geography, such that architecture replicates sacred geography in constructed form: doorways act like caves, pyramids act like mountains (Ashmore 1999; Brady and Ashmore 1999; Taube 1986). Further, the materials used to construct and adorn houses also attest to the conceptual merging of the wild and the tame, and efforts to appease potentially dangerous outside spiritual forces (Harrison-Buck 2012; Royce 2011). Archaeologists, however, are just beginning to come to terms with the likelihood that indigenous peoples (in Mesoamerica and in other parts of the world) do not necessarily make a strong ontological distinction between ritually and spiritually charged natural landscape features and human-constructed space (Harrison-Buck 2012). The result is that both modified and unmodified landscapes, which we distinguish in our survey maps as occupied versus unoccupied lands, are meaningful parts of the animate cosmos (Ingold 2011a); both are alive. Caves are doorways, pyramids are mountains, and all are animate, powerful, and meaningful spaces in ancient human landscapes. People in Mesoamerica likely did not recognize a separation between nature and culture in the same way as it has been constructed in Western epistemologies (Harrison-Buck 2012; López Austin 1984:396). Instead, for Mesoamerican peoples, human and nonhuman worlds and agents were different, but always intricately and delicately interconnected. The actions of humans and nonhumans, taken together, were and are what help to shape both the transformation and creative continuity of past and present communities.

In our Nejapa survey region, at least thirty-one (31/103) sites that we have recorded were important locations where people left visible evidence of having interacted with nonhuman agents and otherworldly spiritual forces. The archaeological evidence in all these cases occurs in important natural landscape features such as caves, rockshelters, the bases of large freestanding boulders, or the bases of cliff faces with appealing characteristics such as interesting shapes, surface modification, or openings. In most cases, architectural enhancement or constructed features are absent at these sites, indicating that they were not typical residential sites but are also obviously closely connected to constructed landscapes.

Eleven sites include rock paintings. The most frequently painted symbols are hands, which were produced either by applying paint by pressing hands onto the surface or by blowing paint and leaving a negative handprint on the surface, typically in red paint (Figure 1.2). Other symbols include circles and dots (though not in specific combinations as typified by Mesoamerican writing systems for numbers). In one large-scale polychrome palimpsest, the paintings include flying monkey–like figures and anthropomorphic beings, including in one instance a traveler walking along a road carrying a bundle on his back using a tumpline, with an animal companion (Figure 1.3). Such panels balance the ritual and realistic into a seamless image, showing no boundaries.

Petroglyphs, which we have recorded at five locations, were either pecked or ground onto rock faces. In most cases, petroglyphs are located on freestanding boulders, and one lies flat in the bed of a seasonal stream. Frequent symbols include crosses, spirals, circles, and other more abstract elements. A carved stone stela was recovered from the site of Nejapa Viejo, a Classic period site (AD 500–800) with a large ceremonial plaza, monumental pyramid architecture, and fine pottery that was in some cases inscribed with Zapotec-language glyphs. This stone had been erected near the central ceremonial plaza at the site. The monument exhibits two phases of carving on either face of the stone. One side looks older and has a different patina than the likely more recent carved surface, which contains a Mesoamerican cosmogram (Figure 1.4).

On side A, the stone's pecked and ground elements are reminiscent of the spirals, circles, lines, and other abstract elements carved onto the freestanding boulder petroglyphs found in other sites across the region. That such symbols overlap in content with those found on freestanding boulders might help to explain why this particular stone was selected for erection in the site's central plaza and deemed suitable for recarving with a Mesoamerican cosmogram. It may have been very much alive. Indeed, the glyph featured in the center of the cosmogram is also present as a petroglyph at a site we recorded in 2013, located high in the hills, on a flat rock outcrop alongside a seasonal waterfall (likely a sacred space) along with dozens of other superimposed, carved elements. The blending of styles on the two faces of the stone seems less surprising after we see the palimpsest of carved symbols and glyphs from various periods of time at the mountaintop site.

Elsewhere we have found small rudimentary ceramic incense burners, offerings left by visitors to particular ritually charged places. In three instances, incense burners were placed at the base of freestanding boulders, remnants of offerings left during rites (Figure 1.5). At Piedra la Boluda, people placed incense burners on an adobe altar at the base of an enormous freestanding boulder near the top of the mountain, accessible only via

FIGURE 1.2. Painted hands, Mano de Gente, San Juan Lajarcia.

a narrow bridge of land. The stone is visible from low in the valley bottom, perched as if it is about to fall off the mountain at any moment. The stone is believed to be a sacred, powerful, and even dangerous place by local residents, though in common post-Catholicized fashion it has been linked with diabolical forces. The large numbers of expedient, low-quality ceramic incense burner fragments found at the site suggest that Piedra la Boluda may have been a frequently visited stop on a pilgrimage circuit in some earlier century. At the archaeological site of Los Picachos, people from a more recent epoch carefully placed complete ceramic *patojo* (boot-shaped) vessels in open-air locations on top of walls at the abandoned archaeological site as votive offerings.

All these locations—the archaeological sites, freestanding boulders, caves, arroyos, springs, waterfalls, and cliff faces—would have been visited as sacred places during pilgrimages or by ritual specialists on occasions that facilitated and acknowledged the direct communication between nonhuman and human agents. In some indigenous communities in Oaxaca, people continue to participate in regular pilgrimages to caves, springs, tops of mountains, old archaeological sites, and boundary markers (Russo 2005; Steele 1997). Many of these kinds of sacred places have now been linked with Christian calendrical events during which people leave offerings, burn candles, drink *mezcal*, eat, and dance to appease spirits as part of regular ritual circuits. Others, such as the modern Cueva del Diablo and the freestanding boulder known as La Mujer Dormida in Mitla, Oaxaca, continue to be visited by people and religious specialists to appease spirits, perform

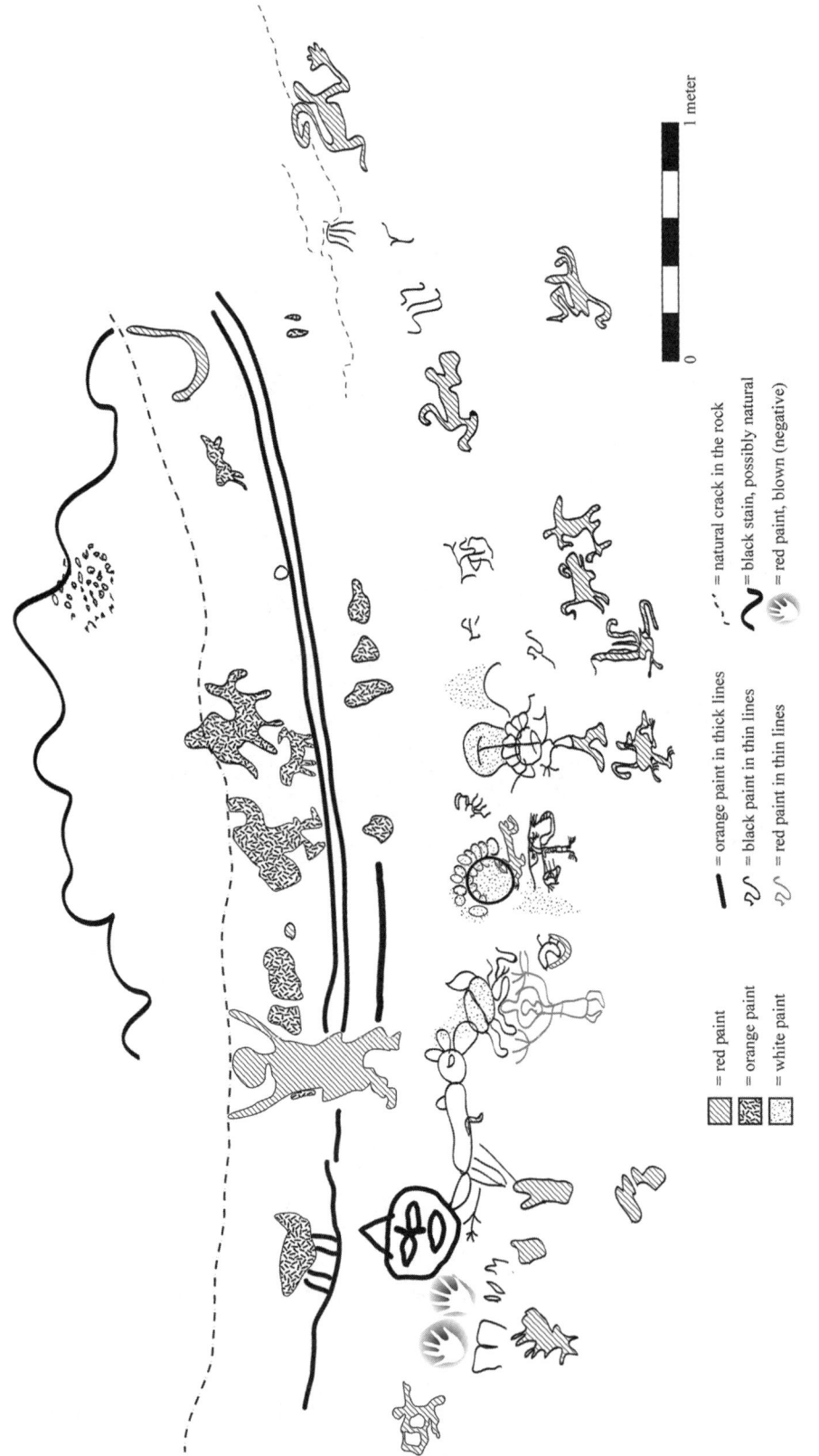

FIGURE 1.3. Drawing of a polychrome, palimpsest panel of rock art, Piedra de los Monos, Nejapa de Madero. Note the repeated zoomorphic flying figures (*lower right*) and the human traveler on a road who is carrying a bundle and is accompanied by an animal (*centered at the top*).

Side A　　　　　　　　　　　Side B

FIGURE 1.4. Carved stone monument recovered from the site of Nejapa Viejo, Nejapa de Madero.

FIGURE 1.5. Ceramic incense burner left as an offering in front of a freestanding boulder, Piedra la Boluda, Santa Ana Tavela.

healing rituals, request gifts, and seek guidance (Barabas et al. 2005). Often such places are simultaneously viewed as dangerous, wild places controlled by animal, ancestral, and diabolical spirits, which humans must treat carefully and demonstrably with respect and appreciation (places described to me in the field as "*delicada*") (Barabas et al. 2005; Brown 2004; Brown and Emery 2008).

At some of the archaeological sites we have documented, there is clear evidence that rituals continue. For example, we documented a possible boundary marker shrine where visitors, now usually only hunters or ranchers, continue to place pine fronds when they pass by. Another site, a small mesa with cliff faces on nearly all sides, is still regularly visited by petitioners seeking health and abundance. People describe it as an enchanted yet scary and somewhat dangerous place. In another instance, we visited a spring ("*ojo de agua*") in the mountains above San Francisco Guichina, which serves at the town's primary supply of drinking water. Here people from Guichina have constructed a small open-air amphitheater where they hold an annual fiesta. In addition to a Catholic mass, the fiesta includes food, drink, dance, a live band, and a formal procession back to town. Lit candles and saint images adorn the constructed altars built into niches in the stone above the spring, while the tattered remains of plastic bunting from last year's fiesta flutter in the breeze overhead.

One of the greatest challenges in the study of such sites is that they are often very difficult to date. The characteristics that make these places special have existed for thousands of years, and people likely visited these places intermittently over the course of many centuries. For example, painted hands are some of the oldest forms of rock art in the Americas, dating to as early as the earliest migrants to the New World. However, this does not mean that all painted hands are very old—the example of multiple, blown painted hands alongside the negative blown painting of a Historic period gun at the site of Bolsón de Mapimí in northern Mexico shows us that the style and image cannot be attributed to a specific or even single time and place (Turpin 2002). Handprints are easy designs to make. In some cases, judging by the sizes of handprints alone, it is obvious that some of the Nejapa region hands were produced by children. Even if children did not do the actual production (blowing the paint), they were clearly involved in the rituals surrounding the handprint production.

We have had long discussions in the field about what these handprints might indicate. Some Mesoamericanist scholars argue that hands were symbols of power or were important symbols of curing and health (Escalante Gonzalbo 2005). Most studies mention that they were probably produced as part of rituals, but of what kind and for what purposes remains speculation (e.g., Palka 2005). Although anecdotally we know that there are examples of painted hands from other regions of Oaxaca and across Mesoamerica, no one has yet done a study of painted hands that systematically evaluates their locations, associations, and distribution. The ceramic offerings found at the base of such rock art panels in most cases are generic incense burners that cannot be directly correlated with the production of the art itself.

I would argue, however, that the initial moment of production is only one part of the interpretation. If we look at all the sites where we have found paintings, carvings, and offerings (caves, springs, freestanding boulders, arroyos, mountains, and "abandoned" archaeological sites), we find that part of what makes these sites important and meaningful are their particular and unique locations, landscape, and sensory characteristics (see Brown Vega, this volume; Romain, this volume; Skousen, this volume). Such locations derive their meaning not only because of where they are (on a mountaintop) and how they look (shaped like an animal or human) but because of how they feel. In most cases, there is a clear association with water, air, and light; they are places with unique air patterns and moisture conditions, where brightness and darkness commingle. The rocks literally breathe from their mouths (caves), painted hands appear to climb, and mountains give birth to water. The painted rock faces are frequently found along narrow fissures in the mountains, in precisely the same places where seasonal water flows, vegetation is unusually lush and humid, and sound and smells are changed. Some sites are hidden, dark, shady, and moist, as in the case of rockshelters, while others are visible, exposed, windy, and light, as in the case of freestanding boulders perched on hills or peaks of mountains. During the rainy season in Oaxaca, these same hilltops often lie in the clouds, subject to torrential rains, lightning, and thunder, all of which were considered to have been made by animate beings.

These locations are visited and marked precisely because the weather, colors, moisture, and pungent smells confirm their life. The evidence of ongoing visits shows us that these animate places transcend time and fit into already well-established historical sets of entanglements that help to give them meaning (cf. Hodder 2012). Visitors from as soon as one year later to as many as thousands of years later would have seen these marked locations on their journeys, pilgrimages, and movements through the world either as part of group activities and processions or as individuals (Romain, this volume; Skousen, this volume). Such visits, as repetitive actions, confirm the enduring vitality of the animate world; at the same time, these types of activities underscore the problematic nature of differentiating occupied versus unoccupied spaces. To which period of human settlement should we assign these sites? Do we add them to all the settlement distribution maps, to one, or to none? To exclude them is to erroneously eliminate those spaces from the meaningful world of people and to ignore the webs of relationships in which they were and continue to be entangled, and to include them in all iterations of site maps is to perhaps to overemphasize or overconcretize their meaning, influence, and value.

Discussion and Conclusion

What, then, do survey data tell us about changing human landscapes? How can we better account for change through time in human worlds when we interpret archaeological survey data? All places, including those that lie outside the boundaries of constructed space, were *inhabited* (Buchanan, this volume). "Unoccupied" land is connected to living communities and constructed settlements throughout time and space in intricate and enduring ways. The drawings and interpretations that we produce as part of settlement surveys, when we depict and discuss all sites that were constructed or elaborated in particular time periods, will never accurately represent all of what was visited, revered, feared, and propitiated, or all of what was inhabited space. Many places, whether wild/tame, forest/town, dark/light, wet/dry, or dangerous/safe (or *both*), were likely considered part of the meaningful, sentient, animate world of people in the past. Conversely, when people (even new migrants) make decisions to construct and modify space within and close to already charged locations, it involves a renegotiation with an already animate, meaningful world. For example, when people in Nejapa moved into the hills and mountains or decided to alter and fortify mountaintop sites closer to long-propitiated, painted rock art panels, the reconfiguration of space and settlement choices says something powerful about the needs and wishes of both Nejapa residents *and* nonhuman agents.

Settlement pattern studies in Mesoamerica, premised as they are on structural/functional notions of categorization and boundedness, do not do an effective job of incorporating the possibility and ontological reality of interdigitation and relational complexity. We would do much better to think of *all* places as part of ancient inhabitants' living world. Using ethnographic and ethnohistoric texts on Mesoamerican cosmologies and body ideologies, we can begin to rethink how people saw themselves and experienced life, and how they wove their own paths among the enduring vestiges of past peoples. Whether positive or negative, safe or dangerous, these already animate places required respect and regular action on the part of people in the form of pilgrimage, ritual, and propitiation. We might do well to think about what people would have seen and felt during the years, decades, or centuries when sites were being constructed; we should take special note of previously occupied sites and places that have been marked in some way because they channeled otherworldly beings. We must also do a better job of conveying sensory characteristics and experiential information in our presentation of survey data; we should not strip our work of such phenomenological experience, leaving only our maps with dots or site-boundary "amoebas," structure counts, and population estimates. Ignoring the "doing" of survey not only removes ourselves from the production of data but also weakens our interpretations of the past people's lives and their choices to elaborate, modify, and inhabit particular spaces. We should collect stories and place

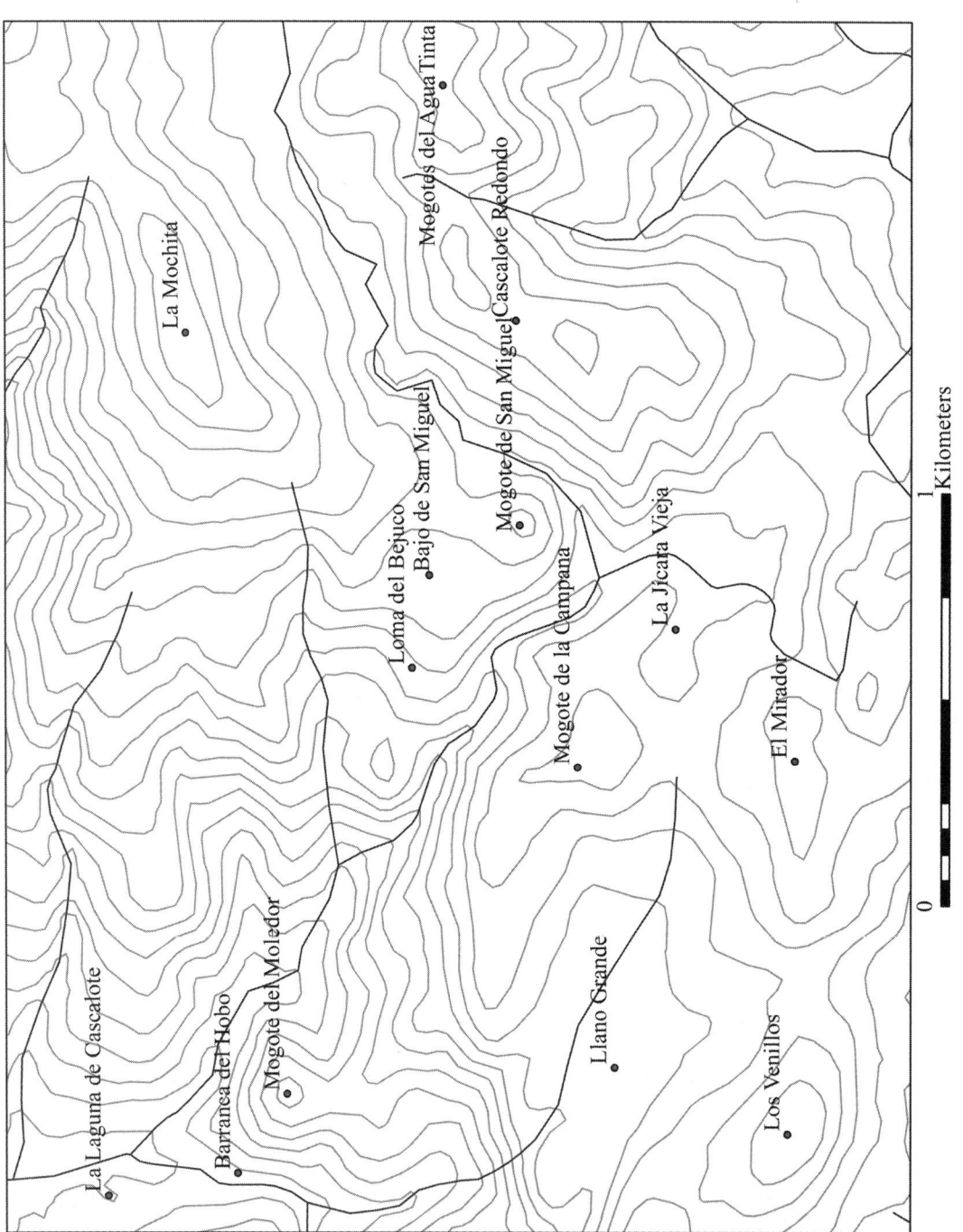

FIGURE 1.6. A recent version of our continuously updated place-name map, depicting territory that belongs to Santa Ana Tavela and San Juan Lajarcia.

names in addition to ceramic densities and architectural measurements, and include those stories and names as part of our data presentations and interpretive framework.

One of the maps we have been making and continually updating is a map of modern and historical place names (Figure 1.6). Sometimes the data are difficult to process, such as when two different names are given to us for the same place (by different guides or in different languages, which in our case are usually Zapotec and Spanish), or when two different communities use different names for the same hilltop (whose label do we apply?). But it is often this map that generates the most conversation in our public presentations. The conversation usually involves extensive discussions about the past and is inherently both "archaeological" and "interpretive." Our updated place-name map is also dynamic and more inclusive than a typical site map in terms of its production and sources of knowledge.

We must also remain aware that webs of entanglement are just as present in our scientific and humanistic enterprise as they were for indigenous Mesoamericans, and we need to try not to emplace such a great gulf between the two. Ingold's (2007, 2011a, 2011b) framework helps to highlight the problems in settlement survey information (boundedness and oversimplified categorization across both time and space) but also helps to guide us in considering alternative approaches to understanding change. For example, change through time might be better understood by more systematically recording and integrating a broader range of data; by expanding the scope of such data to include place names, oral histories, marked and unmarked living spaces, sensory characteristics, and experiential information; and by carefully noting the ways in which constructed and modified spaces gradually moved and changed. During our 2013 field season, we made the conscious shift in methodology to solicit and include more oral history in our descriptive data, to ask about historical land-use patterns in areas that do not have evidence of past human habitation, and even sometimes to record stories with a voice recorder. We made a systematic effort to record and plot all place names, and we began to keep daily GPS tracks of our own footsteps and paths. We also continued to map and note the locations of rockshelters, caves, large freestanding boulders, and springs, in addition to all the more typical, basic site documentation.

In the end, in presenting these data, I feel far more comfortable skipping the step of creating regional site maps organized by time period and through time. Rather, in my work, I prefer to discuss particular sites and landscapes that seem to have played especially important roles for people at different points in time, and place them within broader, purposefully nondelimited regional and interregional contexts. As exemplars, these sites demonstrate particular elements of what life may have been like for certain groups of people at specific points in time, but do so without creating false boundaries or clear delimitations. When considering relational ontologies, we are forced to think beyond the lines—and take into account precisely that which in traditional settlement survey would be outside the lines—inevitably opening up the realm of interpretation to a deeper account of meaning through time and space.

Acknowledgments

The data included in this chapter derive from my ongoing work in the Nejapa region of Oaxaca, Mexico. First and foremost, I thank the many government officials and community members with whom we have worked in the municipalities of Nejapa de Madero, Santa Ana Tavela, San Juan Lajarcia, San Bartolo Yautepec, and San Carlos Yautepec. I also express my gratitude to the Consejo de Arqueología of the Instituto Nacional de Antropología e Historia and the Centro INAH Oaxaca in Mexico for continued support of the Nejapa project. My research has been generously funded by several grants from Indiana University's New Frontiers in the Arts and Humanities program, as well as the National Science Foundation (grant #1015392). Finally, I thank the coeditors of this volume for inviting me to participate in the original Society for American Anthropology symposium, as well as the other contributors for their thought-provoking presentations. My work has been much improved based on reviewer comments and suggestions made throughout the editorial process. Nonetheless, and as always, any errors contained within the text are my own.

Note

1. The site counts included in this chapter reflect 2009 and 2011 data. Data from the 2013 field season are still being compiled but show similar patterns.

References Cited

Ashmore, Wendy
1999   Mesoamerican Landscape Archaeologies. *Ancient Mesoamerica* 20:183–187.

Barabas, Alicia M., Marcus Winter, María del Carmen Castillo, and Nallely Moreno
2005   La Cueva del Diablo: Creencias y rituales de ayer y de hoy entre los Zapotecos de Mitla, Oaxaca. *Cuadernos del Sur* 22:21–34.

Brady, James E., and Wendy Ashmore
1999   Mountains, Caves, Water: Ideational Landscapes of the Ancient Maya. In *Archaeologies of Landscape: Contemporary Perspectives*, edited by Wendy Ashmore and A. Bernard Knapp, pp. 124–145. Blackwell, Malden, Massachusetts.

Brown, Linda A.
2004   Dangerous Places and Wild Spaces: Creating Meaning with Materials and Space at Contemporary Maya Shrines on El Duende Mountain. *Journal of Archaeological Method and Theory* 11:31–58.

Brown, Linda A., and Kitty F. Emery
2008   Negotiations with the Animate Forest: Hunting Shrines in the Guatemalan Highlands. *Journal of Archaeological Method and Theory* 15:300–337.

Carrasco, David
1990   *Religions of Mesoamerica: Cosmovision and Ceremonial Centers*. Waveland Press, Long Grove, Illinois.

Escalante Gonzalbo, Pablo
2005   Manos y pies en Mesoamerica: Segmentos y contextos. *Arqueología Mexicana* XII:20–27.

Gosden, Chris
1994   *Social Being and Time*. Blackwell, Oxford.

Greenberg, James B.
1981   *Santiago's Sword: Chatino Peasant Religion and Economics*. University of California Press, Berkeley.

Harrison-Buck, Eleanor
2012   Architecture as Animate Landscape: Circular Shrines in the Ancient Maya Lowlands. *American Anthropologist* 114:64–80.

Hill, Jane H.
1992   The Flower World of Old Uto-Aztecan. *Journal of Anthropological Research* 48:117–144.

Hodder, Ian
2012   *Entangled: An Archaeology of the Relationships between Humans and Things*. Wiley-Blackwell, Malden, Massachusetts.

Ingold, Timothy
2007   *Lines: A Brief History*. Routledge, New York.
2011a *Being Alive: Essays on Movement, Knowledge, and Description*. Routledge, New York.
2011b *The Perception of the Environment: Essays on Livelihood, Dwelling and Skill*. Routledge, London.
2013   *Making: Anthropology, Archaeology, Art and Architecture*. Routledge, London.

Johnson, Matthew H.
2012   Phenomenological Approaches in Landscape Archaeology. *Annual Review of Anthropology* 41:269–284.

King, Stacie M.
2010   Informe final: Proyecto Arqueológico Nejapa/Tavela, 2009. Final report submitted to the Instituto Nacional de Antropología e Historia, Mexico City.
2012   Hidden Transcripts, Contested Landscapes, and Long-Term Indigenous History in Oaxaca, Mexico. In *Decolonizing Indigenous Histories: Exploring Prehistoric/Colonial Transitions in Archaeology*, edited by Maxine Oland, Siobhan M. Hart, and Liam Frink, pp. 230–263. University of Arizona Press, Tucson.

King, Stacie M., Elizabeth Konwest, and Alex Elvis Badillo
2012   Informe final: Proyecto Arqueológico Nejapa/Tavela, Temporada II, 2011. Final report submitted to the Consejo de Arqueología and the Centro INAH Oaxaca of the Instituto Nacional de Antropología e Historia, Oaxaca, Mexico.

López Austin, Alfredo
1984   *Cuerpo humano e ideología*. Universidad Nacional Autónoma de México, Mexico City.

Maldonado Alvarado, Benjamín
2002   *Geografía simbólica: Una materia para la educación intercultural en escuelas indias de Oaxaca*. Dirección General de Culturas Populares e Indígenas, Documentos del Centro de Información y Documentación, Mexico City.

Marcus, Joyce
1989   Zapotec Chiefdoms and the Nature of Formative Religions. In *Regional Perspectives on the Olmec*, edited by Robert J. Sharer and David C. Grove, pp. 148–197. Cambridge University Press, Cambridge.

Monaghan, John
1998   Dedication: Ritual or Production? In *The Sowing and the Dawning: Termination, Dedication, and Transformation in the Archaeological and Ethnographic Record of Mesoamerica*, edited by Shirley Boteler Mock, pp. 47–52. University of New Mexico Press, Albuquerque.

Palka, Joel
2005 Rock Paintings and Lacandon Maya Sacred Landscapes. *PARI Journal* V (3): 1–7.

Parsons, Elsie Clews
1936 *Mitla, Town of the Souls, and Other Zapotec-Speaking Pueblos of Oaxaca, Mexico*. University of Chicago Press, Chicago.

Royce, Anya P.
2011 *Becoming an Ancestor: The Isthmus Zapotec Way of Death*. State University of New York Press, Albany.

Russo, Alessandra
2005 *El realismo circular: Tierras, espacios, y paisajes de la cartografía indígena novohispana, siglos XVI y XVII*. Instituto de Investigacioneds Estéticas, Universidad Nacional Autónoma de México, Mexico City.

Steele, Janet Fitzsimmons
1997 Cave Rituals in Oaxaca, Mexico. Paper presented at the 62nd Annual Meeting of the Society for American Archaeology, Nashville, Tennessee.

Taube, Karl A.
1986 The Teotihuacan Cave of Origin: The Iconography and Architecture of Emergence Mythology in Mesoamerica and the American Southwest. *RES: Anthropology and Aesthetics* 12:51–86.

2004 Flower Mountain: Concepts of Life, Beauty, and Paradise among the Classic Maya. *RES: Anthropology and Aesthetics* 45:69–98.

Tilley, Christopher
1994 *A Phenomenology of Landscape*. Routledge, New York.

Turpin, Solveig A.
2002 Rock Art as Propaganda: Spanish and Native Inscriptions in the Bolsón de Mapimí, Northern Mexico. In *Rock Art and Cultural Processes*, edited by Solveig A. Turpin, pp. 91–117. Special Publication No. 3. Rock Art Foundation, San Antonio, Texas.

2

Moonbeams, Water, and Smoke

Tracing Otherworldly Relationships at the Emerald Site

B. Jacob Skousen

One of the best-known origin stories of the Choctaw Indians of southeastern North America tells of an epic journey taken by their ancestors, who left their home in the west and headed east in the direction of the rising sun (Swanton 1931). They traveled day after day, carrying the bones of their deceased relatives, being led by a medicine man with a special pole that, at the beginning of each day, pointed out the path they were to follow. At long last, and just at the onset of winter, the pole instructed them to settle at the junction of three rivers, a place rich with resources. After enjoying a comfortable winter there and recalling the difficulty of their journey, the Choctaw decided to make this settlement their permanent home. To show their thanks to the sacred pole for safely guiding them on their journey, they constructed a mound to serve as the pole's final resting place. They called this mound *Nanih Waiya*. Other versions of the origin story similarly emphasize a place called Nanih Waiya (e.g., Brescia 1985; Swanton 1931) but claim that it was a hill or a hole in the ground from which several groups of people, including the Choctaw, emerged from the belly of the earth. According to these versions, these groups eventually left Nanih Waiya and settled in other regions, which led to the formation of separate native tribes throughout the Southeast (Swanton 1931).

Modern Choctaw Indians believe Nanih Waiya is a specific mound site located in present-day Mississippi. The site consists of two mounds. One is a rectangular platform mound with an associated earthen rampart, and the second is a conical mound penetrated by a moderate-sized hole (Brescia 1985; Swanton 1931). More importantly, modern Choctaw still see this site as an important, sacred part of their heritage (Carleton 1996; Nabokov 2006:47–51). For example, one origin account notes that those who emerged from the earth at Nanih Waiya "ever afterwards remembered the hill from the summit of which they first beheld the light of the sun" (Brescia 1985:12), and a more recent Choctaw writer described Nanih Waiya as "the center of the Choctaw Universe" (cited in Nabokov 2006:50). Furthermore, many Choctaw have returned to this site to remember and celebrate its place in their history. More ancient journeys to Nanih Waiya are implied by the remnants of "two broad, deeply worn roads or highways" that converged at the site's mounds (Swanton 1931:9). Sometime during the eighteenth and nineteenth centuries, unknown persons (presumably Choctaws) visited the site and left offerings on the mounds (Carleton 1996). Today local Choctaws periodically travel to Nanih Waiya to remember and revere its role as their "Mother" and recall the events that took place there (Carleton 1996; Nabokov 2006:47).

Clearly, journeys to Nanih Waiya had and continue to have significance and power for many Choctaws (and for many non-Indians as well; e.g., Nabokov 2006:47–51). Indeed, journeys of all kinds often have profound effects on the lives of travelers and nontravelers alike in that they afford encounters with a myriad of people, places, things, and memories (Basso 1996; Oetelaar 2012, this volume; Romain, this volume; Zedeño and Stoffle 2003). Following this vein, in this chapter I argue that repeated journeys to and from the Emerald site, an outlying mound center contemporaneous with the pre-Columbian city of Cahokia, generated a series of relationships that continually constituted Cahokia from AD 1050 to 1200.

This chapter is divided into four sections. In the first I introduce Tim Ingold's notion of meshwork (Ingold 2011) and "ghostly lines" (Ingold 2007:47–50). In the second I contend that these concepts illustrate how relationships were created during Native American journeys as well as how these relationships were variable, dynamic, and ever-changing. The third section draws on archaeological and ethnographic data to show that individuals repeatedly traveled or returned to the Emerald site, where they encountered elemental, ghostly traces—specifically moonbeams, water from a spring, and smoke from sacred fires—that linked and relinked individuals, otherworldly realms and beings, and temporalities. In the final section I argue that recurrent journeys, along with the continually negotiated and transformative relationships they engendered, were a crucial part in the rise and ongoing re-creation of Cahokia (e.g., Pauketat 2001). This process involved a view of the cosmos in which individuals from diverse regions, backgrounds, religions, and ethnicities could experience multiple dimensions and beings in special places (Baltus, this volume; Pauketat 2013a).

Meshworks, Lines, and "Ghostly" Lines

In the past decade Tim Ingold has developed a way of viewing the world that considers life to be a web of interconnected entities that is fluid, relational, and ever-changing (Ingold 2000, 2007, 2011, 2013). These entities are not static or singular, isolated from the rest of the world; instead, each is a line of "movement or growth" with no beginning or end (Ingold 2011:69). As individual lines issue forth, they pass, cross over, collide with, run alongside, and become intertwined with other lines, trails, and conglomerations of lines. The result is a field not "of interconnected points but of interwoven lines; not a network but a meshwork" (Ingold 2011:70). Since all entities within the world are caught up in a meshwork of relationships, each is actually a knot, bundle, field, or accumulation of multiple lines that is always in the process of becoming (Baires et al. 2013; Ingold 2011, 2013; Pauketat 2013b; Zedeño 2008). These entanglements of lines are inherently temporal in that past entanglements influence future ones. In Ingold's words, "the past is with us as we press into the future" (Ingold 2007:119), meaning that the links to and citations of past experiences and memories always contextualize the present in unique ways (e.g., Ingold 2000:238–240; Mills and Walker 2008; Van Dyke and Alcock 2003). Therefore, the key to understanding an entity or experience is to know which lines and movements are part of the entanglement, how they became entangled within other relational webs, the transformations caused by these entanglements, and how these transformations facilitate, enable, and afford ongoing movements and rebirth.

Adopting such a perspective demands a deeper inspection of the individual lines that constitute entities and experiences (Ingold 2007:41–52, 2013:132–139). Ingold provides a classification of lines to better comprehend their nature and effects. He distinguishes between two primary types: threads and traces. A thread is "a filament of some kind, which may be entangled with other threads or suspended between points in three-dimensional space" (Ingold 2007:41). A trace, on the other hand, is "any enduring mark left in or on a solid surface by a continuous movement" (Ingold 2007:43). Other kinds of lines include cuts, cracks, and creases, all of which have to do with the "materiality" of the surface and how it is disrupted or ruptured through movement (Ingold 2007:44). Ingold admits that these are not mutually exclusive categories, and we can further argue that lines within the same class are qualitatively dissimilar; each thread has a unique thickness, density, texture, and trajectory, and traces are etched in different surfaces at varying depths and orientations. Moreover, lines move at different speeds, have different histories, are multidimensional, and never entangle the same way twice. And, as expected, all these qualities change through time, space, and circumstance.

"Ghostly lines," according to Ingold, are distinct from the lines described above (Ingold 2007: 47–50). While threads and traces have "a real phenomenal presence in the environment, or in the bodies of those organisms that inhabit it" (Ingold 2007:47), ghostly lines do not. They are metaphysical and often invisible (e.g., the lines that connect stars in a constellation or the unmarked boundaries between territories) (Ingold 2007:47–49). Some ghostly lines may be "materialized" at first, but their presence is fleeting because they do not endure on or within certain surfaces, substances, and mediums (e.g., tracks in the snow melt, lightning bolts disperse, trails of smoke evaporate, and ripples in water diffuse). In a sense, then, ghostly lines are ephemeral, immaterial, or quasi-material, and are always in flux. While these lines defy classification into the primary groups mentioned above (they are traces of a kind but have no solid surface on which they can be carved [Ingold 2007:50]), I suggest that they provide a useful metaphor for viewing and understanding relationships created during Native American journeys: their ephemeral, not-quite-material quality indicates that the nature of the relationships themselves continually changes, as do their traces in the physical world. Later in the chapter I further argue that ghostly lines provide a useful way of visualizing and tracing the unpredictable, seemingly intangible, and constantly negotiated relationships between visitors, otherworldly realms, deities, and memories at the Emerald site.

Native American Journeys

Journeys were and still are an incessant and necessary part of Native American life, culture, and myth. Ethnohistoric and contemporary accounts reveal that Native American journeys are extremely varied, as are their meanings, importance, and effects (Blaeser 2003; Cave 2006; Hall 1997; Momaday 1969; Nabokov 2006; Oetelaar 2012; Zedeño and Stoffle 2003). Clearly, hunting, scouting, movements of war parties, migrations, trade, and forced removals or relocations—frequent occurrences in the recent past—qualify as journeys (Zedeño and Stoffle 2003). Some journeys, however, were deemed sacred due to the kinds of encounters and entanglements they generated (Blaeser 2003; e.g., Pauketat 2013a). One kind of sacred journey involved the physical travel of a person or group of people to a place where an important person lived or significant event occurred (Cave 2006; Deloria 2003; Nabokov 2006; Pauketat 2013a). An example of such a journey is recounted by Alfred Cave (2006), who describes the traveling of large groups of Native Americans from throughout the Southeast and Midwest to Prophetstown, a Native American town, to see Tenskwatawa, an early nineteenth-century Shawnee prophet. Visitors heard his teachings and participated in public gatherings and ceremonies, and many were converted to the new religious ideals and practices he taught (Cave 2006). Vision quests were another type of sacred journey practiced by many Native American groups, during which lone individuals traveled long distances in the hope of obtaining visions, advice, and power from guardian spirits, deities, or ancestors (Gill 2005; Hultkrantz 1987). Francis La Flesche recorded a narrative telling how two men from different clans, after being chosen for the office of chief, left the village to "seek for some sign of approval from the Supernatural"; "for seven days and six nights the men fasted and cried to Wa-kon-da" (Bailey 1995:72). Eventually, each man was visited by a stranger who offered his assistance. One of the men was taught how to make medicines for pains and ailments; the other received feathers as a symbol that his people would reach old age. In short, during their journey these men received special knowledge that ensured the strength and longevity of their tribe (Bailey 1995:73). In other cases, vision quests accompanied rites of passage or were meant to have a healing effect on sick patients (Kelly and Brown 2012; Zedeño and Stoffle 2003:66).

Perhaps most importantly, American Indian sacred journeys usually involve returning, remembering, and retelling (Blaeser 2003). Individuals return to certain places to remember people, practices, and events of the past, and it is only through these memories that the importance and sacredness of the journey becomes evident (Blaeser 2003; Deloria 2003; Gill 2005; Momaday 1969; Nabokov 2006; Oetelaar 2012, this volume). Furthermore, remembering, according to many Native American groups, is closely associated with physical movement. Not only does physically returning to places recall memories, but remembering itself is a movement through time and space (see Basso 1996; Blaeser 2003; Deloria 2003; Momaday 1969; Oetelaar 2012). For instance, Gerald Oetelaar (2012; this volume) argues that the Blackfoot Indians of the Northern Plains view their homeland as a series of places, each of which was the site of specific actions performed by an ancestral being. These places are marked and remembered through narratives that describe these actions. The Blackfoot have visited these places during annual pilgrimages for generations, and returning to these places allows them to remember and retell the narratives as well as perform specific ceremonies associated with each place. This process appeases the ancestral spirits, which ultimately ensures the well-being of the entire community. Thus, Blackfoot pilgrimages are not only the physical travels between places but also a process of remembering past events in the present.

Similarly, some Apache place names, formulated by Apache ancestors, describe specific places (Basso 1996). Thus, simply speaking a place name cites the ancestors and the reasons they made the name, and "gives a picture" of the place "just as it was a long time ago" (Basso 1996:12). Other place names reference events that occurred there. One place, called "Men Stand Above Here and There," was named after a man who unwisely forgot his Apache roots and instead adopted American mannerisms (Basso 1996:54). This place and its associated story were used to teach the importance of Apache heritage and tradition. One young Apache woman, for example, was told this story after she had violated traditional dress etiquette by wearing curlers to an Apache puberty ceremony. The effect of this story was so profound that whenever the young woman returned to or passed by this place, she remembered the story, her infraction, and the lesson she learned (Basso 1996:57). For the Apache, then, speaking place names or physically returning to the place itself evokes memories of the past, which in turn reinforces Apache morals and tradition.

In addition, the movements that define Native American sacred journeys—both the physical movements between specific places and the act of remembering past events and doings—are generative of unique kinds of entanglements and subsequent transformations. Indeed, ethnographies describe sacred journeys that merged all sorts of entities—including human and non-human persons, things, ancestors, otherworldly realms, and temporalities—which inevitably had profound impacts on those involved (Bailey 1995; Blaeser 2003; Cave 2006; Hall 1997; Momaday 1969; Nabokov 2006; Oetelaar 2012, this volume; Zedeño and Stoffle 2003; see also Baires et al. 2013; Lepper 2006; Pauketat 2013a). Each journey enabled a unique convergence of "fields" of relationships that included beings of all kinds, worlds, and temporalities, which when entangled caused significant transformations (e.g., Baires et al. 2013; Pauketat 2013a). Additionally, these convergences were continual, as many sacred journeys were often repeated in association with celestial events, annual hunting rounds, or changes in the seasons; some journeys may have been a regular part of everyday life that brought balance to the cosmos or facilitated community harmony (Blaeser 2003; Oetelaar 2012; Pauketat 2013a; Zedeño and Stoffle 2003). The relationships that were generated during sacred journeys were dynamic and ongoing—even each return journey facilitated engagements that were always slightly different than those of previous journeys. Furthermore, because these sacred journeys facilitated encounters with otherworldly dimensions, persons, and temporalities, the ensuing relationships were often seen as mysterious, immaterial, and volatile (Bailey 1995; Baires et al. 2013; Blaeser 2003; Lepper 2006; Momaday 1969). Thus, many of the relationships formed during some Native American sacred journeys resembled a ghostly line—they were fleeting, seemingly intangible, and renegotiated with each subsequent journey. While these relationships may not have always persisted as an enduring trace in the visible world, they lived on in the memories of travelers, who were likewise always in the process of becoming.

I argue that contemporary and ethnographic accounts of Native American journeys, such as those mentioned above, are suggestive of Native American journeys that took place in the past. Although using ethnographies to directly infer the meanings of ancient practices is problematic, it is likely that some broad themes, ideas, and views of the cosmos were common to many native peoples in the Eastern Woodlands (see Emerson 1997; Hall 1997; Lankford 2007a). In short, while each person would have interpreted a single journey differently, I maintain that ethnographies can allude to the sorts of general themes that may have affected an individual's experience. In this case, I suggest that the themes of returning to special places and encountering memories, human and nonhuman persons, and otherworldly dimensions—evident in more recent accounts of Native American sacred journeys—are revealing of sacred journeys to the Cahokia region about one thousand years ago. Again, while each individual's experiences during a journey were undoubtedly unique, such insights are useful when we try to comprehend and appreciate the experiences of those who traveled to the Emerald site.

Cahokia and the Emerald Site

The pre-Columbian city of Cahokia, located in the American Bottom just east of present-day St. Louis, was constructed at or around AD 1050 during what Timothy Pauketat (1997) has called the "Big Bang" (Figure 2.1). Within a few decades Cahokia spread to cover an area of over 13 sq km, a process that involved widespread landscape modification and the construction of more than one hundred earthen mounds, all as part of a planned city (Dalan et al. 2003; Fowler 1997; Romain 2015). New pottery, tool, and house construction styles appeared (Alt 2012). Additionally, Cahokia's population burgeoned to between 10,000 and 15,000 people, in part due to an influx of immigrants, particularly in the uplands east of Cahokia (Alt 2002, 2006; Pauketat 2003; Pauketat and Lopinot 1997). Cahokians traveled to, traded with, or somehow associated with groups throughout the Midwest; some Cahokians established settlements or outposts at distant places like Aztalan and Trempealeau in Wisconsin (Benden et al. 2010, 2011; Emerson and Lewis 1991; Richards 2003; Stoltman 1991). A new suite of supernatural themes, myths, ancestors, and worlds were co-opted by the Cahokian elite (Emerson 2003; Emerson et al. 2003; Hall 2006; Pauketat 2013a).

Pauketat has argued that Cahokia's abrupt and unprecedented rise was due to the constant engagement, citation, and entanglement of persons, spaces, objects, myths, and celestial movements and events (Pauketat 2008, 2010, 2013a; Pauketat and Emerson 2008). Building on Pauketat, I propose that sacred journeys were crucial in these configurations, as they mediated intersections between Cahokians, nonlocal visitors, otherworldly beings and domains, and memories. Individuals traveled to a number of special places in the greater Cahokia region to experience, become acquainted with, or remember these worlds, beings, and events (Pauketat 2005, 2010). Their experiences reinforced the power, grandeur, and mystique of Cahokia as well as altered their view of the cosmos, particularly as they moved through purposefully constructed landscapes that referenced or permitted encounters with these beings, places, and events (Dalan et al. 2003; Emerson 1997; Pauketat 2005). The stories and experiences of these visits almost certainly prompted additional movements of people into the region, especially during large gatherings, feasts, renewal ceremonies, and public mortuary spectacles (e.g., Fowler et al. 1999; Goldstein 2000; Pauketat 2010, 2013a; Pauketat and Alt 2003; Pauketat et al. 2002). In short, the sacred journeys of pilgrims, emissaries, traders, and individuals on vision quests may have paved the way for new groups to migrate to or visit the region, themselves contributing to Cahokia's continual formation.

The Emerald site, located 24 km east of Cahokia, was one of the special places where people, deities, otherworldly realms, and temporalities converged (Figure 2.1). The site consists of a two-tiered platform mound, plaza, and two lines of conical mounds situated atop a high ridge, all of which align to lunar standstill events that occur every 18.6 years (Pauketat 2013a; see also Finney 2000) (Figure 2.2). The uniqueness of this alignment suggests that people may have returned to or visited Emerald throughout its history. Recent archaeological evidence also supports this idea. First, the excavation of a number of structures by the Illinois State Archaeological Survey in 1998 shows that Emerald's primary occupation occurred from AD 1000 to 1150 (Pauketat 2013a:171). However, my recent analysis of these features and their pottery assemblages suggests that the occupation was somewhat sporadic. For instance, a number of seemingly contemporaneous, single-post structures were constructed several decades before AD 1050 (Figure 2.3). Occupation span estimates and structure rebuilds imply that some structures were continuously occupied for twenty to thirty years (approximately AD 1030 to 1050), while others were dismantled and abandoned after being used for less than a year. Later (around AD 1100) a few apparently contemporaneous wall trench structures were constructed near the ear-

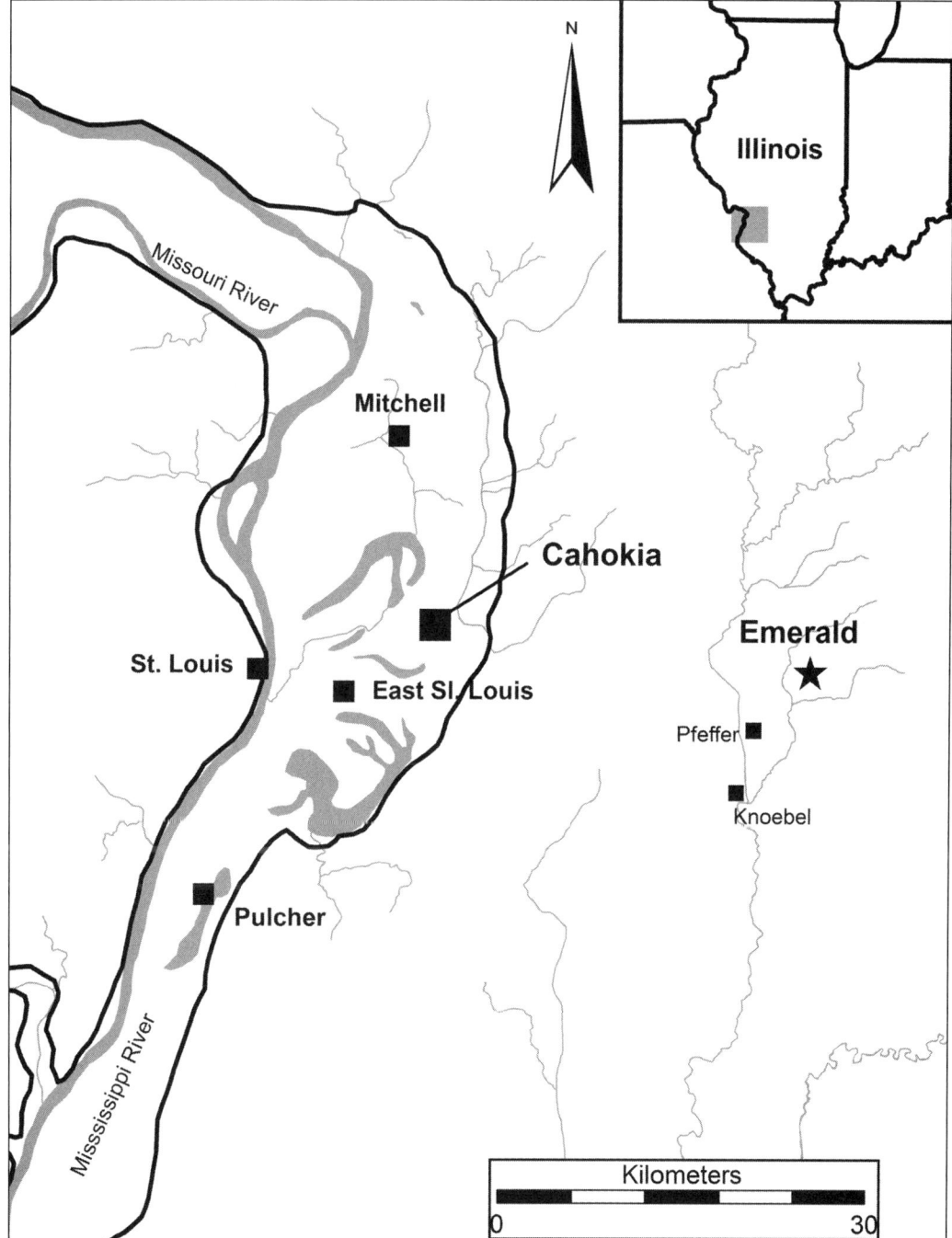

FIGURE 2.1. Cahokia, Emerald, and other selected sites in the American Bottom region.

lier structures (Figure 2.3). Occupation span estimates and rebuilds suggest that these later structures were inhabited for ten to twenty years. Once these structures were dismantled, however, the site was abandoned. After a seventy-year settlement hiatus, the site was again reoccupied around AD 1200 (Koldehoff et al. 1993; Woods and Holley 1991; Winters and Struever 1962). This final occupation, however, consisted solely of special structures on top of Mound 12 and limited

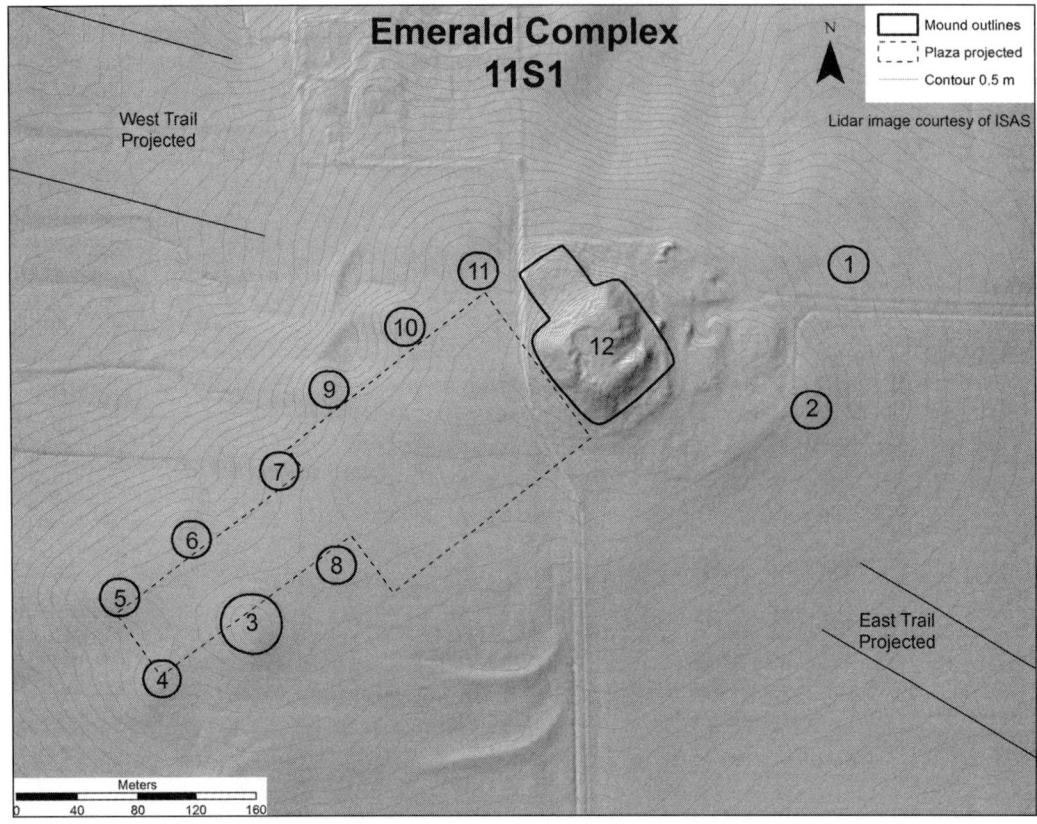

FIGURE 2.2. Overview of the Emerald site with mounds and possible plaza labeled (LiDAR image courtesy of the Illinois State Archaeological Survey).

additions to Mounds 2 and 12 (Skousen and Pauketat 2013; Winters and Struever 1962).

A second line of evidence for continued visits to Emerald is that many of the structures mentioned above contained the remnants of nonlocal pottery vessels made in southern Indiana and Illinois and as far south as Louisiana and Mississippi, implying that some of Emerald's population consisted of traders, pilgrims, or visitors from these distant regions. Third, Mound 12 was built in numerous stages, many of which were left open to the elements long enough for layers of laminated, water-washed silt to develop on the open mound surfaces before being covered again (Pauketat 2000; Skousen and Pauketat 2013). Finally, and perhaps most importantly, my own excavations have revealed the presence of an early nineteenth-century roadway that converges at Emerald (Skousen 2014). These excavations, as well as historical accounts and aerial photos, suggest that this roadway was once a pre-Columbian road or trail that connected Emerald to Cahokia (Skousen 2014; see also Moorehead 2000 [1922]:22; Porter 1974:34; Pauketat 2013a:Figure 7.9; Walton 1962:259). The presence of a pre-Columbian roadway not only indicates regular movements to and from Emerald but suggests that moving along it would have retraced and recalled earlier journeys.

This evidence suggests that people journeyed to Emerald many times throughout its history—visitors, pilgrims, and perhaps local residents likely came and went along formal roads and entryways, and while there built and rebuilt houses, constructed and renewed mounds referencing celestial phenomena, and witnessed rare lunar standstill events. For the remainder of this chapter, I focus on how relationships were formed and renegotiated between these visitors and otherworldly dimensions and entities during these repeated journeys to Emerald. In short, I suggest that these relationships were created by the continual encounters with and movements of

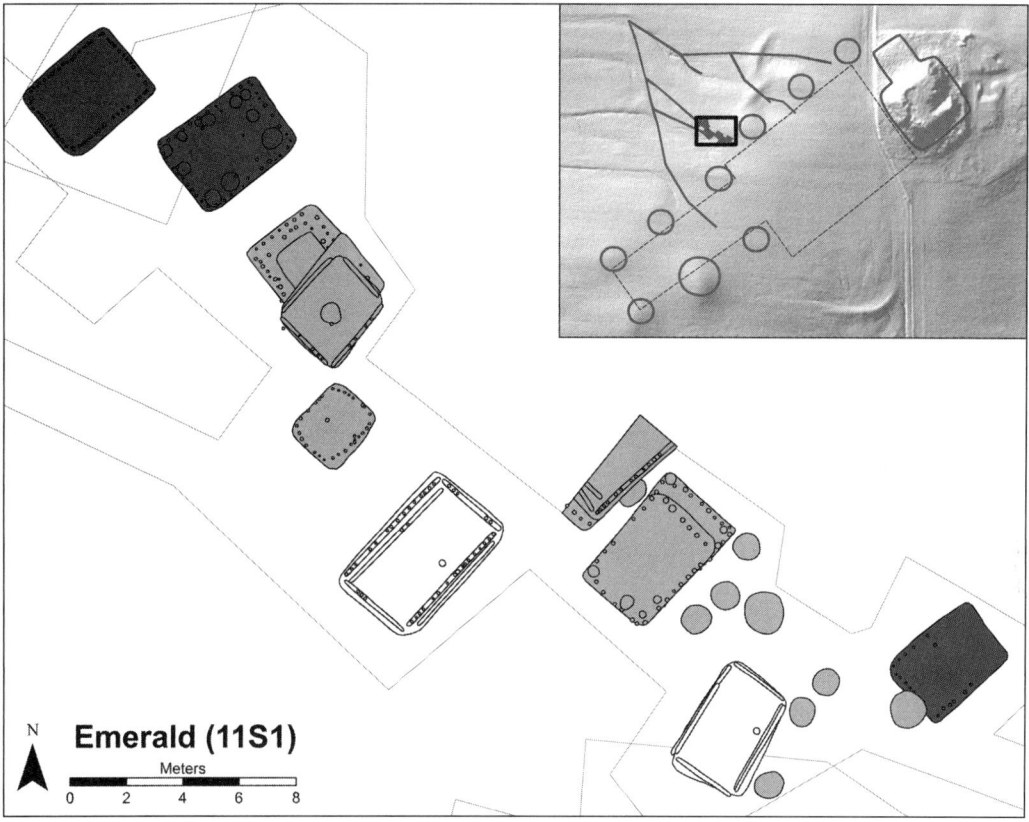

FIGURE 2.3. Plan view of structures excavated at the Emerald site: dark gray features represent structures built around AD 1030 that were occupied for less than a year; light gray features represent structures built between AD 1030 and 1050, with each group of structures representing an occupation of twenty to thirty years; white features represent structures built around AD 1100 that were occupied for ten to twenty years.

moonbeams, watery traces from a spring, and smoke from sacred fires. This notion of elements as agents of transformation parallels Baltus and Baires's (2012) argument that fire fashioned, mediated, and transformed relationships of power among and between people, places, and things in eleventh-century Cahokia, particularly transdimensional spheres and supernatural beings and ancestors. Moreover, these elemental traces mimicked Ingold's ghostly lines: they were momentary, unpredictable, and not quite tangible. Nevertheless, they created vital relationships that fueled Cahokia's rise and, due to their fleeting nature, had to be reformed again and again through subsequent journeys. Such relationships stimulated changes that profoundly affected the history of Cahokia and the entire Midwest; indeed, they constituted and spread a new view of the cosmos in which multiple deities and worlds could be experienced simultaneously at certain places and times.

Emerald's Ghostly Lines
Moonbeams

The moon was significant to the builders and inhabitants of Emerald and Cahokia (Pauketat 2013a; Romain 2015, this volume for a Hopewell example). Lunar standstill events were repeatedly cited through the purposeful construction of Emerald's landscape (Pauketat 2013a). For instance, Mound 12, two rows of small conical mounds, and a possible plaza were built to align to 53 degrees of azimuth, or where the moon reaches its maximum rising and setting position every 18.6 years (Pauketat 2013a:144). Even the natural ridge on which the site was built references this alignment and was probably further sculpted in ancient times to exaggerate this link (Pauketat 2013a:144).

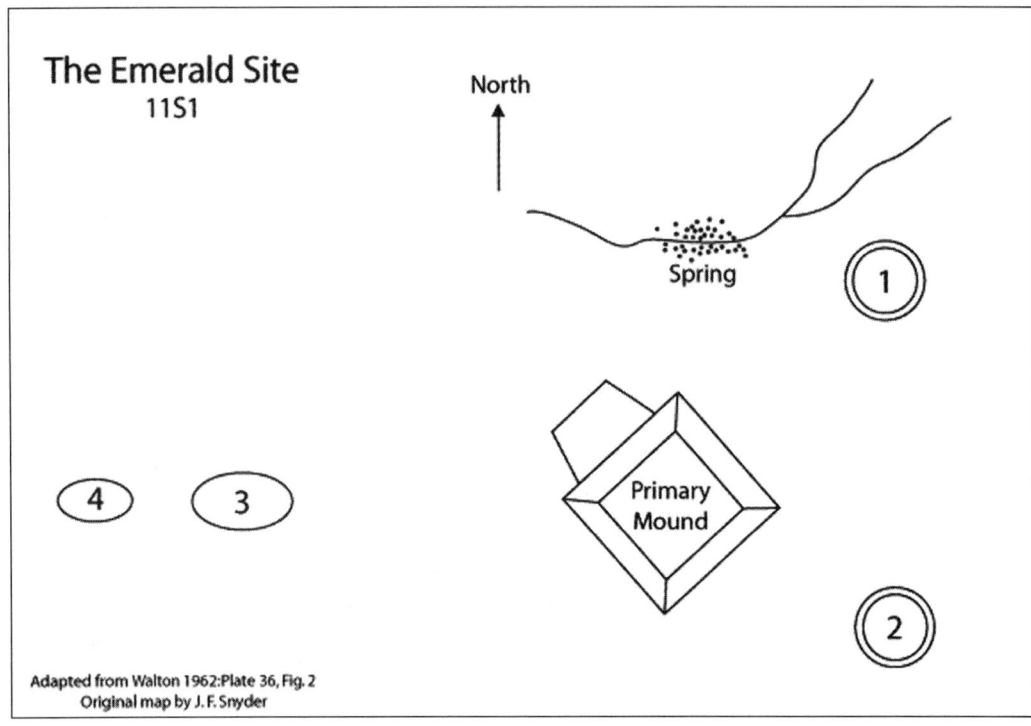

FIGURE 2.4. Plan map of the Emerald site emphasizing the location of the now-defunct spring, adapted from a sketch by John F. Snyder (courtesy of the Abraham Lincoln Presidential Library & Museum).

Furthermore, the nearby Brown Mound, located on a high knoll about 1.5 km northwest of Emerald, is perpendicular to Emerald's 53-degree axis; moreover, this small conical mound lies directly in line with the face of Emerald's Mound 12 (Pauketat 2013a:147), meaning it would have been visible from either terrace. Even structures at the site, mentioned earlier, generally conformed to the 53-degree alignment (Pauketat 2013a:146; see Figure 2.3). In short, the citation of lunar standstill events through mounds, the surrounding landscape, and domestic houses created a clear connection between earth and sky, and the moon in particular (Pauketat 2013a; see also Lepper 2004).

Referencing the moon in this way likely had to do with the fact that like many Midwestern and Southeastern native groups, some Cahokians saw celestial bodies, including the moon, as ancestors, deities, or powerful beings (e.g., Hall 1997; Lankford 2007b; McCleary 1997). Through the orchestrated construction of Emerald, the Cahokian elite created a new and poignant way for Cahokians and visitors alike to commune with, visit, or remember these beings through moonbeams, memories, and earthworks. More importantly, this link is reminiscent of Ingold's ghostly line. The moonbeams did not necessarily make a physical trace but consisted of threads of light that penetrated the darkness and illuminated and cast shadows along features etched in the landscape. Furthermore, these links between earth and sky were rare, as they occurred only once every 18.6 years. Still, these events were remembered when people traveled to Emerald, and specifically when people built or rebuilt structures, constructed or added to mounds, or moved through the landscape. Even memories of past journeys to Emerald were ghostly lines in that they were immaterial and also reconstructed the links between earth and sky each time they were recalled.

Springs and Watery Traces

At the base of the natural ridge on which Emerald was built, and next to a small stream feeding Silver Creek, laid a now-defunct spring or seep (Figure 2.4). It was first described by John Francis Snyder in 1909: "Near the bank of that rivulet, beneath the spreading branches of stately old elms and oaks, there gushed from the earth...a bold spring of clear, cold water in the days before the era of well-digging and corn-raising. It furnished the water supply of the colony of mound builders whose lodes were pitched all around it on both sides of the branch, as attested by the numerous hut rings and fire-places, obliterated only after many years of annual plowing" (Walton 1962:260). While Snyder's description suggests that the spring was used for subsistence purposes, it is likely that it was also a watery trace of special significance and, along with the natural orientation of the ridge (see Pauketat 2013a:145), may have been the reason that Emerald was constructed at this specific place.

According to ethnohistoric accounts, many native groups in the Southeast and Midwest saw springs, rivers, and caves as portals to the underworld and a place to attain spiritual power (Hudson 1976:128–130; Wagner et al. 2000). Through these conduits, underworld beings and creatures (e.g., the Horned Serpent and Underwater Panther) could visit the middleworld, and persons from the middleworld could access the underworld (Lankford 2004, 2007c; Reilly 2004). Thus, the water that flowed from the Emerald spring was a fluid trace that united these worlds and, like moonbeams, was a ghostly line. The water was quasi material, and its trace would not have been permanent due to variations in precipitation or modifications to the nearby catchment area; the volume and strength of water flow undoubtedly waxed and waned, likely disappearing altogether during the dry season and reappearing during the wet season, carving new traces in the landscape. As a result, the relationship between the underworld and middleworld was always in flux. Thus, the relationship between these visitors, worlds, and supernatural beings could be rekindled only through continual visits to Emerald or the recalling of memories of past journeys and encounters with the spring. Seeing the changes in the spring during a return visit would have likely altered people's perception of their relationship with the underworld and its associated entities.

Smoke and Sacred Fires

Two large, formal hearths were unearthed during excavations at Emerald. One of these hearths was identified on the summit of Mound 12 by Robert Hall in 1964 (Hall 1965:535). Recent excavations have shown that this hearth was associated with or possibly inside one of two religious structures, one of which was oriented to Emerald's 53-degree axis (Skousen and Pauketat 2013) (Figure 2.5). This rectangular-shaped hearth measured approximately 45 by 40 cm, and the heat oxidized the surrounding earth to a red color. The hearth contained charcoal, burned bone, and a few ceramic sherds (Robert Hall, 1964, excavation notes on file at the University of Illinois North American Archaeology Lab). Another hearth was discovered directly beneath Mound 2 during salvage excavations in 1961 (Winters and Struever 1962) (see Figure 2.2). The hearth was circular in shape and measured approximately 1 m in diameter (Winters and Struever 1962:86). The excavators claimed that "the walls had been lined at least twice with carefully smoothed clay" (Winters and Struever 1962:86), which suggests that the hearth was specially prepared. This hearth contained ash, the shells of two young turtles, the partial remains of a fawn, and pottery sherds (Winters and Struever 1962:87). Interestingly, the pottery recovered suggests that both hearths date to AD 1200, long after the original occupation of the site (Winters and Struever 1962; Skousen and Pauketat 2013).

The placement, construction, and contents of these hearths suggest that they were special, much like the sacred fires of Historic era native groups in the Eastern Woodlands (e.g., Hudson 1976:126, 371–372). Sacred fire represented the sun and upperworld and contrasted with underworld symbols such as rivers and springs (Hudson 1976:128; Treat 2005:194). Some groups believed sacred fire was sent by upperworld beings to the people below through lightning; additionally, smoke from these fires was a vaporous trace through which individuals could commune with upperworld beings and vice versa (Baltus and Baires 2012; Hudson 1976:126–127; Pauketat 2008:63). In some cases, smoke from sacred fires was seen as a "witness" or force that carried prayers to other realms, much like smoke from sacred pipes (Baires et al. 2013; Baltus and Baires 2012; Hudson 1976:318). In short, smoke was a temporary link between worlds and may have provided a way to communicate with otherworldly beings; fire itself was a transformative element through which this could occur (Baltus and Baires 2012). Fire and

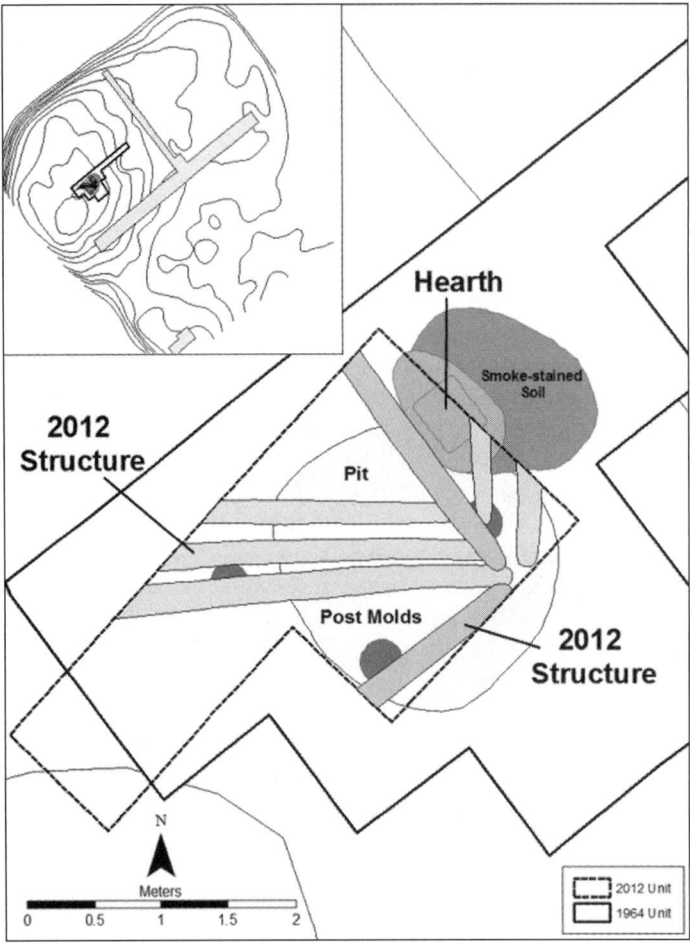

FIGURE 2.5. Plan map of 1964 and 2012 excavations on Emerald's Mound 12 (the inset shows the entire mound terrace).

smoke were both a kind of ghostly line that linked dimensions and beings. Like moonbeams, fire and smoke were immaterial traces in a sense; the fire burned and the smoke dissipated differently depending on the weather, the time of day, and the fuel that was consumed, meaning that these links between the worlds were always in flux. Additionally, the fact that these hearths date to Emerald's later occupation may suggest that those who returned attempted to renew or reenact the connections to otherworldly beings and places that were established there nearly two hundred years earlier, albeit through different means. Thus, kindling, feeding, and experiencing these fires and their smoke drew visitors into an ever-changing association with otherworldly places and beings that cited the activities of earlier visitors.

Discussion

The impact of recurrent journeys to Emerald as well as other special places throughout the greater Cahokia region is significant. From a relational perspective, Cahokia was continually constructed from the convergence and entanglement of people, practices, places, things, and their associated fields of relations (Alt 2006, 2012; Pauketat 2001, 2008, 2010, 2013a). Contrary to evolutionary, adaptationalist, and elite-centered models, there was never just one cause or founding event that caused Cahokia's emergence (e.g., Milner 1998; Smith 1978). Cahokia was always a work in progress, a place continually made through the movements, practices, and representations of people (including residents, visitors, captives, pilgrims, deities, and ancestors), places, things, temporalities, and dimensions, each constituted by diverse contexts, circumstances, and entanglements (Alt 2002, 2006, 2008; Pauketat 1997, 2001, 2003, 2008, 2010, 2013a; Pauketat and Emerson 2008; Baltus, this volume). Sacred journeys also mattered in Cahokia's emergence. Even if the number of a visiting party was relatively small, its movements may have prompted the travel of larger groups, all of which would become part of the relational webs that created Cahokia. In the end, revisiting special places within the Cahokian sphere (such as Emerson's [1997] civic and ceremonial "nodes"; see also Alt 2006), recounting the memories of past journeys to these places, and displaying the knowledge, rituals, and objects obtained during these journeys undoubtedly re-created Cahokia time and time again.

The Emerald site was clearly special, purposefully established at a place where worlds, beings, and memories merged (e.g., Lepper 2004). Thus, at Emerald and similar places, Cahokian elite were able to construct a new view of the cosmos while individuals, through their subsequent interpretations, reactions, practices, and movements, reconstructed Cahokia. Journeys to these special places—particularly when coupled with a suite of co-opted superhuman beings and mythical ancestors (e.g., forerunners of Red Horn, Corn Mother, or the Morning Star deity) (Baltus and Baires 2012; Emerson et al. 2003; Hall 1989, 2006; Pauketat 2005, 2010; Prentice 1986); Cahokia's unique city plan with lunar referents (Romain 2015; see also Dalan et al. 2003; Emerson 1997; Fowler 1997); the construction of mounds, monumental posts, and temples that doubled as portals to other worlds (see Hall 1997; Knight 1989; Skousen 2012; Wittry 1996); and special objects that embodied these persons and places (e.g., Ramey Incised jars, long-nosed god masks, rock art sites, flint-clay figurines, basalt celts) (Diaz-Granados and Duncan 2000; Emerson et al. 2003; Hall 1997; Kelly and Brown 2012; Pauketat and Emerson 1991)—created complex entanglements that have never occurred before or since, and thus comprised the foundation of Cahokia itself (Pauketat 2013a).

Conclusion

I have argued that journeys afford the convergence and entanglement of unique phenomena into a web of relationships that inevitably cause transformations. According to ethnographies and contemporary accounts, Native American sacred journeys are transformative primarily because of entanglements with human and nonhuman persons, otherworldly dimensions, and temporalities. The relationships created between these phenomena are comparable to Ingold's concept of ghostly lines in that the relationships are ephemeral, continually renegotiated, and seemingly immaterial (Ingold 2007:47–49). Such relationships were a crucial part of the Emerald site, a unique place in the greater Cahokia region that was regularly visited for nearly two hundred years. Visitors experienced a landscape that referenced multiple worlds, beings, and temporalities all at once—moonbeams and mounds cited the upperworld, water from a spring carved traces to the underworld, and sacred fires and smoke renewed links with upperworld beings. However, these traces and the relationships they created constantly changed; thus, each journey to Emerald brought about a unique convergence of worlds, beings, and memories that not only denoted a specific Cahokian cosmological order but continually changed how individuals viewed their place in the world. And just as these relationships were renegotiated with every journey, Cahokia was likewise renegotiated and re-created. Consequently, the return of visitors and the accompanying transformations that resulted from their journeys stimulated the spread of Mississippian practices, materials, and ideas that dramatically affected the historical trajectory of North America (Pauketat 2005).

Acknowledgments

Many thanks to Meghan Buchanan, Tim Pauketat, Bill Romain, Sarah Baires, Andrew Jones, and an anonymous reviewer for their helpful comments on an earlier draft of this chapter. The reanalysis of Robert Hall's 1964 excavations at Emerald Mound was funded by a summer research grant from the University of Illinois Urbana-Champaign's Department of Anthropology. Support for the 2012 excavations on Emerald Mound was provided by the Boston Historical Society's Religion and Innovation in Human Affairs Program, funded by the John Templeton Foundation. The excavations on the roadway and analysis of the 1998 excavations by the Illinois State Archaeological Survey (ISAS) were supported by the National Science Foundation under grant no. 1349157. And finally, thanks to Tom Emerson and ISAS for the use of the 1998 Emerald data. I take full responsibility for any omissions, errors, or misinterpretations.

References Cited

Alt, Susan M.
2002 Identities, Traditions, and Diversity in Cahokia's Uplands. *Midcontinental Journal of Archaeology* 27:217–235.
2006 Cultural Pluralism and Complexity: Analyzing a Cahokian Ritual Outpost. Unpublished Ph.D. dissertation, Department of Anthropology, University of Illinois, Urbana.
2008 Unwilling Immigrants: Culture, Change, and the "Other" in Mississippian Societies. In *Invisible Citizens: Captives and Their Consequences*, edited by C. M. Cameron, pp. 205–222. University of Utah Press, Salt Lake City.
2012 Making Mississippian at Cahokia. In *The Oxford Handbook of North American Archaeology*, edited by T. R. Pauketat, pp. 497–508. Oxford University Press, New York.

Bailey, Garrick A. (editor)
1995 *The Osage and the Invisible World: From the Works of Francis La Flesche*. University of Oklahoma Press, Norman.

Baires, Sarah E., Amanda J. Butler, B. Jacob Skousen, and Timothy R. Pauketat
2013 Fields of Movement in the Eastern Woodlands. In *Archaeology after Interpretation: Materials, Relations, Becomings*, edited by Benjamin Alberti, Andrew M. Jones, and Joshua Pollard, pp. 197–218. Left Coast Press, Walnut Creek, California.

Baltus, Melissa R., and Sarah E. Baires
2012 Elements of Ancient Power in the Cahokian World. *Journal of Social Archaeology* 12:167–192.

Basso, Keith H.
1996 *Wisdom Sits in Places: Landscape and Language among the Western Apache*. University of New Mexico Press, Albuquerque.

Benden, Danielle M., Timothy R. Pauketat, and Robert F. Boszhardt
2010 Early Mississippian Colonists in the Upper Mississippi Valley: 2009 Investigations at the Fisher Mounds Site Complex. *Wisconsin Archeologist* 91:131–132.
2011 The Mississippian Initiative: Year Two at Trempealeau. *Wisconsin Archeologist* 92:73–75.

Blaeser, Kimberly M.
2003 Sacred Journey Cycles: Pilgrimage as Returning and Re-telling in American Indigenous Literatures. *Religion and Literature* 35:83–104.

Brescia, William, Jr.
1985 Choctaw Oral Tradition Relating to Tribal Origin. In *The Choctaw before Removal*, edited by Carolyn Keller Reeves, pp. 3–16. University Press of Mississippi, Jackson.

Carleton, Kenneth
1996 Nanih Waiya: Mother Mound of the Choctaw. *Common Ground* 1 (1). http://www.nps.gov/archeology/cg/vol1_num1/mother.htm, accessed January 10, 2014.

Cave, Alfred A.
2006 *Prophets of the Great Spirit: Native American Revitalization Movements in Eastern North America*. University of Nebraska Press, Lincoln.

Dalan, R. A., George R. Holley, William I. Woods, H. W. Watters Jr., and J. A. Koepke
2003 *Envisioning Cahokia: A Landscape Perspective*. Northern Illinois University Press, DeKalb.

Deloria, Vine, Jr.
2003 *God Is Red: A Native View of Religion*. 3rd ed. Fulcrum, Golden, Colorado.

Diaz-Granados, Carol, and James R. Duncan
2000 *The Petroglyphs and Pictographs of Missouri*. University of Alabama Press, Tuscaloosa.

Emerson, Thomas E.
1997 *Cahokia and the Archaeology of Power*. University of Alabama Press, Tuscaloosa.
2003 Materializing Cahokia Shamans. *Southeastern Archaeology* 22:135–154.

Emerson, Thomas E., Randal Hughes, Mary Hynes, and Sarah U. Wisseman
2003 The Sourcing and Interpretation of Cahokia-Style Figures in the Trans-Mississippi South and Southeast. *American Antiquity* 68:287–314.

Emerson, Thomas E., and R. Barry Lewis (editors)
1991 *Cahokia and the Hinterlands: Middle Mississippian Cultures of the Midwest*. University of Illinois Press, Urbana.

Finney, Fred A.
2000 Theodore H. Lewis and the Northwestern Archaeological Survey's 1891 Fieldwork in the American Bottom. *Illinois Archaeology* 12:244–276.

Fowler, Melvin L.
1997 *The Cahokia Atlas: A Historical Atlas of Cahokia Archaeology*. Studies in Archaeology No. 2. Illinois Transportation Archaeologi-

cal Research Program, University of Illinois, Urbana.

Fowler, Melvin L., Jerome Rose, Barbara Vander Leest, and Steven A. Ahler
1999 *The Mound 72 Area: Dedicated and Sacred Space in Early Cahokia*. Reports of Investigations No. 54. Illinois State Museum, Springfield.

Gill, Sam D.
2005 *Native American Religions: An Introduction*. 2nd ed. Wadsworth, Belmont, California.

Goldstein, Lynne
2000 Mississippian Ritual as Viewed through the Practice of Secondary Disposal of the Dead. In *Mounds, Modoc, and Mesoamerica: Papers in Honor of Melvin L. Fowler*, edited by Steven R. Ahler, pp. 193–206. Scientific Papers Vol. 28. Illinois State Museum, Springfield.

Hall, Robert L.
1965 Current Research. *American Antiquity* 30: 535–341.
1989 The Cultural Background of Mississippian Symbolism. In *The Southeastern Ceremonial Complex*, edited by Patricia Galloway, pp. 239–278. University of Nebraska Press, Lincoln.
1997 *An Archaeology of the Soul: North American Indian Belief and Ritual*. University of Illinois Press, Urbana.
2006 Exploring the Mississippian Big Bang at Cahokia. In *A Pre-Columbian World*, edited by Jeffrey Quilter and Mary Miller, pp. 187–230. Dumbarton Oaks Research Library and Collection, Washington, D.C.

Hudson, Charles
1976 *The Southeastern Indians*. University of Tennessee Press, Knoxville.

Hultkrantz, Åke
1987 *Native Religions of North America*. Harper and Row, San Francisco.

Ingold, Tim
2000 *The Perception of the Environment: Essays on Livelihood, Dwelling and Skill*. Routledge, London.
2007 *Lines: A Brief History*. Routledge, London.
2011 *Being Alive: Essays on Movement, Knowledge and Description*. Routledge, London.
2013 *Making: Anthropology, Archaeology, Art and Architecture*. Routledge, London.

Kelly, John E., and James A. Brown
2012 In Search of Cosmic Power: Contextualizing Spiritual Journeys between Cahokia and the St. Francois Mountains. In *Archaeology of Spiritualities*, edited by Kathryn Rountree, Christine Morris, and Alan Peatfield, pp. 107–129. Springer, New York.

Knight, Vernon James, Jr.
1989 Symbolism of Mississippian Mounds. In *Powhatan's Mantle: Indians in the Colonial Southeast*, edited by Peter H. Wood, Gregory A. Waselkov, and M. Thomas Hatley, pp. 279–291. University of Nebraska Press, Lincoln.

Koldehoff, Brad, Timothy R. Pauketat, and John E. Kelly
1993 The Emerald Site and the Mississippian Occupation of the Central Silver Creek Valley. *Illinois Archaeology* 5:331–343.

Lankford, George E.
2004 World on a String: Some Cosmological Components of the Southeastern Ceremonial Complex. In *Hero, Hawk, and Open Hand: American Indian Art of the Ancient Midwest and South*, edited by Richard F. Townsend, pp. 207–218. Art Institute of Chicago, Chicago; Yale University Press, New Haven.
2007a Some Cosmological Motifs in the Southeastern Ceremonial Complex. In *Ancient Objects and Sacred Realms: Interpretations of Mississippian Iconography*, edited by F. Kent Reilly III and James F. Garber, pp. 8–38. University of Texas Press, Austin.
2007b *Reachable Stars: Patterns in the Ethnoastronomy of Eastern North America*. University of Alabama Press, Tuscaloosa.
2007c The "Path of Souls": Some Death Imagery in the Southeastern Ceremonial Complex. In *Ancient Objects and Sacred Realms: Interpretations of Mississippian Iconography*, edited by F. Kent Reilly III and James F. Garber, pp. 174–212. University of Texas Press, Austin.

Lepper, Bradley T.
2004 The Newark Earthworks: Monumental Geometry and Astronomy at a Hopewellian Pilgrimage Center. In *Hero, Hawk, and Open Hand: American Indian Art of the Ancient Midwest and South*, edited by Richard F. Townsend, pp. 72–81. Art Institute of Chicago, Chicago; Yale University Press, New Haven.
2006 The Great Hopewell Road and the Role of the Pilgrimage in the Hopewell Interaction Sphere. In *Recreating Hopewell*, edited by Douglas K. Charles and Jane E. Buikstra, pp. 122–133. University Press of Florida, Gainesville.

McCleary, Timothy P.
1997 *The Stars We Know: Crow Indian Astronomy and Lifeways*. Waveland Press, Prospect Heights, Illinois.

Mills, J. Barbara, and William H. Walker (editors)
2008 *Memory Work: Archaeologies of Material Practices*. School for Advanced Research Press, Santa Fe, New Mexico.

Milner, George R.
1998 *The Cahokia Chiefdom: The Archaeology of a Mississippian Society.* Smithsonian Institution Press, Washington, D.C.

Momaday, N. Scott
1969 *The Way to Rainy Mountain.* University of New Mexico Press, Albuquerque.

Moorehead, Warren K.
2000 [1922] *The Cahokia Mounds.* University of Alabama Press, Tuscaloosa.

Nabokov, Peter
2006 *Where the Lightning Strikes: The Lives of American Indian Sacred Places.* Penguin, New York.

Oetelaar, Gerald A.
2012 The Archaeological Imprint of Oral Traditions on the Landscape of Northern Plains Hunter-Gatherers. In *The Oxford Handbook of North American Archaeology*, edited by Timothy R. Pauketat, pp. 336–346. Oxford University Press, New York.

Pauketat, Timothy R.
1997 Cahokian Political Economy. In *Cahokia: Domination and Ideology in the Mississippian World*, edited by Timothy R. Pauketat and Thomas E. Emerson, pp. 30–51. University of Nebraska Press, Lincoln.
2000 Early Cahokia Project Excavations at the Emerald Site (11-S-2). Report submitted to Illinois Historic Preservation Agency, Springfield.
2001 Practice and History in Archaeology: An Emerging Paradigm. *Anthropological Theory* 1:73–98.
2003 Resettled Farmers and the Making of a Mississippian Polity. *American Antiquity* 68:39–66.
2005 The Forgotten History of the Mississippians. In *North American Archaeology*, edited by Timothy R. Pauketat and Diana DiPaolo Loren, pp. 187–211. Blackwell, Oxford.
2008 Founders' Cults and the Archaeology of Wa-Kan-da. In *Memory Work: Archaeologies of Material Practices*, edited by Barbara J. Mills and William H. Walker, pp. 61–79. School for Advanced Research Press, Santa Fe, New Mexico.
2010 The Missing Persons in Mississippian Mortuaries. In *Mississippian Mortuary Practices: Beyond Hierarchy and the Representationist Perspective*, edited by Lynne P. Sullivan and Robert C. Mainfort, pp. 15–28. University Press of Florida, Gainesville.
2013a *An Archaeology of the Cosmos: Rethinking Agency and Religion in Ancient America.* Routledge, London.
2013b Bundles in/of/as Time. In *Big Histories, Human Lives: Tackling Problems of Scale in Archaeology*, edited by John Robb and Timothy R. Pauketat, pp. 35–56. School for Advanced Research Press, Santa Fe, New Mexico.

Pauketat, Timothy R., and Susan M. Alt
2003 Mounds, Memory, and Contested Mississippian History. In *Archaeologies of Memory*, edited by Ruth Van Dyke and Susan Alcock, pp. 151–179. Blackwell Press, Oxford.

Pauketat, Timothy R., and Thomas E. Emerson
1991 The Ideology of Authority and the Power of the Pot. *American Anthropologist* 93:919–941.

Pauketat, Timothy R., Lucretia S. Kelly, Gayle J. Fritz, Neal H. Lopinot, Scott Elias, and Eve Hargrave
2002 The Residues of Feasting and Public Ritual at Early Cahokia. *American Antiquity* 67:257–279.

Pauketat, Timothy R., and Neal H. Lopinot
1997 Cahokia Population Dynamics. In *Cahokia: Domination and Ideology in the Mississippian World*, edited by Timothy R. Pauketat and Thomas E. Emerson, pp. 103–123. University of Nebraska Press, Lincoln.
2008 Star Performances and Cosmic Clutter. *Cambridge Archaeological Journal* 18:78–85.

Porter, James W.
1974 Cahokia Archaeology as Viewed from the Mitchell Site: A Satellite Community at AD 1150–1200. Unpublished Ph.D. dissertation, Department of Anthropology, University of Wisconsin, Madison.

Prentice, Guy
1986 An Analysis of the Symbolism Expressed by the Birger Figurine. *American Antiquity* 51:239–266.

Reilly, F. Kent
2004 People of Earth, People of Sky: Visualizing the Sacred in Native American Art of the Mississippian Period. In *Hero, Hawk, and Open Hand: American Indian Art of the Ancient Midwest and South*, edited by Richard F. Townsend, pp. 125–137. Art Institute of Chicago, Chicago; Yale University Press, New Haven.

Richards, John D.
2003 Collars, Castellations, and Cahokia: A Regional Perspective on the Aztalan Ceramic Assemblage. *Wisconsin Archeologist*, special issue: *A Deep-Time Perspective: Studies in Symbols, Meaning, and the Archaeological Record; Papers in Honor of Robert L. Hall* 86 (1–2):139–153.

Romain, William F.
2015 Moonwatchers of Cahokia. In *Medieval Mississippians*, edited by Timothy R. Pauketat and Susan M. Alt, pp. 33–41. School for Advanced Research Press, Santa Fe, New Mexico.

Skousen, B. Jacob
2012 Posts, Places, Ancestors, and Worlds: Dividual

Personhood in the American Bottom Region. *Southeastern Archaeology* 31:57–69.
2014 Ground-Truthing the Emerald Avenue. Paper presented at the 60th Annual Meeting of the Midwest Archaeological Conference, Urbana, Illinois.

Skousen, B. Jacob, and Timothy R. Pauketat
2013 Preliminary Report of the 2012 Excavations on the Primary Mound at the Emerald Site (11S1), Lebanon, Illinois. Report submitted to Illinois Historic Preservation Agency, Springfield.

Smith, Bruce D.
1978 Variation in Mississippian Settlement Patterns. In *Mississippian Settlement Patterns*, edited by Bruce D. Smith, pp. 479–503. Academic Press, New York.

Stoltman, James B. (editor)
1991 *New Perspectives on Cahokia: Views from the Periphery*. Monographs in World Archaeology No. 2. Prehistory Press, Madison, Wisconsin.

Swanton, John Reed
1931 *Source Material for the Social and Ceremonial Life of the Choctaw Indians*. U.S. Government Printing Office, Washington, D.C.

Treat, James
2005 *Around the Sacred Fire: Native Religious Activism in the Red Power Era*. Palgrave Macmillan, New York.

Van Dyke, Ruth, and Susan Alcock (editors)
2003 *Archaeologies of Memory*. Blackwell Press, Oxford.

Wagner, Mark J., Bethany J. Myers, and Charles A. Swedlund
2000 The Power of Place and Rock Art in Southern Illinois: The Austin Hollow Rock Site. *Illinois Archaeology* 12:161–198.

Walton, Clyde C.
1962 *John Francis Synder: Selected Writings*. Illinois State Historical Society, Springfield.

Winters, Howard D., and Stuart Struever
1962 The Emerald Mound Group and Village. *Living Museum* 23:86–87.

Wittry, Warren L.
1996 Discovering and Interpreting the Cahokia Woodhenges. *Wisconsin Archeologist* 77:26–35.

Woods, Williams I., and George R. Holley
1991 Upland Mississippian Settlement in the American Bottom Region. In *Cahokia and the Hinterlands: Middle Mississippian Cultures of the Midwest*, edited by T. E. Emerson and R. B. Lewis, pp. 46–60. University of Illinois Press, Urbana.

Zedeño, Maria Nieves
2008 Bundled Worlds: The Roles and Interactions of Complex Objects from the North American Plains. *Journal of Archaeological Method and Theory* 15:362–378.

Zedeño, María Nieves, and Richard W. Stoffle
2003 Tracking the Role of Pathways in the Evolution of a Human Landscape. In *Colonization of Unfamiliar Landscapes: The Archaeology of Adaptation*, edited by Marcy Rockman and James Steele, pp. 59–80. Routledge, London.

3

Adena-Hopewell Earthworks and the Milky Way Path of Souls

William F. Romain

In this chapter I consider Adena-Hopewell earthworks from a relational perspective. For decades, archaeologists have focused a great deal of attention on individual sites. But what if it was found that the full significance of certain sites unfolded in their relationships to other earthworks and even other dimensions? What if it was found that certain sites were entangled with each other and nonmaterial realms in such a way as to give rise to emergent properties that contribute to the deep meaning of these places and made such places special to their builders? Would that change how we think about Adena-Hopewell? Would that change the questions we ask?

In what follows, I propose that the Newark Earthworks, Great Hopewell Road, Sugarloaf Mountain, Serpent Mound, and others were part of a dynamic relational web. These sites span a distance of about 89 miles (143 km) across south-central Ohio. But the relational web I am referring to consisted of more than just a handful of prehistoric sites. It included nonhuman agents such as the sun and moon, Milky Way, and star constellations, as well as souls of the dead, living people, spirit entities, and special places in the Otherworld. Moreover, this relational field was not static, but rather, to quote Skousen and Buchanan (Chapter 1, this volume), was "encountered, experienced, and constructed through practices, performances, movements, and relationships of all kinds."[1] In this, the deep significance of any one site was contingent on others as well as celestial and nonhuman agents.

I suggest that the Newark Earthworks were a portal to the Otherworld that allowed for interdimensional movement of the soul during certain solar, lunar, and stellar configurations; that the Great Hopewell Road was the terrestrial equivalent of or a metaphor for the Milky Way Path of Souls, providing a directional component for soul travel to the Realm of the Dead; that Sugarloaf Mountain in Chillicothe was an axis mundi connecting cosmic realms; that multiple sites in the Chillicothe area were entangled with Sugarloaf Mountain, thus expanding the relational web temporally and spatially; and that Serpent Mound was a cognate for the Great Lowerworld Serpent, which guarded the Realm of the Dead. Each site was more than a cosmic symbol. Rather, each site "did" something in the sense of enabling, facilitating, guiding, constraining, or otherwise affecting the movements and experiences of people, living and dead. Each site was part of a "transdimensional relational matrix" (after Baires et al. 2013:212) wherein living people, souls of the dead, celestial bodies, and other agents moved in trajectories that intersected and entangled with one another, unfolded, and opened into new realms.

The idea that things are entangled, interconnected, and interdependent is not new. Written Buddhist teachings dating back to at least 200 BC explain: "Three cut reeds can stand only by leaning on one another. If you take one away, the other two will fall." The original sutra explaining the concept of *pratītya-samutpāda* (or dependent co-origination) is a bit more involved (Bodi

2000:607–609, Book of Causation, Sheaves of Reeds 67[7]); but one gets the idea.

Similar, and cutting against the grain of reductive and deterministic thinking, are recent efforts to understand the world in relational ways as expressed by ideas of nonlocality in quantum physics, emergent properties in complexity theory, neural networks in cognitive science, and holism in deep ecology. In anthropology and archaeology, a number of scholars have developed relational approaches, including networks (Latour 2005), material entanglement (Hodder 2006, 2012), meshworks (Ingold 2007, 2011), complex objects (Zedeño 2008, 2013), assemblages (Harris 2014; Fowler 2013 and others), and bundles (Pauketat 2013a, 2013b). There are subtle differences among these metaphors, but the underlying concepts are similar—things are entangled at the deepest ontological levels, and relational fields are in a continuous state of flux, resulting in new configurations.

In support of what I am proposing, I draw on astronomical data, LiDAR imagery,[2] computer planetarium simulations, aerial photographs, and archaeological and ethnohistoric data. Before proceeding further, however, I place things in context with a brief introduction to Adena and Hopewell and a consideration of individual sites. Then I demonstrate how together these bits and pieces made up a relational field that was greater than the sum of its parts.

Adena-Hopewell Earthworks

Our focus is with the Adena and Hopewell of south and central Ohio. There are taxonomic issues concerning the terms *Adena* and *Hopewell* (Applegate and Mainfort 2005; Brown 1992; Otto and Redmond 2008; Swartz 1971). For purposes of this discussion, however, and to maintain continuity with other literature, *Adena* and *Hopewell* are used as heuristic terms of convenience.

Adena flourished from about 500 BC to AD 100. It encompassed southern Ohio and parts of Kentucky, West Virginia, Indiana, and Pennsylvania, as well as occasional outposts farther east. Hopewell flourished from about 100 BC to AD 400. Hopewellian "cultures" are found across the Eastern Woodlands (Crab Orchard, Havana, Marksville, etc.), but classic Hopewell is situated in south and central Ohio.

There are recognizable differences between Adena and Hopewell. At the same time, however, there is considerable temporal and spatial overlap between the two, and it appears that Adena and Hopewell shared certain core beliefs and practices (Romain 2009), even if sometimes expressed in different ways.

The most visible and dramatic expressions of Adena and Hopewell are their monumental earthworks (Squier and Davis 1848; Thomas 1894). Adena mounds, which are conical in shape, range from barely noticeable rises on the landscape to enormous structures reaching roughly 70 feet (21 m) in height and more than 200 feet (60 m) across. Some mounds include burials, others do not. Where burials are found in Adena mounds it is often the case that more than one individual is interred. "Sacred circles" are another kind of Adena earthwork. These structures range from more than 200 feet (60 m) in diameter to much smaller. Most are simple earthen circles with an interior ditch and single opening through the perimeter wall. Some have a burial mound in the center of the circle. Often Adena circle earthworks are found in groups.

In many ways, Hopewell appears to be an elaboration of Adena, but there are differences. Hopewell earthworks are generally larger and more complicated than Adena. Hopewell submound mortuary structures are different from Adena, and Hopewell artifacts have a greater variety and complexity. The most concentrated and greatest number of Hopewell earthworks were located near the present-day city of Chillicothe, Ohio. The most intricate and complex group was at Newark, Ohio. Other major earthwork centers were situated at the present-day cities of Marietta, Portsmouth, and Cincinnati.

Hopewell earthworks include several kinds of mounds, such as conical, truncated pyramid, and loaf-shaped. Many mounds have one or more burials within. Another kind of earthwork built by the Hopewell were hilltop enclosures. This designation is something of a misnomer. Most are better described as flat promontories enclosed by perimeter walls.

Lastly, the Hopewell built geometrically shaped enclosures. Made of walls 5–10 feet (1.5–3 m) or more in height and 20–30 feet (6–9 m) wide at their base, Hopewell geometric earthworks

William F. Romain

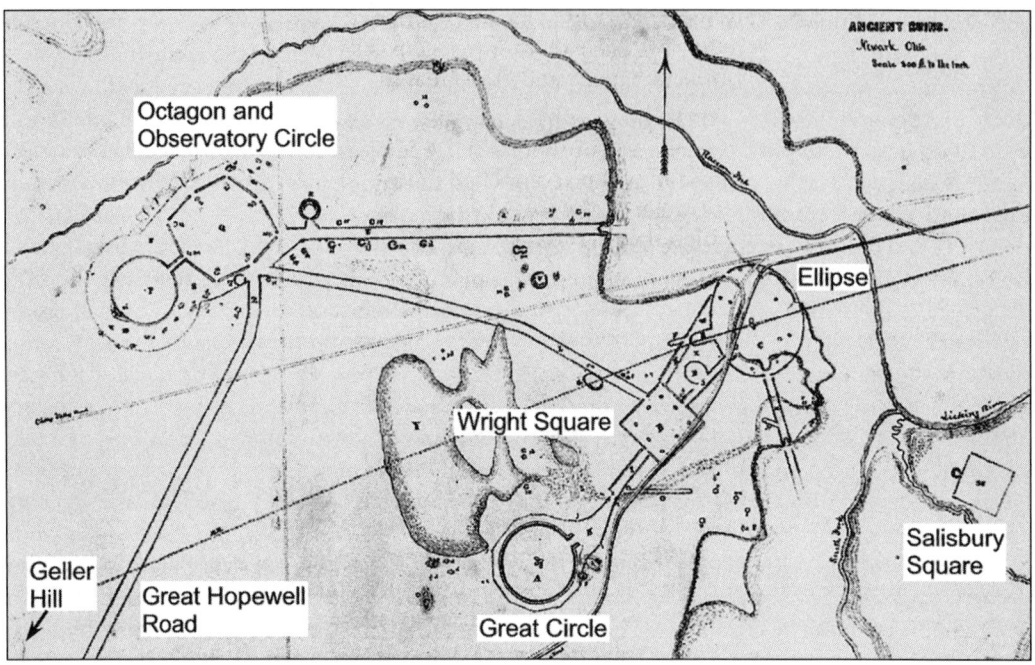

FIGURE 3.1. Annotated Salisbury 1862 map of the Newark Earthworks (image courtesy of the American Antiquarian Society).

typically enclose 15 to 50 acres (6–20 ha), with a couple that are even larger. Hopewell geometric earthworks come in different shapes, the most common of which are circles and squares. Some squares, such as the Liberty Earthworks, have relatively sharp right-angle corners, whereas others, such as Mound City, have rounded corners and ballooned-out sides, making their shape more ambiguous. Geometric earthworks can be single shapes, as at Mound City, or more complex designs that include a circle and square or a circle and octagon, as at Hopeton and High Bank, respectively.

Very large oval or ellipse-shaped earthworks occur at Newark and Turner. Also found in Hopewell are rectangles, irregular polygons, and a few shapes we have no technical name for. Several major earthworks are composed of three or more geometric shapes. Hopewell geometric earthworks incorporate specific design principles, including alignments to the sun and moon, the use of selected geometric shapes, and special units of length (e.g., DeBoer 2010; Eddy 1978; Hively and Horn 1982, 1984, 2010; Romain 1991, 1996, 2000, 2009).

As we see below, mensuration is significant.

For now, suffice it to say that every Hopewell earthwork I have assessed incorporates a unit of length I refer to as the Hopewell measurement unit (HMU), or an iteration thereof. This length is equal to about 1,054 feet (321.26 m). The length was first noted by Cyrus Thomas (1894:464) for the diameter of the Newark Observatory Circle. It was further applied to the earthworks around a century later (Hively and Horn 1982, 1984; Romain 1991, 1996, 2000; Romain and Burks 2008a). In addition to this length, greater and lesser multiples of the HMU were sometimes used.

The Newark Earthworks Complex

The Newark Earthworks Complex is located about 32 miles (51.5 km) northeast of Columbus, Ohio. It covers more than 4 square miles (1000 ha²) of a broad river valley at the confluence of Raccoon Creek and the North and South Forks of the Licking River. Most of the Newark complex has been obliterated by urban development, but from old maps, remaining earthwork remnants, and other clues, it is possible to gain a sense of what was. An early map of the Newark earthworks made by James and Charles Salisbury is shown in Figure 4.1. Although it is not an earthwork, we begin with Geller Hill, an important feature central to the design of the complex.

Geller Hill

Geller Hill is located about 1 mile (1,610 m) southwest of the Observatory Circle and Octagon earthwork (Figures 3.1 and 3.2). The feature is a glacial kame, about 35 feet (10.7 m) in height, 1,150 feet (350.5 m) in length, and 700 feet (213.4 m) in width at its base. In Hopewell times, Geller Hill would have been the most prominent feature on the flat plain where the earthworks are built. There are several knolls on the top of Geller Hill that in Hopewell times could have provided excellent vantage points of the earthworks and celestial events.[3]

As plotted from one of these vantage points (i.e., VP1 at the north end of Geller Hill), an isosceles triangle can be drawn between VP1, the center of the Octagon, and the center of the Great Circle (Figure 3.2b). This triangle has two sides each equal to 7 HMU (or 7,378 ± 10 feet) in length. The northwest leg of the triangle extends along an azimuth that is parallel to the Great Hopewell Road—the significance of which will become evident later.

From VP2 on Geller Hill (Figure 3.2a), on the night of the moon's maximum north rise, an observer would have seen the moon rise in the northeast, balanced between the Octagon and Great Circle. Further, this sightline would have intersected a sizeable lake or bog (ca. 150 acres [60 ha.], per Atwater 1820:Plate II) that appears to have been part of the original complex before it was drained in the 1800s. Together, observers at VP2, along with the lake-bog, moon, and earthworks, would have been entangled in a geometric relationship that unfolded in its full relational significance at celestially determined times. In this, trajectories of space, time, and human perceptions intersected and opened into new relational webs, as discussed below.

The Ellipse

The Ellipse earthwork (Figure 3.1) is part of the Newark complex. The earthwork has been mostly destroyed by urban development, and accounts differ as to how many mounds were originally located in the enclosure. David Wyrick's (1866) map made in 1860 shows seventeen mounds. We do not know how many people were buried in these mounds, as few records were made when the mounds were cleared away during the 1800s. An early report (Squier and Davis 1848:72) records that fourteen skeletons and large quantities of mica were found in one of the Ellipse mounds. Additional information comes from James and Charles Salisbury (1862:12–13), who reported that a mound situated in the northeast section of the Ellipse contained mica and "numerous skeletons." They further reported that an area in the southwest part of the Ellipse contained "many skeletons in a good state of preservation," and within the conjoined mounds at the center of the Ellipse was found a "tier of skeletons" accompanied by mica and copper objects. Given the large number of burial mounds and burials within the Ellipse, it is reasonable to presume that this enclosure was used as a burial ground.

As mentioned, many Hopewell earthworks use the HMU (or 1,054-foot) length in their design. The Newark Observatory Circle, for example, is 1 HMU in diameter (Thomas 1894:464), and the Octagon is designed around a square that is 1,054 feet, or 1 HMU, on each side (Hively and Horn 1982:S8). Where this becomes interesting is in the observation that if instead of drawing an octagon around a 1-HMU square, we draw an ellipse, the resulting figure will have the same shape and size as the Newark Ellipse as represented by the Salisbury map (Figure 3.3a–b).[4] Further, if we take the ellipse and square design just drawn and rotate it so its orientation is the same as that represented by the Salisbury map, one of the diagonal axes of the square will point to the summer solstice sunset while the other will point to the ground trajectory of the Milky Way on the night of the summer solstice, just after sunset (Figure 3.3b). Thus the Newark Ellipse burial ground is oriented and connected to celestial phenomena. Given its celestial orientation and significant numbers of burial mounds and burials, it may be that the Newark Ellipse was something of a staging area for the deceased before they began their journey to the Otherworld.

The observation that the Newark Ellipse is oriented to the summer solstice sunset and Milky Way and that the earthwork may also be implicated in the movement of souls from one realm to another might be dismissed as overly speculative

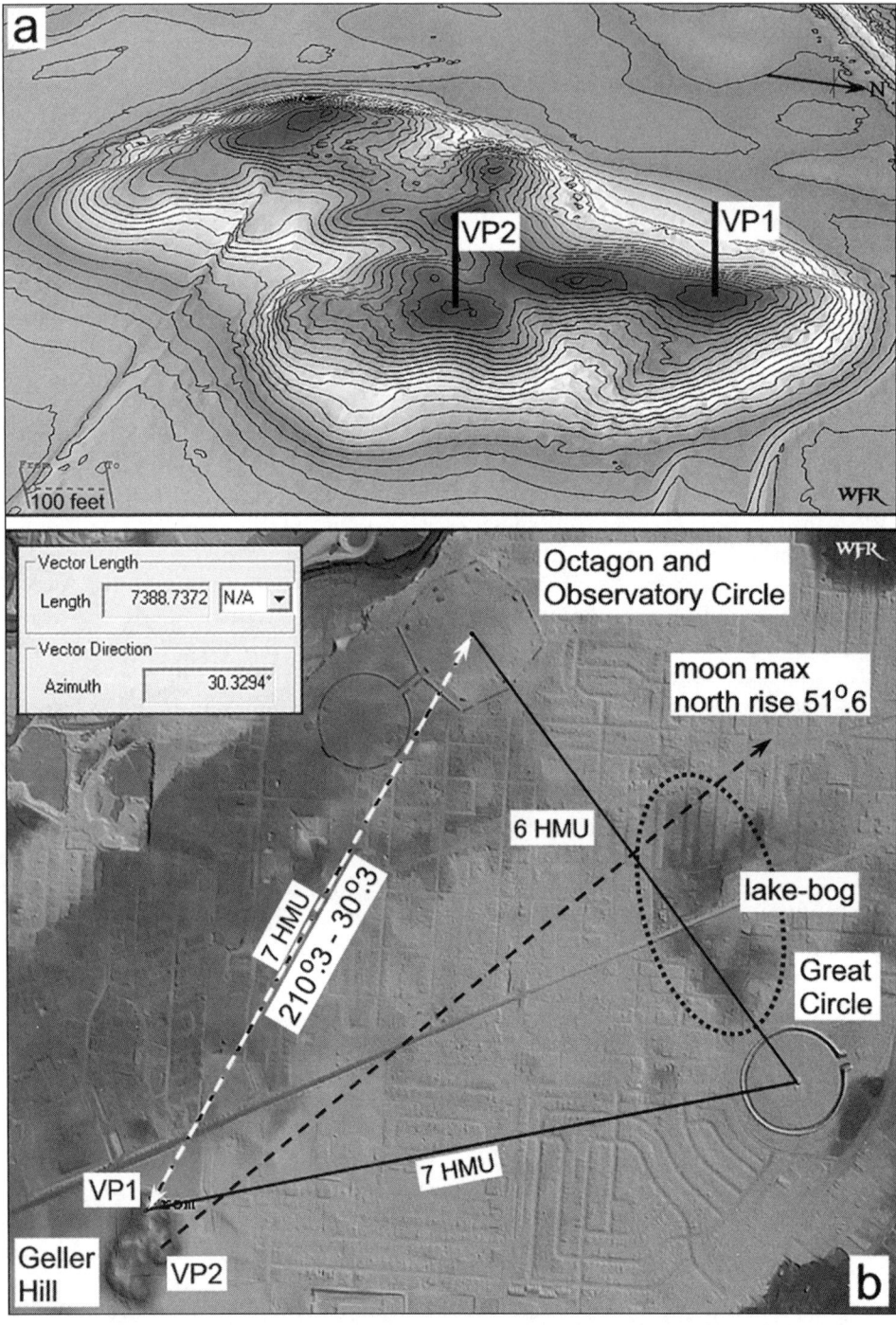

FIGURE 3.2. (*a*) LiDAR image showing locations for VP1 and VP2; (*b*) LiDAR image showing isosceles triangle between VP1, Great Circle, and Octagon. Lake-bog shown by dotted line, as indicated by lower LiDAR elevation represented by dark gray area.

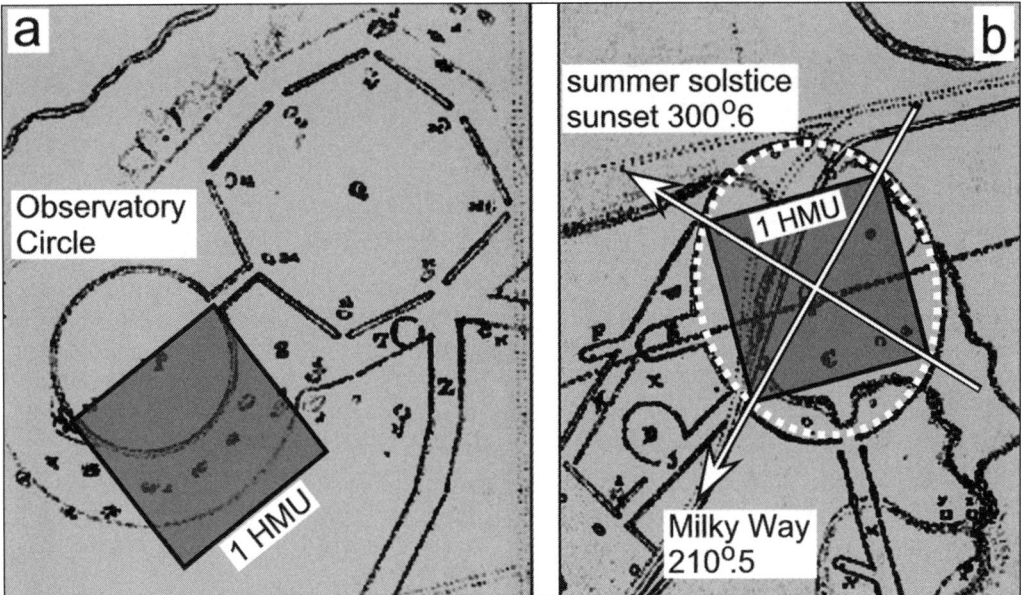

FIGURE 3.3. (*a*) Detail of the Salisbury 1862 map. The Salisburys (1862:23) give the diameter of the Observatory Circle as 1,060 feet. This is to within 4 feet of the Hopewell Measurement Unit (HMU) of 1,054 feet. Using the diameter of the Observatory Circle as a guide, we can draw a square with sides equal to that length. (*b*) Detail of Salisbury map. When an ellipse is drawn around a square that is 1,060 feet on each side (or ca. 1 HMU square), the result matches the shape and size of the Newark Ellipse, as shown. Further, the diagonal axes of the resulting ellipse are oriented to the celestial events shown (Salisbury map image courtesy of the American Antiquarian Society).

except for similar findings at other Hopewell burial grounds. The Turner Earthworks near Cincinnati, for example, feature a large Ellipse earthwork roughly 1,500 feet (457 m) by 1,000 feet (305 m), within which were found dozens of graves and more than a dozen burial mounds (Willoughby 1922). Analyses of aerial photos showing an extant section of the Turner Ellipse finds that the major axis of that earthwork was oriented along the Milky Way trajectory and its minor axis was oriented to the summer solstice sunset (Romain 2015a).

At Mound City, which is about 55 miles southwest of Newark, we find an earthwork best described as a square with rounded corners and ballooned-out sides (perhaps on its way to becoming an ellipse). Ground survey and photographic evidence (Romain 2000:127, 2009:92) show that the southeast-to-northwest diagonal axis across Mound City points to the summer solstice sunset. In addition, the northeast-to-southwest diagonal axis is aligned to the Milky Way trajectory. Like the Newark Ellipse, Mound City uses the 1 HMU in its design. More to the point, Mound City is sometimes referred to as a "city of the dead" in recognition of the large number burial mounds (~ 22) that have been identified within its perimeter walls (Brown 2012).

Octagon and Observatory Circle

By any standard, the Newark Octagon and Observatory Circle earthwork (Figure 3.4a) is an impressive monument. When observed in the 1890s by Thomas (1894:464), the southern part of the Octagon was mostly in original forest. Other sections had been plowed, but in no place were the walls less than 2.5 feet (76 cm) in height. The walls of the Observatory Circle averaged 1–5 feet (1.2–1.5 m) high. In the late 1800s the embankment walls of both features were built up by the Ohio National Guard in order to restore the earthwork to its height as recorded by Squier and Davis (1848).

No known burials are associated with the Octagon and Observatory Circle. Mounds are

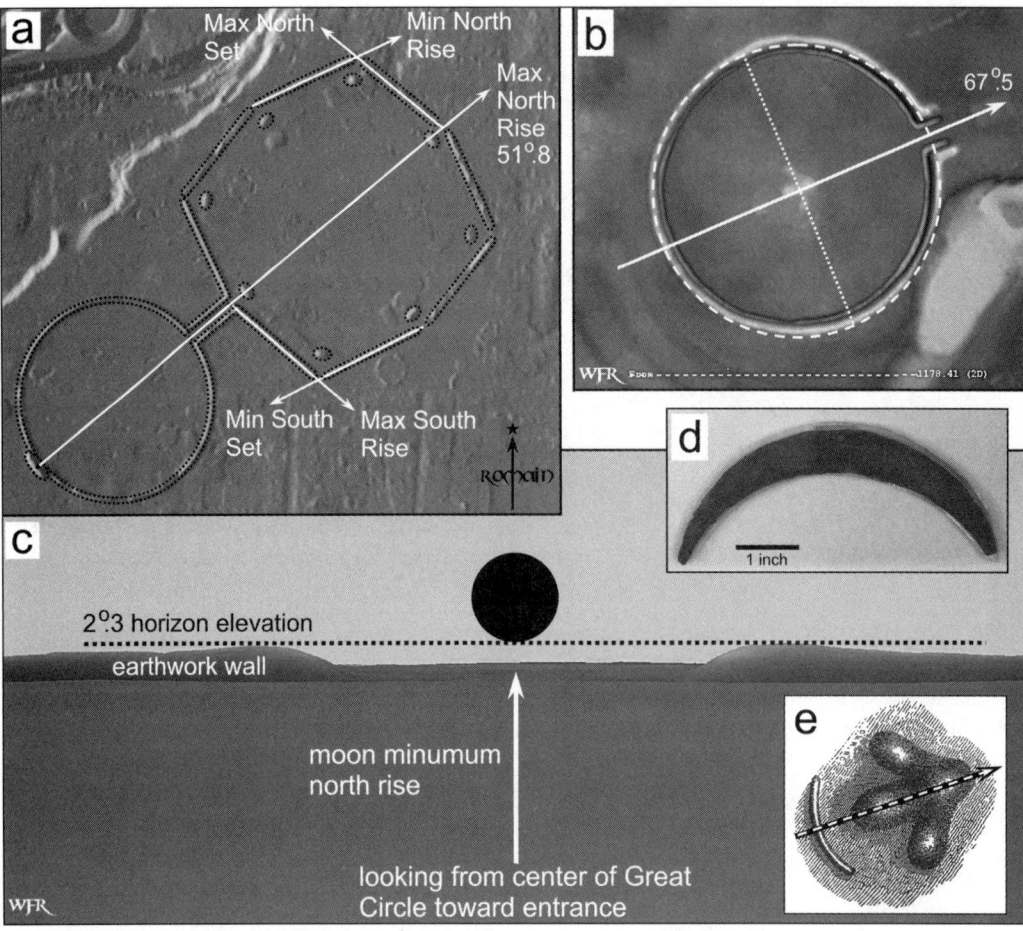

FIGURE 3.4. (*a*) LiDAR image of Newark Observatory Circle and Octagon showing core lunar alignments (after Hively and Horn 2013:Figure 2). (*b*) LiDAR image of Newark Great Circle showing south design circle (dotted line) and lunar alignment. (*c*) LiDAR image showing view from center of the Great Circle (wall heights as rendered by LiDAR program). (*d*) Crescent-shaped copper object found in Eagle Mound. (*e*) Squier and Davis's (1848:Figure 12) illustration of the crescent-shaped and Eagle mounds at center of Great Circle. Arrow added to show lunar alignment.

located at the vertices of the Octagon. However, coring into two of the mounds at multiple locations failed to reveal any evidence for burials, special soils, or man-made features within (Romain 2005).

The Octagon incorporates multiple lunar alignments in its design. Figure 3.4a shows several of the core alignments.[5] The most dramatic of these—the alignment of the earthwork's major axis to the moon's maximum north rise—was discovered by astronomer John Eddy (1978:149). The others were found by Ray Hively and Robert Horn (1982).

The Great Circle

Figure 3.4b shows the Newark Great Circle. This earthwork is about 1,178 feet (395 m) in diameter with a deep interior ditch. When surveyed in the late 1800s, the perimeter walls ranged from 5 to 14 feet (1.5–4.3 m) in height (Thomas 1894:461). Some minor, mostly cosmetic restoration work has been done to the earthwork. Located in the center of the Great Circle is a mound that some people believe looks like a bird—hence the name "Eagle Mound."

Eagle Mound was dug into in the late 1800s by Isaac Smucker. Smucker (1881:266) reported finding an "altar" (likely a crematory basin) at the center of the mound containing "ashes, charcoal, and calcined bones." A more thorough excavation was made in 1928 by Emerson Greenman. Greenman found that the mound covered a series of postholes outlining what seems to have been a temple structure at its base. Situated in the center of the floor of this structure was a clay basin of the type typically used for cremations. Greenman (1928) did not report finding anything in the basin. However, he did note finding bits of mica, lithic debitage, projectile points, charred matting, a crescent-shaped object made of copper, and bone fragments on the floor. It is not known if the bone fragments reported by Smucker and Greenman are human, and unfortunately their present whereabouts is unknown. Given the occurrence of confirmed human remains associated with similar clay basins in other mounds (e.g., Mound City—see Squier and Davis 1848), however, it seems possible that the bone was human.

The major axis of the Great Circle is aligned to the moon's minimum north rise (using the center of the south design circle as the point of origin for the sightline). This alignment takes into account the height of the earthwork's walls on either side of the entrance (Figure 3.4c).[6] Based on nineteenth-century records of pre-restoration wall heights, the artificial horizon created by these walls likely reflects what was seen in ancient times to within tenths of a degree. Further, as Figure 3.4e shows, the longitudinal axis of the Eagle Mound and the underlying temple structure are both oriented to the moon's minimum north rise.

In addition to the lunar alignment of the Great Circle, Eagle Mound, and temple structure, two other findings support a lunar association for this earthwork. As mentioned, a copper crescent was found on the floor of the Eagle Mound temple. The object is about 5.5 inches (14 cm) in length (Figure 3.4d). While it is impossible to know with certainty, it may be that the object is a crescent moon symbol.

It is also the case that a low, crescent-shaped embankment or mound was originally situated to the immediate southwest of the Eagle Mound (Figure 3.4e). The longitudinal axis of the Eagle Mound bisects the crescent mound. And again, the crescent shape suggests a lunar association.

Great Circle: Observatory Mound Alignment

The core lunar alignments for the Octagon and Observatory Circle and Great Circle have been noted. There is an additional alignment between earthworks, however, that is relevant. That alignment extends between the inside entrance to the Great Circle and a feature known as the Observatory Mound. The Observatory Mound is located on the major axis of the Observatory Circle, at its southwest terminus (Figure 3.5a–d). As Figure 3.5a shows, the sightline between the Great Circle entrance and Observatory Mound is aligned to the summer solstice sunset to within three-tenths of one degree.[7]

The Observatory Mound is basically a platform mound built into the perimeter embankment of the Observatory Circle. The mound is about 10 feet (3 m) in height—which is several feet higher than walls of the Observatory Circle and about 3 feet (0.9 m) higher than the gateway mounds at the inside entrances of the Octagon. With reference to its pre-restoration height, Squier and Davis (1848:69) note that the mound was "eight feet higher than the general line of the embankment." According to Squier and Davis (1848:69), explorations into the mound found only "an abundance of rough stones." Since the Observatory Mound is situated on the major axis of the Octagon and Observatory Circle earthwork, a good view of the enclosure is offered from its summit. The height of the mound, however, may have served an additional purpose. LiDAR line-of-sight analysis (Figure 3.5d) shows that the height of the Observatory Mound allows it to be seen from the inside entranceway of the Great Circle, over the intervening perimeter wall of the Great Circle. Further analysis shows that the summer solstice sunset would have been visible over the Observatory Mound as viewed from the inside entrance of the Great Circle (Figure 3.5a.)[8]

The Great Hopewell Road

Another important feature of the Newark Complex is the Great Hopewell Road (Lepper 1995, 2006; Romain and Burks 2008b). Most of the road has been obliterated by plowing and urban development, although a small section survives today in a woodlot just north of the Newark-Heath airport. The Great Hopewell Road consists of

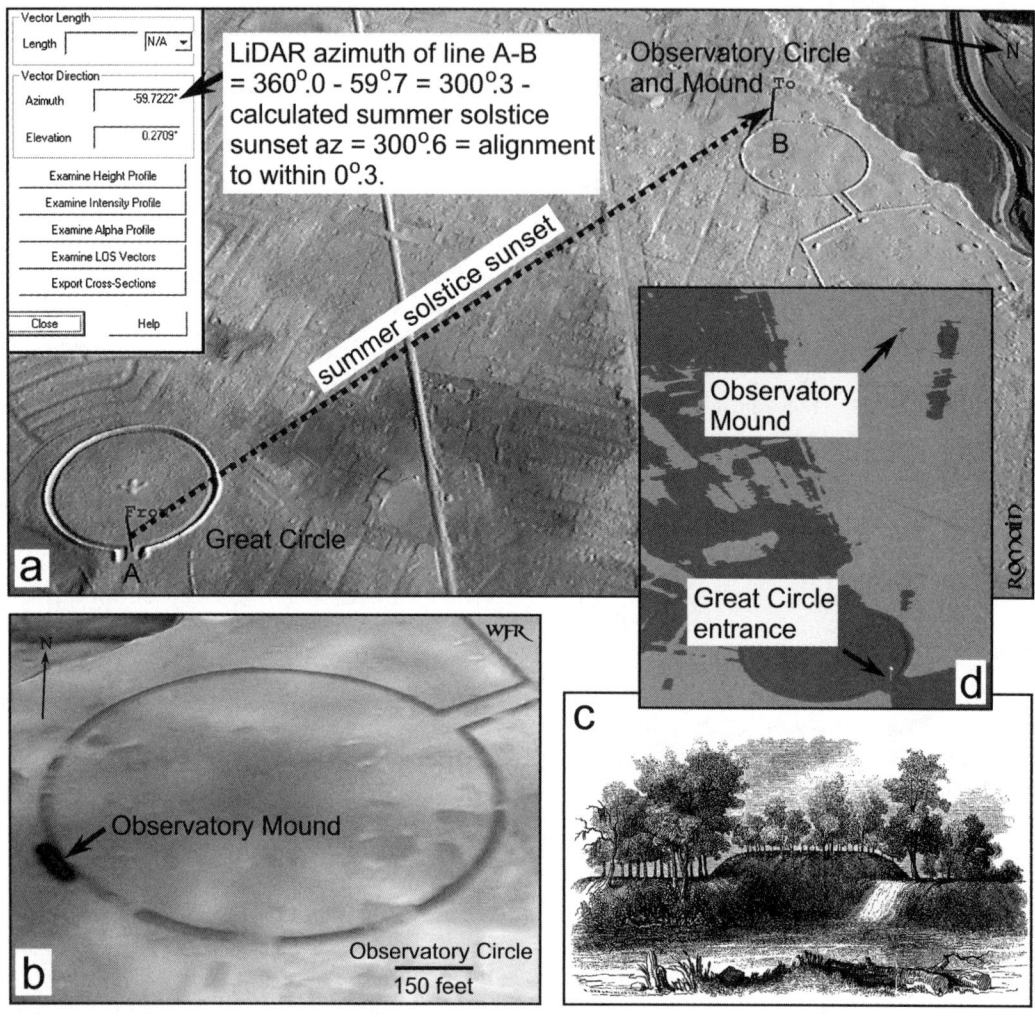

FIGURE 3.5. (*a*) LiDAR view of the Great Circle–Observatory Mound solstice alignment. (*b*) LiDAR image showing the Observatory Mound and Circle. (*c*) Squier and Davis's (1848:Figure 16) sketch of the Observatory Mound. (*d*) LiDAR line-of-sight analysis. Dark areas are visible from the inside entrance of the Great Circle.

two parallel embankments, each about 1.5–2 feet (50–60 cm) in height and 19–30 feet (6–9 m) in width, separated from each other by about 150 feet (50 m) (center to center). The embankments originally extended from near the Octagon to at least as far as Ramp Creek, about 2.5 miles (4,023 m) distant (Figure 3.6a–c). The Great Hopewell Road is not a road in the modern sense. LiDAR cross-section shows that it is concave in shape with parallel walls on either side of the concavity (Romain and Burks 2008b). Similar parallel-walled causeways are found at the Portsmouth, Marietta, High Bank, Hopeton, and Fort Ancient sites. In every instance that can be assessed by LiDAR or ground-truthed data, the parallel wall features at these sites extend along solstice azimuths (Romain 2000, 2004, 2015a).

In 1820 Caleb Atwater (1820:17) suggested that the parallel walls might connect to an earthwork on the Hocking River, roughly 30 miles (48 km) distant. More recently, Bradley T. Lepper (1995, 1998) suggested that the Great Hopewell Road may have connected to Chillicothe. The Salisbury brothers (1862) claimed to have traced the road for a total distance of 6 miles (9.6 km). And in 1931 aviator Warren Weiant Jr. reported seeing

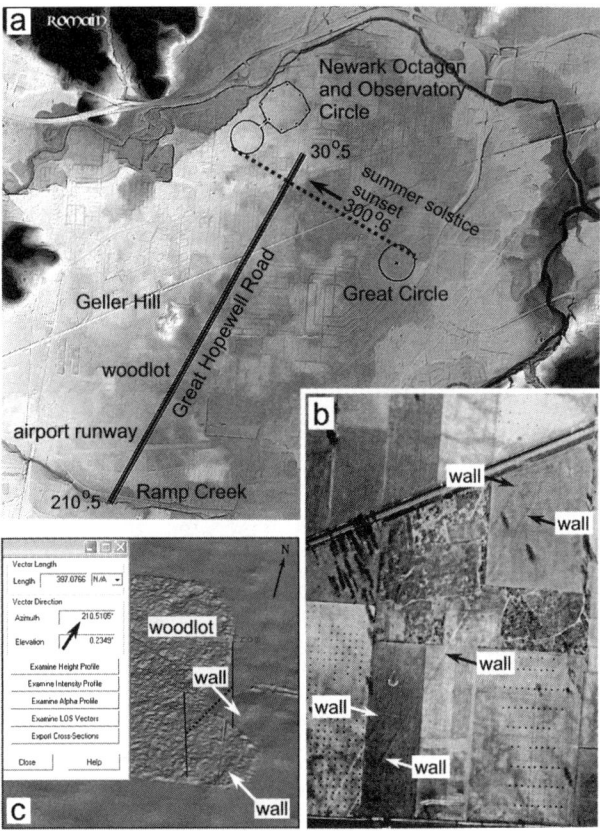

FIGURE 3.6. (*a*) LiDAR image showing trajectory of the Great Hopewell Road. (*b*) Dache Reeves aerial photo from 1934 showing section of Great Hopewell Road north of Ramp Creek. (*c*) LiDAR analysis of extant section of Great Hopewell Road in woodlot north of Newark-Heath airport showing that the road extends along an azimuth of 210.5 degrees.

what he thought was a road extending from Newark toward Millersport (Lepper 1998:129).

The idea is intriguing. However, no ground-truthed excavations, LiDAR, or geophysical data have found evidence for the road south of Ramp Creek, which is about 2.5 miles from the Octagon.[9] The Squier and Davis (1848:Plate XXV) map includes the notation "Parallels 2 1/2 miles long," which is the distance from the Octagon to Ramp Creek. This suggests that Squier and Davis did not survey the area south of Ramp Creek, or if they did, they found no evidence for the road. In contrast, and as already shown, old aerial photographs reveal long sections of the road north of Ramp Creek (even after plowing) (Figure 3.6b), a small section of the road is still visible on the ground and in LiDAR data north of Ramp Creek, and sections of the road can be seen as soil discolorations in Google Earth imagery.

That said, a physical connection between Newark and Chillicothe is not necessary to what follows. LiDAR analysis of the extant section of the Great Hopewell Road in the woodlot north of the Newark-Heath airport shows that the road extends along a trajectory of 210.5 degrees (Figure 3.6c). Several lines of evidence suggest that this trajectory was intentional. First, the trajectory of the road is parallel to a line that extends from VP1 on Geller Hill to the center of the Octagon earthwork (Figure 3.7d). As demonstrated earlier, VP1 appears to have been an important design point given its location at the apex of an isosceles triangle that connects two of the complexes' most important earthworks through their centers. Moreover, what this parallel-line relationship does is bring the road into a geometric relationship with the Octagon and Geller Hill.

Second, the trajectory of the road is orthogonal to the earlier-discussed summer solstice sunset sightline between the Great Circle and Observatory Mound to within one-tenth of one degree. The solstice azimuth between the earthworks is 300.6 degrees, while the trajectory of the road is 210.5 degrees (Figure 3.7d). The likelihood that the road would be oriented 90 degrees perpendicular to a solstice sightline that links two major earthworks due to chance is remote. More likely is that by making the trajectory of the road perpendicular to the solstice sightline, the designers of the road intentionally brought it into a right-angle relationship with the solstice sunset and earthworks.

The geometric relationship between the Great Hopewell Road and the solstice sightline is interesting. But there is a related alignment that may be just as significant—and that is to the Milky Way. In ancient times, before light pollution caused by modern cities, the Milky Way was one of the most prominent features of the night sky. We know that the Milky Way comprises billions of stars. But to the naked-eye observer it looks more like a hazy band of white light arcing across the sky. The Milky Way is about 30 degrees in width.

The trajectory of the Milky Way changes during the course of the year. As astronomer Edwin Krupp (1996:411) explains, "It connects one side of the horizon with another by vaulting over the earth...the angle it makes with the ground depends on where you are located and how the spinning Earth has lifted the Milky Way into the sky." During summer months the Milky Way extends in an arc from northeast to southwest (Figure 4.7a). During the winter it arcs in the opposite direction, from northwest to southeast.

The Milky Way is brightest during the summer months. Moreover, during Hopewell times, on the night of the summer solstice sunset the trajectory of the Milky Way extended in the same direction as the Great Hopewell Road. As Figure 3.7a–d shows, on the night of the summer solstice, at nightfall, the Milky Way would have been seen rising in the northeast at an azimuth of about 30 degrees,[10] arcing across the sky, and plunging to the southwest at an azimuth of about 210 degrees. If the beginning and end azimuths for the solstice Milky Way are connected by a straight line on the ground, then the ground trajectory for the Milky Way is found to extend along the same trajectory as the Great Hopewell Road—that is, from 30 degrees east of north, through Newark, to an azimuth of 210 degrees (Figure 3.7a).

From the foregoing what seems suggested is a spatial-temporal countdown of sorts that could have worked in the following way: relevant years were determined by alignments of either the Octagon or Great Circle with the moon. A significant year occurred about every nine and one-half years when either the Octagon or Great Circle came into alignment with the moon's maximum north or minimum north limit, respectively. The date of the summer solstice narrowed the target time down to the month and day within the designated lunar year. Nightfall on the date of the summer solstice sunset was the final tick of the clock—at which time the Great Hopewell Road–Milky Way alignment occurred. In those moments the trajectories of sun, moon, stars, and earthworks converged to create a special geometric and astronomic relationship in ritual space. As I discuss below, it may be during this liminal time that souls of the dead (perhaps escorted by living people) began their movement from the Ellipse burial ground (and perhaps other locations) toward the Milky Way–Great Hopewell Road entrance and Realm of the Dead. Perhaps it was believed that as the moon rose from the northeast horizon at these special times, that celestial entity transported or otherwise assisted the soul in making the transitional leap from This World to the Otherworld Milky Way Path.

Presumably, the movements of souls (and living people, if present) were further guided by the parallel-walled causeways between earthworks, maybe in a manner similar to that shown in Figure 3.8. Like the Great Hopewell Road, several of these causeways and causeway sections were apparently oriented along celestial azimuths. Aerial photos from the 1930s, for example, show that a then-visible section of causeway 1 near the Octagon (Figure 3.8) was oriented to within one degree of a due east-west line, or basically in the direction of the equinox rise and set. U.S. Geological

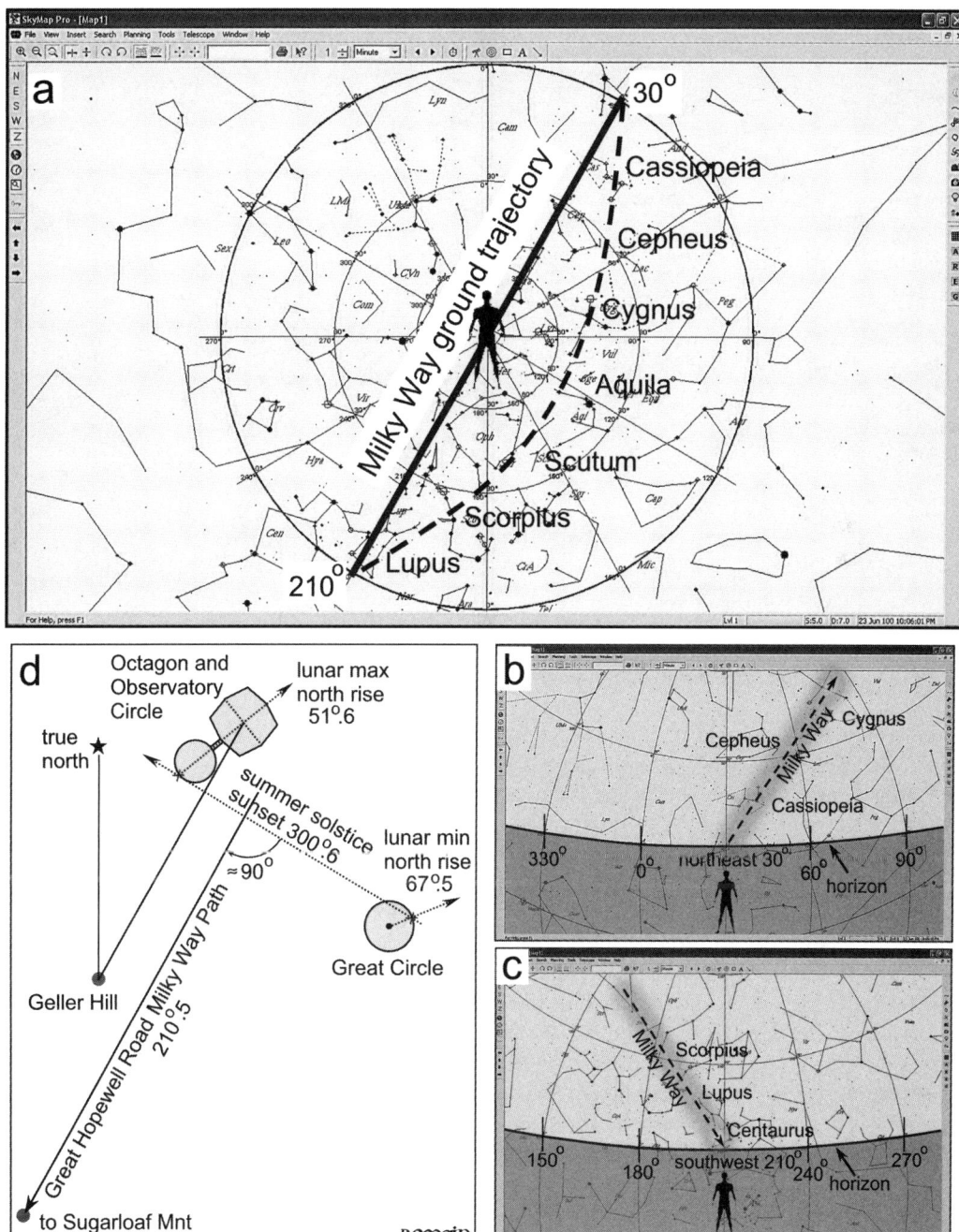

FIGURE 3.7. (*a*) Annotated sky map showing ground trajectory of the Milky Way at nightfall, AD 100, on the date of the summer solstice. (*b*) Central Ohio observer looking northeast at nightfall on the date of the summer solstice, any year between 100 BC and AD 200. (*c*) Same as 4.7b with observer looking southwest (sky maps by SkyMap Pro, annotation added). (*d*) Schematic plan showing relationships between Newark Earthworks and Milky Way trajectory.

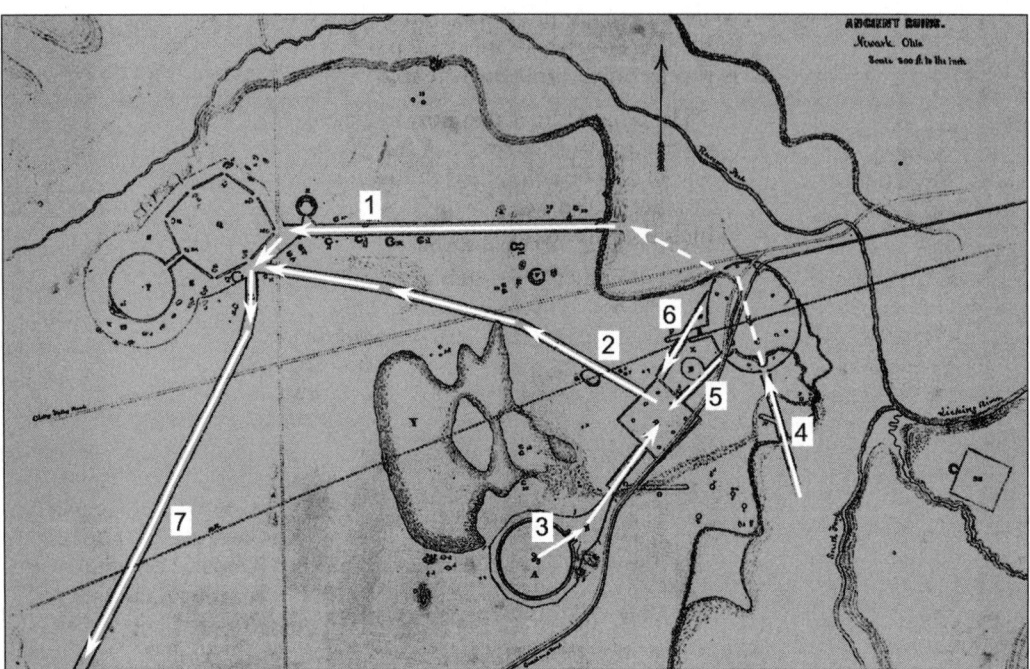

FIGURE 3.8. Hypothetical spirit paths associated with the Newark Earthworks. Salisbury map of 1862 (courtesy of the American Antiquarian Society, annotation added).

Survey map analysis suggests that as it exited the Wright Square, causeway 2 was oriented to the moon's north minimum set before it curved around the former lake-bog, continuing to the area of the Great Hopewell Road's point of beginning. Earlier it was shown how the major axis of the Great Circle—which is oriented to the moon's minimum north rise—leads into a walled walkway. In Figure 3.8 this vector is identified as causeway 3. Causeway 4 is aligned along the same azimuth as the major axis of the Ellipse, which brings it into a geometric relationship with the solstice and Milky Way–oriented design square around which the Ellipse was built. The causeway 5 entrance begins at an opening in the Ellipse situated at the intersection of the Ellipse perimeter wall and the Milky Way axis of the Ellipse design square (Figure 3.3b). Lastly, if the Salisbury map is approximately correct, then causeway 6 extends to within a couple of degrees of the Great Hopewell Road (i.e., causeway 7) and the Milky Way trajectory.

If the celestial-aligned causeways of the Newark Earthworks guided souls and/or people to the entrance of the Great Hopewell Road, the next question is, exactly where does the Great Hopewell Road lead? As Figures 3.1 and 3.8 show, the road initially extends south. At a distance of several hundred feet from the Octagon, however, the road turns southwest and for the rest of its length is perfectly straight.[11] I believe there is good reason for this. When the trajectory of the Great Hopewell Road is plotted, it is found to intersect Sugarloaf Mountain in Chillicothe—52 miles (84 km) distant (Figure 3.9a–d).[12]

The likelihood that the intersection of the Great Hopewell Road trajectory with Sugarloaf Mountain is due to chance is slim. Had the azimuth for the road been even slightly different, it would not intersect Sugarloaf. Similarly, if the straight line section of the road originated at any other point east or west of where it actually begins, then again the road's trajectory would miss Sugarloaf. If the 210.5-degree trajectory (controlled by the perpendicular relationship to the solstice sightline) and the intersection of the road with Sugarloaf Mountain were conditions that had to be met, then the road had to begin where we find it. For reasons I explain below, the Great Hopewell Road and Sugarloaf Mountain were intentionally linked in the ritual space of the Hopewell, if not physically on the ground.

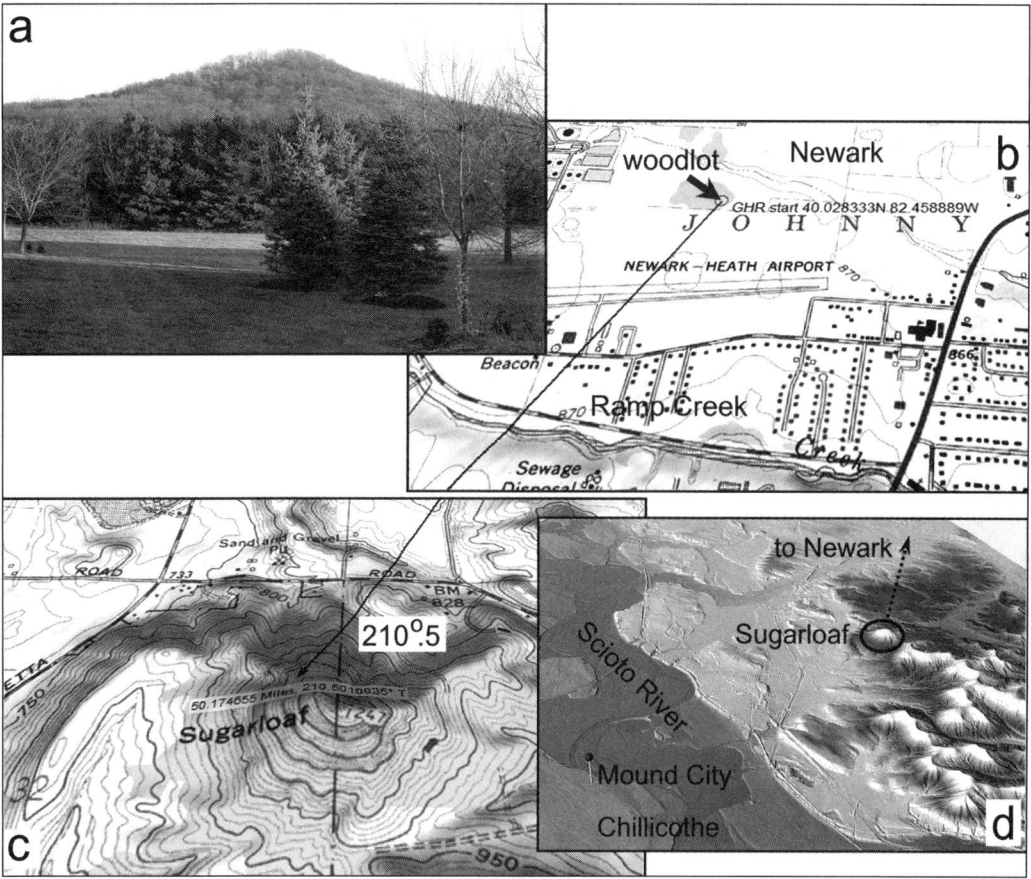

FIGURE 3.9. (*a*) View of Sugarloaf Mountain. (*b*) Starting point for plotting the trajectory of the Great Hopewell Road. (*c*) End point for plotting the Great Hopewell Road (maps by MyTopo). (*d*) LiDAR image showing the location of Sugarloaf Mountain relative to the Scioto River Valley.

Sugarloaf Mountain

Sugarloaf Mountain is situated immediately northeast of the modern-day city of Chillicothe. Sugarloaf is a moderately high mountain compared with others in Ohio. But it is not a matter of height that makes the mountain special. What makes Sugarloaf special is that it is an outlier, meaning it is somewhat separated from others in the group that flank the eastern horizon of Chillicothe. It is in fact the most northern mountain of the group composed of Bald Hill, Sand Hill, Bunker Hill, Mount Ives, and Mount Logan. Because it is an outlier, however, its conical shape is quite distinct and the mountain stands out against the distant horizon. Approached from any of several directions, Sugarloaf is a sure sign that the traveler has arrived in the Hopewell heartland.

Of considerable interest is the relationship between Sugarloaf Mountain and several surrounding Adena and Hopewell sites. At least five major sites in the immediate vicinity are situated so that a significant solar or lunar event will appear over Sugarloaf Mountain when viewed from each respective site (Figure 3.10).[13] Viewed from the Stitt Mound (likely Adena in cultural affiliation), the winter solstice sunrise will appear over Sugarloaf Mountain. Viewed from Mound City, the moon's minimum north rise will appear over Sugarloaf. Viewed from the southeast gateway or from the south small circle of the Hopeton earthwork, the summer solstice sun will rise over Sugarloaf. The summer solstice sun will also rise over Sugarloaf when viewed from the Shriver Circle. And viewed from the namesake Adena Mound, the moon's maximum north rise will appear over Sugarloaf. With the exception of Hopeton, what

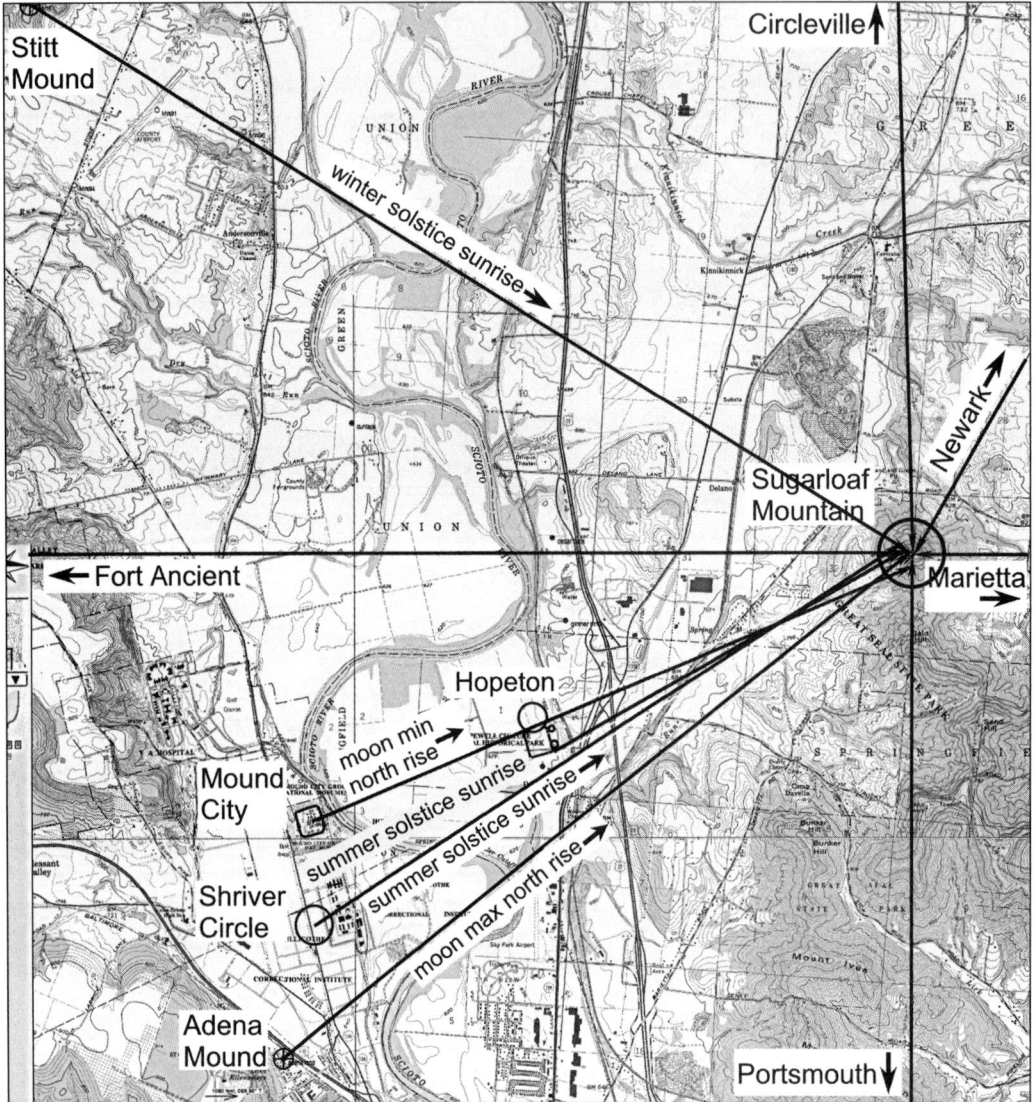

FIGURE 3.10. Several important Chillicothe-area mounds and earthworks as well as major outlier sites are astronomically linked to Sugarloaf Mountain. The map shows celestial events that would have been visible over Sugarloaf Mountain.

Stitt Mound, Mound City, Shriver, and the Adena Mound have in common is that all contained one or more burials. That said, there are several sites in the immediate area that do not demonstrate an obvious celestial link to Sugarloaf Mountain (e.g., Dunlap). The point, however, is that several major sites are linked.

Beyond the Chillicothe area, in addition to the Newark-Sugarloaf connection already discussed, there are other alignments worth noting. For example, a line drawn due west from the summit of Sugarloaf Mountain intersects the Hopewell culture hilltop enclosure known as Fort Ancient at a distance of 62 miles (100 km). The 270-degree azimuth intersects the southern end of the earthwork.

Looking in the other direction, a line drawn due east from Sugarloaf Mountain comes to within 1.5 degrees, or about 10,600 feet (3,231 m), of the Conus mound at the Marietta Earthworks Complex, at a distance of 79 miles (127 km). Looking north from Sugarloaf, a true north line comes to within 1.25 degrees, or 1,520 feet (463 m), of the Circleville earthworks, about 14 miles (22.5 km) distant.

A line drawn due south from Sugarloaf precisely intersects the Biggs mound at a distance of 46 miles (74 km). Situated on the south side of the Ohio River, the Biggs mound was part of the Portsmouth Earthworks Complex and consists of a conical burial mound (resembling Sugarloaf in its shape) surrounded by a ditch and low embankment.

It is interesting that if we add Newark, then these sites generally establish the geographic boundaries of the core south-central Ohio Hopewell territory. That said, I am not suggesting that Circleville, Portsmouth, Fort Ancient, and Marietta were situated where they are in order to form a deliberate relationship to Sugarloaf. Undoubtedly, there were other factors that influenced and constrained the locations of these sites. Still, given the long-distance conceptual link between Newark and Sugarloaf, the possibility needs to be considered that the Adena-Hopewell may have at least recognized the cardinal relationships of these sites to Sugarloaf. If that was the case, then it is reasonable to think that Sugarloaf Mountain was considered the axis mundi for the Ohio Hopewell world. In this view, Sugarloaf Mountain was a place where horizontally extended cardinal, solstice, and lunar directions intersected a vertically oriented landscape feature—a prominent mountain at a geographic location that was central to the Adena-Hopewell world.[14] That is the essence of an axis mundi. As explained by Yi-Fu Tuan (1977:149):

> Human groups nearly everywhere tend to regard their own homeland as the center of the world.... In diverse parts of the world this sense of centrality is made explicit by a geometrical conception of space oriented to the cardinal directions. Home is at the center of an astronomically determined spatial system. A vertical axis, linking heaven to the underworld, passes through it.

The axis mundi concept is integral to many worldviews and can be expressed in different ways (e.g., Eliade 1971 [1954]:12–17). Common axis mundi symbols are trees, poles, columns of smoke, temples, and, significant to the discussion here, mountains. Among the mountains identified as an axis mundi by diverse peoples are Mount Fuji in Japan, Mount Kun-Lun in China, Mount Zion in Jerusalem, Mount Kailash for Hindus, and Mount Calvary for Christians.

From a religious perspective what makes the axis mundi important is not only that it links opposite cosmological realms; it also serves as a vector for ecstatic shamanic journeys to the upper and lower worlds and as a means for souls of the dead to transition to the Otherworld (see also Skousen, this volume).

The Milky Way Path of Souls

From the evidence at hand it appears that at least in part the Newark Earthworks Complex was a place for rituals associated with movement of the dead from This World to the Otherworld. We can speculate that certain of the Hopewell dead were prepared for burial or cremated in special crematory basins situated in the temple structure or spirit house found within the Eagle Mound. It may be relevant to note that in a sense, cremation references a "redistribution of personal substance into the cosmos" (Fowler 2004:74). When timed to solar, lunar, or stellar events, the integration of the deceased into the cosmos becomes a temporally referenced, memorable, and realm-entangling event. During such liminal times, processions might have carried either the prepared bodies or ashes of the dead to staging, holding, or final interment places within the Ellipse. We do not yet understand why some persons were cremated while others were interred as extended burials, especially within the Ellipse. But in either case, it may have been believed that once the corporeal substance of the body was suitably dealt with, the free soul of the deceased would continue to the Land of the Dead.

Many Native American traditions explain that a person has more than one soul (Hultkrantz 1953; also see Lankford 2007c). At the risk of oversimplifying the matter, a person was said to have a physical body that decays after death, a shadow soul that lingers with the body after death and is basically a grave ghost, and a free soul that continues on in a journey to the Realm of the Dead. The Great Hopewell Road may have been the directional corridor that guided the free soul in its journey. In essence, the Great Hopewell Road and Milky Way Path were equivalent expressions of the pathway to the Realm of the Dead.

Along similar lines, Lepper (1998:132) early on proposed that the Great Hopewell Road was the "functional equivalent of a Mayan *sacbe*"—meaning a sacred road. He further noted that in the Mayan language the term *sacbe* not only means "white road" but also is a "Mayan term for the Milky Way" (Lepper 1998:132; also see Keller 2009). Lepper did not pursue the Great Hopewell Road–Milky Way connection further, but I believe he was on the right track.

Part of the road existed in This World, where processions helped guide the deceased person's free soul along the Milky Way trajectory. Beyond where the road physically dissolved into the landscape, the Great Hopewell Road was a spirit path aimed with precision at Sugarloaf Mountain—perhaps the final terrestrial landmark for the soul in This World. One can imagine that having been guided by the trajectory of the Great Hopewell Road to Sugarloaf Mountain, the soul ascended the axis mundi that was Sugarloaf Mountain, connecting This World to the Otherworld. In this the Great Hopewell Road was a "cosmological corridor" (sensu Marshall 1997) that connected the ceremonial earthworks at Newark to the topographic and cosmological axis mundi of the Hopewell world.

By now the reader is perhaps thinking that all this sounds like a just-so story. Maybe that is the case, or maybe not. Certainly there is overwhelming evidence from other pre-Columbian periods and sites to suggest that monumental architecture was often linked to celestial events and religious rituals (e.g., Davis 2012; Malville 2008; Pauketat 2013a; Rolingson 2012; Romain 2012a, 2012b, 2014; Romain and Davis 2013; Sherrod and Rolingson 1987; Skousen, this volume; Sofaer 2008; Van Dyke 2007). Even more to the point, compelling cases have been made for seeing various prehistoric roads and causeways as corridors linking This World to the Otherworld (e.g., Baires 2014; Baires et al. 2013; Marshall 1997; Parker Pearson et al. 2006).

Specific support for identification of the celestial Milky Way as a "Path of Souls" is provided by ethnologist George Lankford (also see Hall 1997:162). As Lankford (2007a:175) explains:

The mortuary belief complex in question manifests variation in ethnographic details from one tribal group to another, as might be expected, but there is a unifying metaphor which argues for a common core of belief across the Eastern Woodlands and Plains, and probably far beyond that area. That unifying notion is an understanding of the Milky Way as the path on which the souls of the deceased must walk.

Lankford (2007a:179–180) further notes:

That identification is virtually universal in the early ethnographic literature of North America. It is recorded from the Ojibwa, Fox, Sauk, Menomini, Miami, Delaware, Shawnee, Powhatan, Cheyenne, Huron, Iroquois, Oglala, Osage, Omaha, Quapaw, Saponi, Caddo, Pawnee, Chickasaw, and Creek, and the designation extends at least as far south as the Andes (Sullivan 1996:58–75), as far north as Siberia (Eliade 1974:188, 248–251, 295, 466), and as far west as California (see Krupp 1996).

To the list of tribes provided by Lankford we can add the Apache (Curtis 1907:134), Paiute (Mooney 1976 [1896]:290), Shoshone (Curtis 1926:82), and Seneca (Wallace 1972:245).

As for the ascension of the soul, we know the dangers of drawing ethnographic analogies between cultures separated by thousands of years and thousands of miles, and in what follows I am not suggesting a direct connection. Rather, the following serves to inform us of the possibilities. Specifically, astronomer Edwin Krupp (1996:416) makes the interesting observation that among the Ajumawi Indians of northeast California, "the dead travel to the summit of Mount Shasta and from there, ascend to the Milky Way." Krupp's (1996:417) account is worth quoting in full:

In the northeastern part of California, Floyd Buckskin, a member of the Pit River Indians Tribal Council, has reported Ajumawi band beliefs about the journey to the land of the dead. Departing from the body at death, the shadow, or soul, migrates southwest. It leaves the Fall River Valley and at the Pit River, it turns west and continues to the Pacific Ocean.... Arriving at the coast, the shadow heads north and soars to the summit of Mount Shasta. From the mountain top, the shadow transfers to the Milky Way. The Ajumawi call the Milky Way "the pathway of spirits." When the Milky Way arcs over Mount Shasta, the shadow is able to travel east and join Hewisi the Creator at sunrise. This itinerary has a seasonal aspect, for the Milky Way climbs out of the northeast before dawn at summer solstice. The Ajumawi say the Milky Way is aligned at this time with the trail followed on the Earth by the dead and aligned with the Sun as well. Because these celestial and terrestrial routes are all so congruent, it is easier for those who die at this time of year to travel to the Creator.

Serpent Mound and the Realm of the Dead

Thus far, we have traced the movement of the soul through the labyrinth passageways of the Newark Earthworks, along the trajectory of the Great Hopewell Road, and upward along the Sugarloaf Mountain axis mundi to the Milky Way Path. But there was more. Most Eastern Woodlands traditions explain that the final destination for the soul was the Realm of the Dead. Accounts differ as to the details of this otherworldly place. Some accounts say the Realm of the Dead is like a "mirror world," where things are the reverse of This World: when it is daytime in This World, it is nighttime in the Realm of the Dead, seasons are reversed, and so on (e.g., Smith 1995:46; also see Hall 1997:133). Generally, though, the Realm of the Dead is a place where souls continue on in an existence similar to their corporeal life (e.g., Landes 1968:196–197; Smith 1995:46).

The location for the Realm of the Dead varies but is usually said to be in the south, southwest, or west (Lankford 2007a:176; 2007b:207, 240); and as already discussed, it is the Milky Way Path of Souls that leads to the Realm of the Dead. Given the widespread occurrence of these beliefs across the Eastern Woodlands, it seems possible that their conceptual origins extend back at least to Adena-Hopewell times (Lankford 2007b:224; Reilly 2004:126).

Where things become intriguing is Lankford's (2007b:213–214) finding from "Ojibwa, Menomini, Miami, Potawatomi, Sauk, Fox, Shawnee, and other Algonkian sources…[that] at the southern foot of the [Milky Way] Path the free-soul encounters the guardian/owner of the realm of the dead souls, sometimes identified as a serpent." Elsewhere Lankford (2007a:178) explains: "The goal of the journey is the Realm of the Dead, which lies at the southern end of the [Milky Way] Path. It is protected by the Great Serpent with the red jewel in its forehead…Scorpio."

The Great Serpent is known throughout the Eastern Woodlands as the master of the Lowerworld (Lankford 2007c; Penny 1985; Reilly 2004, 2011). The Great Serpent is the main antagonist of Upperworld entities such as the Thunderbirds. Although the Great Serpent reigns over the Lowerworld, the creature has celestial attributes as well; in some stories it is visible as a meteor or can be seen during summer months flying across the night sky, from one watery entrance to the Lowerworld to another (Hewitt 1891:384). Moreover, as Lankford suggests, the constellation Scorpius may be a cognate for the Great Serpent.

Back on the ground in Ohio, the iconic Serpent Mound effigy in Adams County (Figure 3.11a) is located precisely where one would expect to find the Lowerworld Serpent: at the end of the Milky Way Path. Serpent Mound is the best-known effigy mound in North America.[15] The effigy is situated on a promontory overlooking Brush Creek; its total length is about 1,370 feet (420 m). The body of the Serpent has seven convolutions and ends in a spiral coil. The head of the Serpent resembles a snake poised to bite or swallow an ellipse-shaped figure (the oval embankment), perhaps intended as a circle sun symbol turned at an angle, similar to the way the Serpent's head is turned to show its profile (Figure 3.12a).

Charles Willoughby (1919) was the first to suggest that the Serpent Mound effigy represents the Great Serpent of Native American mythology. In 1988 I documented a number of physical resemblances between Serpent Mound and ethnographic descriptions of the Great Serpent (Romain 1988). More recently, Lankford (2007c) likewise concluded that Serpent Mound represents the Great Serpent of Native American legend. Perhaps Lankford's most valuable contribution to the discussion, however, has been to connect the Great Serpent of Eastern Woodlands mythology and the Serpent Mound effigy with the constellation Scorpius. Specifically, Lankford

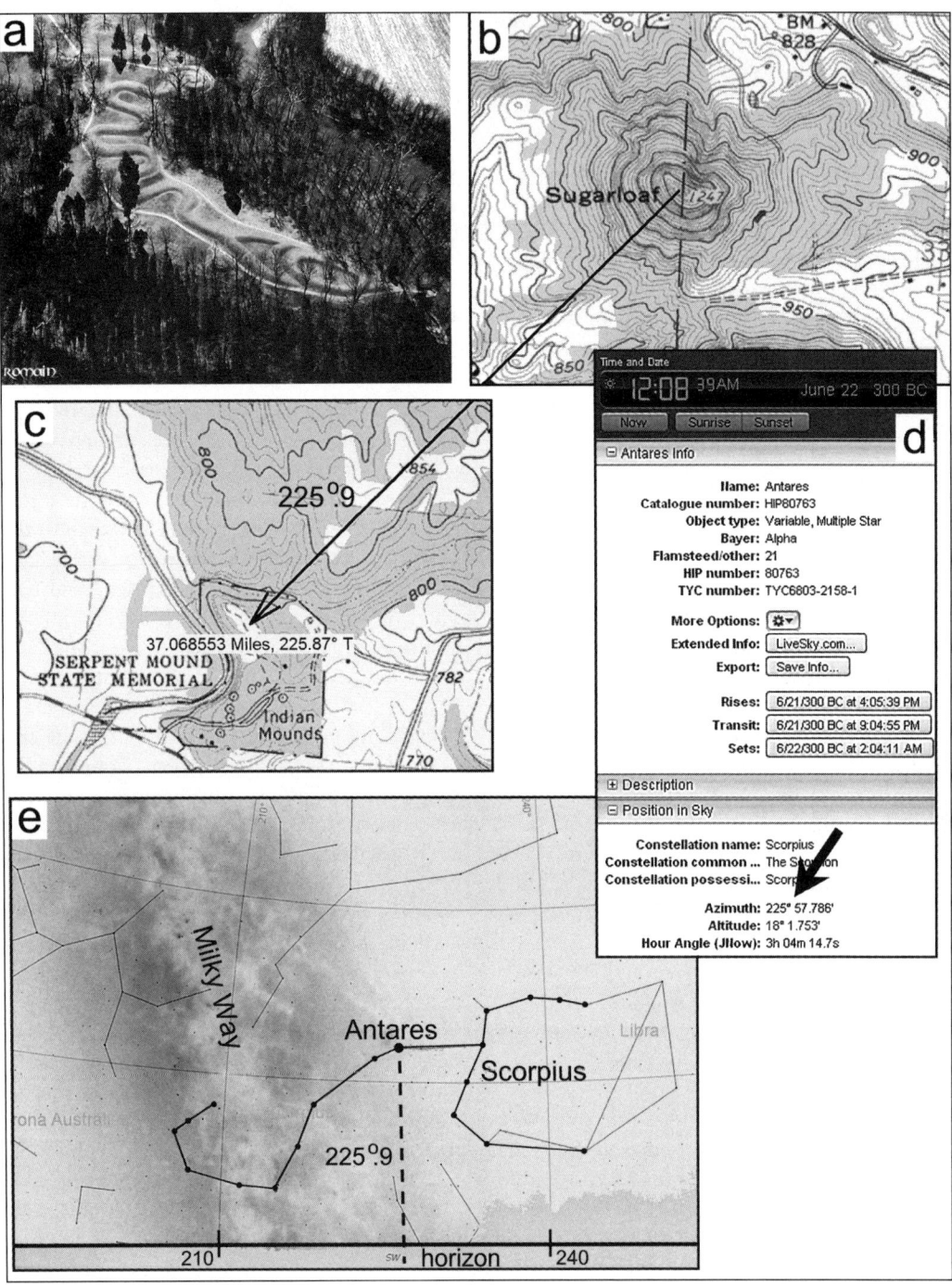

FIGURE 3.11. (*a*) Aerial view of Serpent Mound. (*b*) Starting point for plotting the azimuth between Sugarloaf Mountain and Serpent Mound. (*c*) End point for plotting the azimuth between Sugarloaf Mountain and Serpent Mound (maps provided by MyTopo). (*d*) Starry Night computer data for Antares at midnight on summer solstice, 300 BC. (*e*) Sky map showing Antares and Scorpius at midnight on night of summer solstice, 300 BC (map by Starry Night, annotation added).

(2007c:133) posits: "If the identification of the earthwork is the Great Serpent under discussion, then the oval shape [i.e., the oval embankment] would be readily seen as the red crystal/eye/Antares, and the peculiar globular forms at the base of the head are likely remnants of some feather locative." Further, according to Lankford (2007c:132), "the identification of Scorpio and Antares as the Serpent and his red eye points to a significant ethnoastronomical belief complex which cut across tribal and linguistic lines."

I believe Lankford is correct in his identification of Serpent Mound with Scorpius.[16] I differ from Lankford in how the Serpent may be represented by Scorpius, however. I believe that Antares is better situated to be the heart of the Serpent and that the Serpent's open mouth is found in the Scorpius configuration in the manner suggested by Figure 3.11e. In my interpretation, the Great Serpent in its Scorpius guise is forever in pursuit of the sun. Notably, this comports well with the on-the-ground, visual representation of the serpent attempting to swallow the rotated sun disk, and with the finding that the oval embankment is aligned to the summer solstice sunset through its major axis, thereby directly connecting the oval to the sun (see Figure 3.12b; also see Hardman and Hardman 1987; Fletcher and Cameron 1988; Romain 1992, 2000). Moreover, several stories from the Eastern Woodlands tell of a celestial serpent that tries to bite or swallow the sun (e.g., Hewitt 1891; Mooney 1900). Perhaps best known is the Cherokee story of the monstrous Uktena serpent who attacks the sun (Mooney 1900:252–254, 297–298). In any event, the fundamental idea is the same—that is, Scorpius is the celestial manifestation of the Great Serpent of Eastern Woodlands mythology and is represented on the ground by the Serpent Mound effigy.

To this I would add the following. As viewed from Sugarloaf Mountain on the night of the summer solstice, Scorpius and its bright star Antares are situated at the end of the Milky Way Path, on an azimuth of 225.9 degrees (Figure 3.11b–e).[17] Likewise, as plotted from Sugarloaf Mountain, the Serpent Mound effigy is located on the same 225.9-degree azimuth, at a distance of 37 miles (59.5 km). Given this, it may be that the location for the Serpent Mound was selected based on its azimuthal relationships to Sugarloaf Mountain, the Milky Way, and Scorpius (in addition to its location in the midst of several sinkhole fields—presumably Lowerworld entrances).

Supporting the interpretation for Serpent Mound as a cognate for Scorpius and the Lowerworld Great Serpent is the observation that Scorpius is a summer constellation that appears to rise in the southern sky and then rotate clockwise both during the course of a single night and over the course of the summer months (as viewed at the same time of night at one-month intervals—see Figure 3.12d–g). With regard to the monthly position of Scorpius, as shown by Figure 3.12c–g, the bisectors of each Serpent Mound body convolution reference or correspond to the monthly position of Scorpius when each of the convolution bisectors moves into a horizontal position relative to the observer's horizon. Notable too is that the annual path of the sun (referred to as the ecliptic) passes through the Scorpius serpent's jaws. Hence the appearance of the summer sun at sunset, being pursued by the Great Serpent as the serpent entity becomes visible in the darkening sky.

In summary, it may be that some earthworks in the Adena-Hopewell world were used to facilitate the transition of souls from This World to the Otherworld. The Newark Earthworks served at least in part as a focal point for mortuary ceremonies involving cremation and burial. From this we can speculate the following. Very likely the mortuary ceremonies at Newark—such as occurred within the spirit house in the center of the Great Circle—included measures for dealing with the dual or even multiple souls that a person might have. Perhaps the shadow soul was ritually contained within its designated burial ground while the free soul was helped in its transition to the Otherworld by the moon as that celestial entity rose from the northeast horizon. Having made the transition to the Otherworld, the soul was then guided by spirit barriers and passageways to the beginning of the Great Hopewell Road. For its journey through the Newark Earthworks, the soul may have been accompanied by processional movements of living people: relatives, mourners, psychopomps, and others. It appears that ceremonies were timed to coincide with temporal and spatial intersections involving lunar standstill and solstice events. Maybe it was believed that during such times This World and the Otherworld were

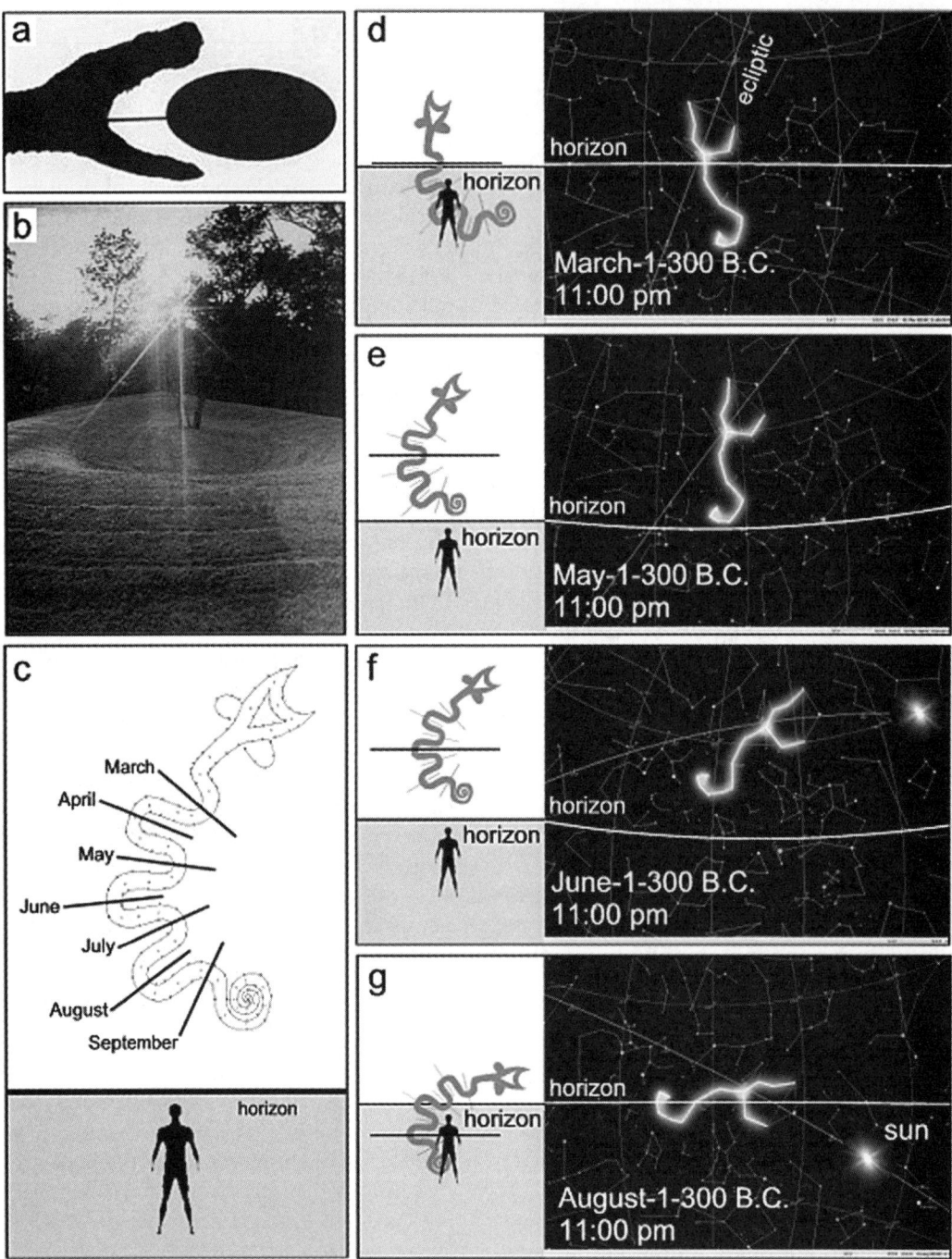

FIGURE 3.12. (*a*) Serpent Mound resembles the side view of a serpent attempting to bite a circle disk that has been rotated in a similar fashion as the serpent's head, thus generating the appearance of an oval. (*b*) Summer solstice sunset along the major axis of the Serpent Mound oval embankment, June 21, 1990. (*c*) The Serpent has been lifted off the flat earth surface and placed in the sky as Scorpius. Each line that bisects a body convolution represents one month of rotation of the Scorpius Serpent. The rising of Scorpius begins in March as the head of the Serpent rises from the Lowerworld. The Serpent continues its movement in an upward and clockwise manner until the end of the summer, when it descends back into the Lowerworld, below the horizon. (*d*–*g*) Views showing how each Serpent Mound convolution references an incremental clockwise turn of the Serpent during the course of the summer at monthly intervals. In each figure the bisector line for each body convolution is parallel to the horizon. Each month a different bisector line moves into the horizontal position and thereby shows the relative position of Scorpius in the sky. Not all summer months shown due to space limitations (maps by SkyMap Pro, annotation added).

at their closest or that the boundaries between realms were blurred, thereby allowing the soul to cross. In any case, once the soul reached its entry point to the Great Hopewell Road, movement along the trajectory of the road provided the soul with the requisite direction for its journey.

Continuing the soul journey, we can imagine that, following the Great Hopewell Road–Milky Way trajectory, the soul (or perhaps multiple souls released in a related group) traveled until reaching Sugarloaf Mountain, the axis mundi and center of the Hopewell world. Following the vertical track of the mountain, the free soul ascended to the Milky Way Path. There the soul may have been joined by others from nearby Chillicothe burial mounds also linked to Sugarloaf along celestial azimuths. Traveling southwest along the Milky Way Path, with the bright red star Antares as its guide, the soul eventually encountered the Great Serpent, guardian of the Realm of the Dead. If the soul was successful in its encounter with the Great Serpent, it joined the ancestors in the Realm of the Dead.

Conclusion

Of course there are possible iterations and scenarios other than what I proposed above. For example, over the course of more than one thousand years and especially in the Southeast, the story likely evolved to include concepts involving the Orion constellation, ogee symbol, and hand-in-eye motif (Lankford 2007a). The important point is that, considered as separate entities, the Newark Earthworks, Great Hopewell Road, Sugarloaf Mountain, Chillicothe sites, and Serpent Mound provide a limited view of what may have been happening in the Adena-Hopewell world. Considered together as part of something bigger, these sites offer a different set of meanings. The sites emerge as part of a relational web that gathered and engaged people (both living and dead), special places in This World and the Otherworld, cosmic forces and entities, landscape features, and celestial events in a dynamic meshwork that evolved in its manifestations over generations.

In this relational web the boundaries between realms were permeable and mutable, and human perceptions, emotions, and memories entangled multiple spaces and dimensions—which is to say, Adena-Hopewell earthworks facilitated movement between worlds and provided a center place for temporally linked rituals that intertwined human sensory experience with the dimension of spirit. This relational web linked sites across a distance of nearly one hundred miles. In this, the Newark–Sugarloaf–Serpent Mound relational web may have been one of the largest religious complexes known to the prehistoric world.

Indeed, it may be that the Milky Way Path as written across the landscape of Ohio was known to people throughout the Eastern Woodlands, and that the Newark–Sugarloaf–Serpent Mound corridor served as a regional ceremonial center intended to provide access to the Realm of the Dead for selected special persons such as powerful chiefs, medicine men, clan leaders, and shamans. In this, Newark and certain of the central Ohio earthworks may have been pilgrimage destinations (also see Lepper 2006). Such a scenario is supported by the many occurrences of large quantities of exotic materials found in central Ohio burial contexts that were brought into the area from far-flung regions (e.g., Indiana hornstone, obsidian from Yellowstone, mica from the Appalachians, copper from the upper Great Lakes, conch shell from the Atlantic or Gulf coasts).

In any event, for the people who were part of it, the relational web I have sought to rematerialize engaged and unfolded into a powerful narrative. This narrative was woven from moonbeams and starlight, landscape features and life events, all on a framework of geometric shapes and symbols that were the earthworks. This narrative, I believe, provided people with answers to life's most perplexing questions: What happens when we die? Where do we go? The Newark–Sugarloaf–Serpent Mound relational web gave an answer to those questions. It was an answer visible in the heavens above and traced across the land for all to see. Generations of people built the earthworks, used them for various purposes, lived, and died. As souls, they ascended to the Milky Way Path, journeyed to the Realm of the Dead, and joined the ancestors. It was all perfectly clear and needed no further proof beyond that which the people could see, feel, and experience. The relational web that the Adena-Hopewell built and were enmeshed in provided a context that was familiar, reassuring, and hopeful. Neither the individual nor the community was destined to perish.

Acknowledgments

I wish to thank B. Jacob Skousen and Meghan E. Buchanan for inviting me to contribute to this book. Thanks also to Jacob and Meghan for useful comments on an earlier version of this chapter. Many thanks to Kimberley C. Vivier for editing. Thank you to Newark Earthworks Center director Richard Shiels for providing me with student volunteers for coring operations at the Octagon; I am grateful to Mike Ranalli, Josh Robison, Darrell McCall, Theresa McManus, and Matthew McClellan. For permission to work at Geller Hill, my sincere thanks to Heath mayor Mark D. Johns and Parks and Recreation Department superintendent Bob Geller.

Thank you to the Ohio Historical Society for permission to work at Serpent Mound and the Newark Octagon. I greatly appreciate the efforts of all those who assisted me with the Serpent Mound Project, including G. William Monaghan, Edward Herrmann, Karen Leone, Matthew Purtill, Tim Schilling, Jarrod Burks, Al Tonetti, Jeff Wilson, and Mike Zaleha. I am especially grateful to Bill Monaghan and Ed Herrmann for Geoprobe coring work at Serpent Mound and Geller Hill, and the Glenn Black Laboratory for use of its equipment.

My thinking about relational webs and the Adena-Hopewell Milky Way Path has been influenced by the work of Tom Emerson, Robert Hall, George Lankford, Tim Pauketat, and Kent Reilly III. I am solely responsible for any shortcomings in this chapter.

Notes

1. Given the temporal range of the Adena and Hopewell earthworks involved in the relational web described, it is clearly not the case that the entire web, or even each site, was built contemporaneously pursuant to a grand master plan. Hundreds of years passed as the web morphed and expanded and eventually came into the form we see today. Most likely, different parts were added in a piecemeal fashion as special places became evident, the narrative became more detailed, or new earthworks and symbols needed to be added. However, as long as the additional constructions incorporated basic shared design principles, and the core narrative was maintained by successive mound builders, the relational web would have continued to work throughout the Adena-Hopewell florescence.

2. LiDAR is an acronym for Light Detection and Ranging. The technology uses reflected near-infrared laser beams aimed at the earth from an aircraft to develop high-resolution images of the ground (Romain and Burks 2008a, 2008b, 2008c). Because of the high density of coordinate point data typically collected and because LiDAR beams have the ability to penetrate some vegetation, accurate representations of the surface topography can be made.

3. The Salisbury (1862) map shows these knolls as mounds. The knolls resemble mounds in shape and size. However, Geoprobe coring by Monaghan, Herrmann, and Romain (Romain 2013) into four of the knolls at multiple locations failed to find any evidence that these features are man-made.

4. There are other maps that show the Ellipse earthwork, such as those by Atwater (1820), Squier and Davis (1848), and Wyrick (1866). The represented shape for the Ellipse differs somewhat between maps. Each map has its unique strengths and weaknesses; for distance, shape, and direction, I consider the Salisbury (1862) map to be the most accurate.

A sense of the accuracy of the Salisbury map can be gained from the following comparison to modern, ground-truthed data: Salisbury diameter for the Observatory Circle is accurate to within 6 feet; Salisbury azimuth for the main axis of the Octagon–Observatory Circle is accurate to within one-half degree; azimuth between Observatory Circle and Great Circle is accurate to within 4 degrees; azimuth of railroad shown by the Salisburys is accurate to within 1.5 degrees; distance between Observatory Circle and Great Circle is accurate to within 100 feet; Salisbury azimuth for the Great Hopewell Road is accurate to within 2 degrees.

5. Lunar azimuths calculated by Romain for AD 100, zero-degree horizon elevations corrected for parallax, refraction, and lower limb tangency. Zero-degree horizon after Hively and Horn (2010), who propose that for this earthwork, lunar azimuths were established by observations made from surrounding hilltops. The difference between azimuths computed using local horizon elevations viewed from the earthwork and zero-degree elevations from hilltops is on average less than one degree—but in the direction favoring the zero-degree hypothesis.

6. The lunar alignment posited here differs from that suggested by Hively and Horn (1982:S15), who used the axis of the entranceway walls leading to the Circle for calculation purposes.

The Newark Great Circle appears to have been laid out on the ground using two slightly overlapping circles, each about 1,178 feet in diameter (perhaps reflective of two different construction episodes). In Figure 3.4b the southern design circle is shown and is used for calculation purposes.

Newark Great Circle moon minimum north rise azimuth calculated for AD 100, with horizon elevation based on an entrance wall height = 15 feet, horizontal distance 589 feet, 0.35-degree refraction correction, 0.25-degree lower limb correction, 0.95-degree parallax correction, which yields a corrected horizon elevation of 2.3 degrees.

7. Newark Great Circle–Observatory Mound summer solstice sunset azimuth calculated for AD 100; map-measured distant horizon elevation corrected for refraction, lower limb tangency, and estimated foresight tree level of 80 feet = corrected horizon elevation = 0.98 degrees.

8. Several design lines between earthworks at Newark involve geometric relationships and multiples of the HMU in such a way that relationships between earthworks are clearly and intentionally established—even though the beginning and end points for many of these lines are not intervisible. The validity of the solstice sightline between the Great Circle and Observatory Mound does not require intervisibility.

9. A considerable number of Eastern Woodlands stories explain that to reach the Realm of the Dead the soul must travel along the Milky Way Path. Before reaching this realm, however, the soul must cross a river. Some souls are able to successfully cross the river, but others fail and are lost (Lankford 2007a:182–183). Coincident with this feature of the soul journey story, it is interesting to note that Ramp Creek cuts across the trajectory of the Great Hopewell Road about 2.5 miles south of the Octagon. Beyond this location, physical traces of the road vanish. It is as though once the soul reached the other side of Ramp Creek, the soul entered a slightly different dimension, a dimension where physical manifestation of the road was no longer needed for directional guidance.

10. In AD 100 the summer solstice sunset occurred on June 23. Nightfall occurred at about 10:05 PM local standard time. Nightfall begins after sunset and after twilight when no visible light is provided by the sun. This occurs when the sun reaches an elevation of about 18 degrees below the horizon.

11. Great Hopewell Road starting point coordinates: Ohio State Plane (NAD83): N 738729 / E 1980066.

12. The observation that the trajectory of the Great Hopewell Road intersects Sugarloaf Mountain was noted in an Internet posting in 1998 by Joseph M. Knapp. To my knowledge, Mr. Knapp's finding has not been reported in the professional literature. I happened on the Knapp (1998) article after independently reaching the same conclusion. Mr. Knapp used USGS maps and aerial photos to determine the azimuth for the road. As indicated, my findings are based on LiDAR data. Our azimuth values are nearly the same.

13. Alignments calculated for AD 100 (although observation dates ± 300 years will not result in azimuth differences discernible to the naked eye). Stitt Mound winter solstice sunrise = 121.8 degrees, map measured horizon elevation corrected for refraction and lower limb tangency = 0.5 degrees, map measured azimuth = 121.5 degrees, and therefore alignment is to within 0.3 degrees; Mound City moon minimum north rise—see Hively and Horn 2010:145; Shriver summer solstice sunrise = 59.7 degrees, corrected h (where h refers to horizon elevation) = 1.1 degrees, map measured azimuth = 59.02 degrees, and therefore alignment is to within 0.7 degrees; Hopeton summer solstice sunrise = 61.1 degrees, corrected h = 2.6 degrees, alignment is to within 0.2 degrees; Adena Mound moon maximum north rise = 52.25 degrees, corrected h = 0.8 degrees, map measured azimuth = 52.12 degrees, alignment is to within 0.2 degrees.

14. Review of the Ohio Archaeological Inventory database reveals no reported prehistoric sites documented on Sugarloaf Mountain. At first this seems peculiar for what is purportedly a central component of the relational web proposed; but in an Adena-Hopewell world, where things were part of a larger web of relationships, there was no real need for humans to mark or designate the mountain as special. As an entity possessing agency in its own right—meaning the capacity, consciously or not, to "alter the trajectory of some other being, phenomenon, or entity" (Pauketat 2013a:29; also see Skousen 2012)—the mountain was already obviously special simply by virtue of its presence.

15. Recent radiocarbon dates (Herrmann et al. 2014; Romain 2014; Romain et al. 2013) suggest that Serpent Mound was built during the Early Woodland period. Five radiocarbon samples extracted by Geoprobe coring from five different locations along the spine of the Serpent at the base of the effigy yielded an OxCal median date of 321 BC, with a 2-sigma range of 381–44 BC. Two additional samples yielded dates about two hundred years earlier. These findings differ from claims made by Fletcher et al. (1996), who, using two radiocarbon dates from an area of the Serpent subject to erosion, assert that the effigy was built by Fort Ancient people. The most parsimonious explanation for the combined data is that Serpent Mound was built by people of the Adena culture and later repaired or renewed by people of the Fort Ancient culture. (For further details, see Herrmann et al.

2014; Romain 2014.) Physical evidence shows that the area to the immediate south of Serpent Mound was occupied by Archaic, Adena, and Fort Ancient peoples.

16. Scorpius is a "Western" constellation in the sense that it was recognized as a scorpion by the Babylonians and Greeks. The constellation was known as a serpent, however, by some Native Americans, including the Skidi Pawnee (Chamberlain 1982:82; Fletcher 1903:15, also see Lankford 2007b:131–132).

17. Azimuths for Scorpius and Antares plotted for midnight ± 10 minutes, June 22, 300 BC, eastern standard time (no daylight saving time correction applied).

Although star declinations change over time, the stars that make up the constellations are, for all practical purposes, fixed relative to each other. Thus Scorpius in 300 BC looked the same as it does today. So, too, in cal AD 1070 (the date that Fletcher et al. [1996:133] posit for Serpent Mound construction) Scorpius and Antares would appear in the southwest sky at the same azimuths as they did in 300 BC, but roughly one hour later, at about 1:00 AM rather than midnight. Given this, the Great Serpent in the guise of Scorpius and Serpent Mound could have been recognized from Historic times back through Fort Ancient and into the Adena period in the same position relative to the Milky Way.

Midnight is the conceptual opposite of noon, and hence it is a symbolically meaningful time. In this regard, recall the earlier discussion that the Realm of the Dead is the reverse of This World.

Antares is the brightest star in Scorpius. It is bright red and is the only red star in the summer sky.

References Cited

Applegate, Darlene, and Robert C. Mainfort Jr. (editors)
2005   *Woodland Period Systemics in the Middle Ohio Valley*. University of Alabama Press, Tuscaloosa.

Atwater, Caleb
1820   Description of the Antiquities Discovered in the State of Ohio and Other Western States. *Archaeologia Americana* 1:105–267.

Baires, Sarah E.
2014   Cahokia's Rattlesnake Causeway. *Midcontinental Journal of Archaeology* 39 (1) :1–18.

Baires, Sarah E., Amanda J. Butler, B. Jacob Skousen, and Timothy R. Pauketat
2013   Fields of Movement in the Ancient Woodlands of North America. In *Archaeology after Interpretation: Returning Materials to Archaeological Theory*, edited by Benjamin Alberti, Andrew M. Jones, and Joshua Pollard, pp. 197–218. Left Coast Press, Walnut Creek, California.

Bodi, Bhikkhu
2000   *The Connected Discourses of the Buddha: A New Translation of the Samyutta Nikāya*. Wisdom Publications, Boston.

Brown, James A.
1992   Closing Commentary. In *Cultural Variability in Context: Woodland Settlements of the Mid-Ohio Valley*, edited by Mark F. Seeman, pp. 80–82. *Midcontinental Journal of Archaeology* Special Paper No. 7. Kent State University Press, Kent.

2012   *Mound City: The Archaeology of a Renown Hopewell Mound Center*. Special Report No. 6. U.S. Department of the Interior, National Park Service, Midwest Archeological Center, Lincoln, Nebraska.

Chamberlain, Von Del
1982   *When Stars Came Down to Earth: Cosmology of the Skidi Pawnee Indians of North America*. Ballena, Los Altos, California.

Curtis, Edward S.
1907   [1970] *The North American Indian, Being a Series of Volumes Picturing and Describing the Indians of the United States and Alaska, Volume 1*. Johnson Reprint Corporation, New York.

1926   [1970] *The North American Indian, Being a Series of Volumes Picturing and Describing the Indians of the United States and Alaska, Volume 15*. Johnson Reprint Corporation, New York.

Davis, Norman L.
2012   Solar Alignments at the Watson Brake Site. *Louisiana Archaeology* 34:97–115.

DeBoer, Warren
2010   Strange Sightings on the Scioto. In *Hopewell Settlement Patterns, Subsistence, and Symbolic Landscapes*, edited by A. Martin Byers and Dee Anne Wymer, pp. 165–198. University Press of Florida, Gainesville.

Eddy, John
1978   Archaeoastronomy of North America: Cliffs, Mounds, and Medicine Wheels. In *In Search of Ancient Astronomies*, edited by Edwin C. Krupp, pp. 133–163. McGraw-Hill, New York.

Eliade, Mircea
1971   [1954] *The Myth of the Eternal Return; or, Cosmos and History*. Translated by Willard R. Trask. Bollingen Series Vol. XLVI. Princeton University Press, Princeton, New Jersey.

1974   *Shamanism: Archaic Techniques of Ecstasy*. Princeton University Press, Princeton, New Jersey.

Fletcher, Alice C.
1903   Pawnee Star Lore. *Journal of American Folklore* 16:10–15.

Fletcher, Robert V., and Terry L. Cameron
1988   Serpent Mound: A New Look at an Old Snake in the Grass. *Ohio Archaeologist* 38 (1) :55–61.

Fletcher, Robert V., Terry L. Cameron, Bradley T. Lepper, Dee Anne Wymer, and William Pickard
1996   Serpent Mound: A Fort Ancient Icon? *Midcontinental Journal of Archaeology* 21 (1): 105–143.

Fowler, Chris
2004   *The Archaeology of Personhood: An Anthropological Approach*. Routledge, London.
2013   Dynamic Assemblages, or the Past Is What Endures: Change and the Duration of Relations. In *Archaeology after Interpretation: Returning Materials to Archaeological Theory*, edited by Benjamin Alberti, Andrew Meirion Jones, and Joshua Pollard, pp. 235–256. Left Coast Press, Walnut Creek, California.

Greenman, Emerson F.
1928   Field Notes on the Excavation of the Eagle Mound. Manuscript on file, Department of Archaeology, Ohio Historical Society, Columbus.

Hall, Robert L.
1979   In Search of the Ideology of the Adena-Hopewell Climax. In *Hopewell Archaeology: The Chillicothe Conference*, edited by David S. Brose and N'omi B. Greber, pp. 258–265. Kent State University Press, Kent.
1997   *An Archaeology of the Soul: North American Indian Belief and Ritual*. University of Illinois Press, Urbana.

Hardman, Clark, Jr., and Marjorie Hardman
1987   The Great Serpent and the Sun. *Ohio Archaeologist* 37 (3): 34–40.

Harris, Oliver J. T.
2014   (Re)assembling Communities. *Journal of Archaeological Method and Theory* 21 (1): 76–97.

Herrmann, Edward, G. William Monaghan, William F. Romain, Timothy M. Schilling, Jarrod Burks, Karen L. Leone, Matthew P. Purtill, and Alan C. Tonetti
2014   A New Multistage Construction Chronology for the Great Serpent Mound, USA. *Journal of Archaeological Science* 50:117–125. http://www.sciencedirect.com/science/article/pii/S0305440314002465, accessed August 3, 2014.

Hewitt, J.N.B.
1891   Kahastinens or the Fire-Dragon. *American Anthropologist* (o.s.) 4 (4): 384.

Hively, Ray, and Robert Horn
1982   Geometry and Astronomy in Prehistoric Ohio. *Archaeoastronomy* (supplement to *Journal for the History of Astronomy* 13) 4:S1–S20.
1984   Hopewellian Geometry and Astronomy at High Bank. *Archaeoastronomy* (supplement to *Journal for the History of Astronomy* 15) 7:S85–S100.
2010   Hopewell Cosmography at Newark and Chillicothe, Ohio. In *Hopewell Settlement Patterns, Subsistence, and Symbolic Landscapes*, edited by A. Martin Byers and Dee Anne Wymer, pp. 128–164. University Press of Florida, Gainesville.
2013   A New and Extended Case for Lunar (and Solar) Astronomy at the Newark Earthworks. *Midcontinental Journal of Archaeology* 38 (1): 83–182.

Hodder, Ian
2006   *The Leopard's Tale: Revealing the Mysteries of Catahoyuk*. Thames and Hudson, London.
2012   *Entangled: An Archaeology of the Relationships between Humans and Things*. Wiley-Blackwell, West Sussex, England.

Hultkrantz, Åke
1953   *Conceptions of the Soul among North American Indians*. Monograph Series No. 1. Museum of Sweden, Stockholm.

Ingold, Tim
2007   *Lines: A Brief History*. Routledge, London.
2011   *Being Alive: Essays on Movement, Knowledge and Description*. Routledge, London.

Keller, Angela H.
2009   A Road by Any Other Name: Trails, Paths, and Roads in Maya Language and Thought. In *Landscapes of Movement: Trails, Paths, and Roads in Anthropological Perspective*, edited by J. E. Snead, C. L. Erickson, and J. A. Darling, pp. 133–157. University of Pennsylvania Museum of Archaeology and Anthropology, Philadelphia.

Knapp, Joseph M.
1998   On the Great Hopewell Road. http://coolohio.com/octagon/onroad.htm, accessed January 15, 2014.

Krupp, Edwin C.
1996   Negotiating the Highwire of Heaven: The Milky Way and the Itinerary of the Soul. *Vistas in Astronomy* 39:405–430.

Landes, Ruth
1968   *Ojibwa Religion and the Midéwiwin*. University of Wisconsin Press, Madison.

Lankford, George E.
2007a   The "Path of Souls": Some Death Imagery in the Southeastern Ceremonial Complex. In *Ancient Objects and Sacred Realms: Interpretations of Mississippian Iconography*, edited by F. Kent Reilly III and James F. Garber, pp. 174–212. University of Texas Press, Austin.

2007b *Reachable Stars: Patterns in the Ethnoastronomy of Eastern North America*. University of Alabama Press, Tuscaloosa.

2007c The Great Serpent in Eastern North America. In *Ancient Objects and Sacred Realms: Interpretations of Mississippian Iconography*, edited by F. Kent Reilly III and James F. Garber, pp. 107–135. University of Texas Press, Austin.

Latour, Bruno

2005 *Reassembling the Social: An Introduction to Network-Actor-Theory*. Oxford University Press, Oxford.

Lepper, Bradley T.

1995 Tracking Ohio's Great Hopewell Road. *Archaeology* 48 (6): 52–56.

1998 The Archaeology of the Newark Earthworks. In *Ancient Earthen Enclosures of the Eastern Woodlands*, edited by Robert C. Mainfort Jr. and Lynne P. Sullivan, pp. 114–134. University Press of Florida, Gainesville.

2006 The Great Hopewell Road and the Role of Pilgrimage in the Hopewell Interaction Sphere. In *Recreating Hopewell*, edited by Douglas K. Charles and Jane E. Buikstra, pp. 122–133. University Press of Florida, Gainesville.

Malville, J. McKim

2008 *A Guide to Prehistoric Astronomy in the Southwest*. Rev. ed. Johnson Books, Boulder, Colorado.

Marshall, Michael P.

1997 The Chacoan Roads: A Cosmological Interpretation. In *Anasazi Architecture and American Design*, edited by Baker H. Morrow and V. B. Price, pp. 62–74. University of New Mexico Press, Albuquerque.

Mooney, James

1900 *Myths of the Cherokee*. 19th Annual Report of the Bureau of American Ethnology for the Years 1897–1898, Part I. Smithsonian Institution, Washington, D.C.

1976 [1896] *The Ghost-Dance Religion and the Sioux Outbreak of 1890*. Abridged ed. University of Chicago Press, Chicago.

Otto, Martha P., and Brian G. Redmond (editors)

2008 *Transitions: Archaic and Early Woodland Research in the Ohio Country*. Ohio University Press, Athens.

Parker Pearson, Mike, Josh Pollard, Colin Richards, Julian Thomas, Christopher Tilley, Kate Welham, and Umberto Albarella

2006 Materializing Stonehenge: The Stonehenge Riverside Project and New Discoveries. *Journal of Material Culture* 11 (1/2): 227–261.

Pauketat, Timothy R.

2013a *An Archaeology of the Cosmos: Rethinking Agency and Religion in Ancient America*. Routledge, London.

2013b Bundles of/in/as Time. In *Big Histories, Human Lives*, edited by John Robb and Timothy R. Pauketat, pp. 35–56. School for Advanced Research Press, Santa Fe, New Mexico.

Penny, David W.

1985 Continuities of Imagery and Symbolism in the Art of the Woodlands. In *Ancient Art of the American Woodland Indians*, edited by David S. Brose, James A. Brown, and David W. Penny, pp. 147–198. Harry N. Abrams, New York.

Reilly, F. Kent III

2004 People of Earth, People of Sky: Visualizing the Sacred in Native American Art of the Mississippian Period. In *Hero, Hawk, and Open Hand: American Indian Art of the Ancient Midwest and South*, edited by R. F. Townsend and R. V. Sharp, pp. 125–137. Art Institute of Chicago, Chicago; Yale University Press, New Haven.

2011 The Great Serpent in the Lower Mississippi Valley. In *Visualizing the Sacred: Cosmic Visions, Regionalism, and the Art of the Mississippian World*, edited by George E. Lankford, F. Kent Reilly III, and James F. Garber, pp. 118–134. University of Texas Press, Austin.

Rolingson, Martha Ann

2012 *Toltec Mounds: Archaeology of the Mound-and-Plaza Complex*. Research Series No. 65. Arkansas Archaeological Survey, Fayetteville.

Romain, William F.

1988 The Serpent Mound Solar Eclipse Hypothesis: Ethnohistoric Considerations. *Ohio Archaeologist* 38 (3): 32–37.

1991 Evidence for a Basic Hopewell Unit of Measure. *Ohio Archaeologist* 41 (4): 28–37.

1992 Summer Solstice Sunset at Serpent Mound [photograph and figure caption]. *Ohio Archaeologist* 42 (2): 3 and front cover.

1996 Hopewellian Geometry: Forms at the Interface of Time and Eternity. In *A View from the Core: A Synthesis of Ohio Hopewell Archaeology*, edited by Paul J. Pacheco, pp. 194–209. Ohio Archaeological Council, Columbus.

2000 *Mysteries of the Hopewell: Astronomers, Geometers and Magicians of the Eastern Woodlands*. University of Akron Press, Akron.

2004 Journey to the Center of the World: Astronomy, Geometry, and Cosmology of the Fort Ancient Enclosure. In *The Fort Ancient Earthwork: Prehistoric Lifeways of the Hopewell in Southwestern Ohio*, edited by Robert. P. Connolly and Bradley T. Lepper, pp. 66–83. Ohio Historical Society, Columbus.

2005 Results of Coring at Newark Octagon Mounds D and E. Report on file, Archaeology Department, Ohio Historical Society, Columbus.

2009 *Shamans of the Lost World: A Cognitive Approach to the Prehistoric Religion of the Ohio Hopewell.* AltaMira Press, Lanham, Maryland.

2012a Moon City: A Lunar Explanation for the Cahokia Offset Grid. Paper presented at the Mississippian Conference, July 28, Cahokia Mounds State Historic Site, Collinsville, Illinois.

2012b Astronomy and Geometry at the Toltec Mounds Site: Implications for Cahokia. Paper presented at the Midwest Archaeological Conference, October 19, Michigan State University, East Lansing.

2013 Field Notes Regarding Geoprobe Coring at Geller Hill, Heath, Ohio, August 14–15, 2013. On file with author.

2014 New Radiocarbon Dates Suggest Serpent Mound Is More Than 2,000 Years Old. http://ancientearthworksproject.org/blog.html, accessed August 3, 2014.

2015a *An Archaeology of the Sacred: Adena-Hopewell Astronomy and Landscape Archaeology.* In preparation.

2015b Moonwatchers of Cahokia. In *Medieval Mississippians: The Cahokian World*, edited by Tim Pauketat and Susan Alt, pp. 32–41. School for Advanced Research Press, Santa Fe, New Mexico.

Romain, William F., and Jarrod Burks

2008a LiDAR Analyses of Prehistoric Earthworks in Ross County, Ohio. Ohio Archaeological Council. http://www.ohioarchaeology.org/Articles-and-Abstracts-2008/lidar-analyses-of-prehistoric-earthworks-in-ross-county-ohio.html, accessed August 22, 2014.

2008b LiDAR Imaging of the Great Hopewell Road. Ohio Archaeological Council. http://www.ohioarchaeology.org/Articles-and-Abstracts-2008/lidar-imaging-of-the-great-hopewell-road.html, accessed August 22, 2013.

2008c LiDAR Assessment of the Newark Earthworks. Ohio Archaeological Council. http://www.ohioarchaeology.org/Articles-and-Abstracts-2008/lidar-assessment-of-the-newark-earthworks.html, accessed August 22, 2014.

Romain, William F., and Norman L. Davis

2013 Astronomy and Geometry at Poverty Point. Louisiana Archaeological Society. http://www.laarchaeology.org/articles.html, accessed August 22, 2014.

Romain, William F., G. William Monaghan, Jarrod Burks, Michael Zaleha, Karen Leone, Timothy Schilling, Matthew Purtill, Edward Herrmann, and Alan Tonetti

2013 Serpent Mound Project Results. Paper presented at the Midwest Archaeological Conference, October 25, 2013, Columbus, Ohio.

Salisbury, James, and Charles Salisbury

1862 Accurate Surveys and Descriptions of the Ancient Earthworks at Newark, Ohio. Transcribed from the original by B. T. Lepper and B. T. Simmons. Manuscript on file, American Antiquarian Society, Worcester, Massachusetts.

Sherrod, P. Clay, and Martha Ann Rolingson

1987 *Surveyors of the Ancient Mississippi Valley: Modules and Alignments in Prehistoric Mound Sites.* Arkansas Archaeological Survey Research Series No. 28. Arkansas Archaeological Society, Fayetteville.

Skousen, B. Jacob

2012 Posts, Places, Ancestors, and Worlds: Dividual Personhood in the American Bottom Region. *Southeastern Archaeology* 31:57–69.

Smith, Theresa S.

1995 *Island of the Anishnaabeg: Thunderers and Water Monsters in the Traditional Ojibwe Life-World.* University of Idaho Press, Moscow.

Smucker, Isaac

1881 Mound Builder's Works near Newark, Ohio. *American Antiquarian* 3 (4): 261–270.

Sofaer, Anna (editor)

2008 *Chaco Astronomy: An Ancient American Cosmology.* Ocean Tree Books, Santa Fe, New Mexico.

Squier, Ephraim G., and Edwin H. Davis

1848 *Ancient Monuments of the Mississippi Valley Comprising the Results of Extensive Original Surveys and Explorations.* Smithsonian Contributions to Knowledge, Vol. 1. Smithsonian Institution, Washington, D.C.

Sullivan, William

1996 *The Secret of the Incas.* Crown, New York.

Swartz, B. K., Jr. (editor)

1971 *Adena: The Seeking of an Identity.* Ball State University, Muncie, Indiana.

Thomas, Cyrus

1894 *Report on the Mound Explorations of the Bureau of Ethnology for the Years 1890–1891.* 12th Annual Report of the Bureau of American Ethnology. Smithsonian Institution, Washington, D.C.

Tuan, Yi-Fu

1977 *Space and Place: The Perspective of Experience.* University of Minnesota Press, Minneapolis.

Van Dyke, Ruth M.

2007 Great Kivas in Time, Space, and Society. In *The Architecture of Chaco Canyon, New Mexico,* edited by Stephen H. Lekson, pp. 93–126. University of Utah Press, Salt Lake City.

Wallace, Anthony F. C.
1972   *The Death and Rebirth of the Seneca*. Vintage, New York.

Willoughby, Charles C. (with Ernest A. Hooton)
1919   The Serpent Mound of Adams County, Ohio. *American Anthropologist* 21 (2): 153–163.
1922   *The Turner Group of Earthworks, Hamilton County, Ohio*. Papers of the Peabody Museum, Vol. 8, No. 3. Harvard University, Cambridge, Massachusetts.

Wyrick, David
1866   Ancient Works near Newark, Licking County, Ohio. [Map from 1860.] In *Atlas of Licking County, Ohio*, edited by F. W. Beers. Beers + Soula, New York.

Zedeño, María N.
2008   Bundled Worlds: The Roles and Interactions of Complex Objects from the North American Plains. *Journal of Archaeological Method and Theory* 15:362–378.
2013   Methodological and Analytical Challenges in Relational Archaeologies: A View from the Hunting Ground. In *Relational Archaeologies: Humans, Animals, Things*, edited by Christopher Watts, pp. 117–134. Routledge, London.

Part II

Spirits and Forces

4

War-Scapes, Lingering Spirits, and the Mississippian Vacant Quarter

Meghan E. Buchanan

In this chapter I discuss the historical developments of peace and war in the Mississippian Midwestern United States and their relationships to a hypothesized region-wide abandonment referred to as the Vacant Quarter. Drawing on Carolyn Nordstrom's (1997) concept of "war-scapes" and Tim Ingold's (2008, 2011) "meshwork," I argue that the period leading up to and during the abandonment of the Vacant Quarter involved entanglements between multiple groups of people, powerful materials, physical boundaries, and spiritual beings. Using recently excavated materials from the Mississippian Common Field site in southeastern Missouri and ethnohistoric accounts of Osage war and peace ceremonies, I propose that in the face of growing regional hostilities the people of Common Field used minerals imbued with spiritual powers to fortify their palisade walls, bundling physical and spiritual protections. When the palisade was breached, the village burned, and victims left behind, some of the lines of the meshwork of life at Common Field were disentangled, while others, like the restless spirits of the deceased, continued to inhabit the village.

Portions of the pre-Columbian Midwest appear to have been largely abandoned during the fourteenth and fifteenth centuries, a phenomenon that has been referred to as the Vacant Quarter (Williams 1990) (Figure 4.1a). Explanations for this regional abandonment of parts of the Mississippi and Ohio river valleys have ranged from environmental degradation and climate change to the inevitable rise and fall of chiefly societies (Anderson 1994; Cobb and Butler 2002, 2006; Dalan et al. 2003; Iseminger 2010; Milner 1998; Williams 1990; Woods 2004). Since Williams's initial proposal that there was a Vacant Quarter, there has been mounting evidence that violence and warfare played a large role in the dissolution of Mississippian period (AD 1000–1400) polities. Warfare has been incorporated into earlier theories about abandonment, positioning violence as the means by which elites competed over lands and resources as they became scarce over time.

Recently, practice-based approaches to the study of warfare have emphasized its role "as an active 'project'" (Pauketat 2009:247) and a historical process rather than the predetermined outcome of politicking elites or land grabs in light of environmental change (Nielsen and Walker 2009). Warfare is not simply an outcome of culture change but an agent of change. In addition to pointing out the recursivity between warfare, daily life, and historical changes, these practice-based approaches draw attention to multiple agents and agencies (beyond elites and warriors) that are entangled in practices of violence and warfare. For example, archaeological analyses of warfare in the southwestern United States point out that nonhumans, supernatural beings, and animated essences played a role in violence-related practices (Walker 1998, 2009).

Ethnohistoric accounts of violence and warfare among Eastern Woodland and Plains Native

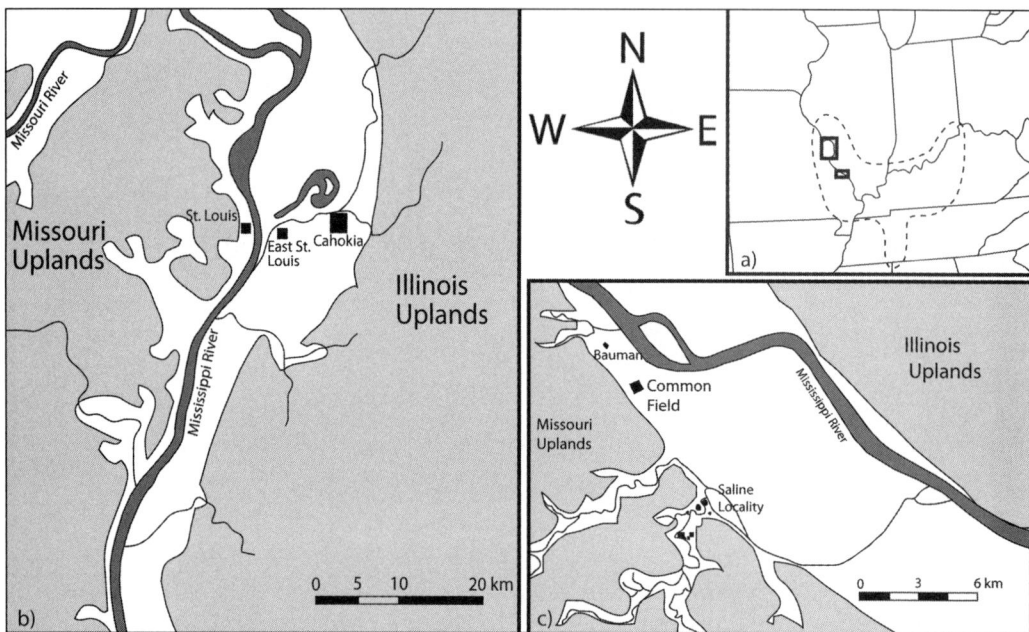

FIGURE 4.1. (*a*) Map of the Midwest with the Vacant Quarter circled (following Cobb and Butler 2002; Williams 1990) and American Bottom and Common Field highlighted. (*b*) Some Mississippian sites located in the American Bottom. (*c*) Common Field and nearby sites.

Americans highlight what Ingold (2008, 2011) refers to as a "meshwork" of movements and relationships between people, places, animals, materials, and animate forces in the universe. Within such relational ontologies, the entanglements between and among actors are transformative, having the potential to cause culture change. Thus, within archaeological analyses of warfare and regional abandonments we must attend to the many movements, entanglements, and disentanglements between agents and agencies that are constitutive of historical processes and disjunctures.

War-Scape Meshworks

Nordstrom (1997) argues that warfare does not take place in circumscribed locations; warfare cannot be isolated to individual sites or battlefields, attributed solely to warriors, or disentangled from the production of daily life (see also Pauketat 2009). She argues instead that war-torn regions are best conceptualized as "war-scapes" in which political boundaries are fluid and multiple groups of actors come together in tangled webs of interactions. Within war-scapes "local and transnational concerns are enmeshed in the cultural construction of conflict that is continually reconfigured across time and space. Each person, each group brings a history that informs action and is negotiated vis-à-vis the various other histories of those with whom they interact" (Nordstrom 1997:37). As boundaries are blurred in war-scapes and groups of people come into contact, new conditions of interaction (whether peaceful, contentious, or neutral) require people to engage with the world around them in novel ways (sensu Alt 2006, 2008; Bhabha 1994).

While Nordstrom's war-scape focuses predominantly on the interactions between human actors, Ingold (2011) argues that the world we inhabit is a meshwork composed of the entangled lines and threads of life and movement. He suggests that "we must stop regarding the world as an inert substratum, over which living things propel themselves about like counters on a board or actors on a stage" (2006:14). Rather than navigate an external reality made up of bounded, exclusionary objects and things, we make our way through and are entangled with the continually transforming world (2008:1802); we inhabit a world that is in flux as actors gain knowledge about the world and construct the world through their engagements with other people, places, spirits, and so on. It is through these movements, through entanglements with others, that things come to be and are continually on the cusp of becoming (sensu Heidegger 1971).

This perspective, in which the world is animate and full of movement, fits well with ethnohistoric accounts of Plains and Eastern Woodlands Native American worldviews, where agency is not the sole domain of humans. While it is problematic to homogenize a singular pan-regional indigenous North American ontology (Harrison-Buck, this volume), many Caddoan- and Siouan-speaking peoples of the Plains, Midwest, and South believe in dispersed powers that inhabit the earth, sky, celestial bodies, substances, and qualities (Bailey 1995; Dorsey 1885; La Flesche 1939).[1] Agency and animacy are distributed among humans, animals, plants, objects, landscapes, weather, and celestial bodies. The boundaries between this world and others, between nature and culture, between humans and the supernatural, are slippery and permeable (see Romain, this volume; Skousen, this volume). For Siouan-speaking peoples of the Plains and upper Midwest, the mysterious life force inhabits earth, fire, water, wind, minerals, pigments, and other substances (Bailey 1995; Hall 1997; La Flesche 1939; Pauketat 2008).

Osage ceremonies surrounding the practice of war invoke the powers of *wa-kon-da* for advice, protection, success in battle, and mourning of the deceased (La Flesche 1939). Ceremonies and religious practices surrounding warfare are not simply "beliefs"; within such a relational perspective, animate beings, powers, and spirits play a role in inspiring war parties, protecting warriors and prophets, animating war trophies and bundles, and seeking retribution (Cave 2006; La Flesche 1939; Pauketat 2013; Zedeño 2008). Humans could attempt to access and tap into these animating powers in order to affect the outcomes of violent encounters and to quell restless or dissatisfied spirits.

Warfare, then, is not just a conflict between discrete groups as part of the predictable fallout from political collapse or climate change. The meshworks of war-scapes involve the actions of many different kinds of actors with their own subjectivities, take place in historicized and animate landscapes, and have ramifications that extend beyond the loci of violent actions (Pauketat 2009; Walker 2009). The war-scape meshwork did not have easily predicted outcomes: actors had to contend with death, destruction, mourning, remembering, and forgetting as some threads of the meshwork were disentangled or reentangled in other ways (Baltus, this volume; Baltus and Baires 2012).

The fragmentation of Mississippian polities in the Midwest, the spread of violence, and the subsequent abandonment of parts of the region provide a window into the meshwork of a pre-Columbian war-scape. In the next section I discuss the development and dissolution of the Cahokian polity, evidence for violent conflict, and the hypothesized Vacant Quarter.

Violence and Conflict in the Mississippian Midwest

The Cahokian polity located in the American Bottom floodplain (near modern-day East St. Louis, Illinois) (Figure 4.1b) was established around AD 1050 in a rapid buildup that included the demolition of earlier villages, reorganization of urban and rural spaces, establishment of the central political-administrative complex (linking Cahokia, the East St. Louis, and St. Louis mound groups), monumental constructions, performance of community-wide feasting and mortuary events, and an influx of immigrants (Alt 2001, 2006, 2008, 2010a; Dalan et al. 2003; Emerson 1997; Pauketat 2004, 2010). As part of this rapid rise, trade envoys and Cahokian missionaries were sent to communities great distances from Cahokia itself. Early Cahokian communities have been found as far north as Wisconsin, where encounters between Mississippians and Late Woodland peoples appear to have been peaceful (Benden et al. 2010, 2011; Green and Rodell 1994; Pauketat 2004). Large portions of the Midwest experienced a Pax Cahokiana, a period of relative peace, punctuated by politically sponsored acts of violence like mass sacrifices and mortuary performances (Brown 2003; Pauketat 2010). Iconographic depictions of violence from this early phase of Cahokia history have traditionally been interpreted as representations of mythic figures (Dye 2009). Others have argued that whether or not these images depict myths, they reveal the concerns and experiences of living peoples (Alt 2008; Cobb and Giles 2009; Emerson 2007).

This period of relative peace ended around AD 1150 with the first construction of the palisade around Cahokia's sacred central precinct as well as the construction of fortifications around elite compounds at the nearby East St. Louis mound site. Recent climatological work in the Cahokia region demonstrates that there were fluctuating wet and dry periods around the same time as this palisade construction (Benson et al. 2009). This unpredictability likely resulted in resource instability and unequal access to goods in some parts of the Midwest. Several of the fortified compounds at East St. Louis were burned in a catastrophic event, leaving behind burned storage huts (or granaries) filled with caches of maize and ceramic vessels (Fortier 2007; Pauketat 2005; Pauketat et al. 2013). During this same period, population at Cahokia dropped from an estimated 10,000–15,000 inhabitants to a few thousand by AD 1200 (Pauketat and Lopinot 1997). While there is no evidence that Cahokia was ever attacked, the burning at East St. Louis and regional emigration implicate contentious politics and a disaffected populace.

Concurrent with these events at Cahokia and East St. Louis, villages in the Illinois River valley constructed palisades. Several of the villages here show evidence of violent conflict. The Orendorf site palisade was rebuilt multiple times, and osteological data have revealed violence-related mortuary patterns, including evidence of scalping, blunt-force cranial trauma, and skeletal elements with embedded arrow points (Steadman 2008). As Oneota groups moved into the Illinois River Valley around AD 1300, there is considerable evidence for violence at the Norris Farms #36 cemetery (Milner 1999; Milner et al. 1991). Other villages in the Illinois valley were similarly palisaded and may have suffered from violent attack (Conrad 1991).

The Vacant Quarter

Stephen Williams (1990) proposed that large Mississippian towns and villages throughout portions of the central Mississippi, lower Ohio, Tennessee, and Cumberland river valleys were depopulated around AD 1450–1550 (Figure 4.1a). While the exact timing and scale of this regional abandonment has been debated (Cobb and Butler 2002; Morse and Morse 1983), there is mounting evidence that mound centers, villages, and hamlets from Williams's proposed Vacant Quarter were abandoned by Mississippian peoples by approximately AD 1450 (and even earlier in some regions). Cahokia, the largest Mississippian polity, was abandoned sometime during the early fourteenth century (Emerson and Hargrave 2000; Milner 1998). Mississippian political centers in the lower Ohio River valley, such as Kincaid and Angel, were similarly depopulated. Following the abandonment of Kincaid Mounds in southern Illinois, people moved to interior upland regions and then left those villages by the mid-fifteenth century (Butler and Cobb 2012; Cobb and Butler 2002, 2006). Angel Mounds in southern Indiana was also abandoned in the mid-fifteenth century (Monaghan and Peebles 2010). As in the relocation and reorganization seen in southern Illinois, former Angel inhabitants moved downstream to form new communities (referred to as Caborn-Welborn) that persisted into the Historic period (Pollack 2004). Palisaded villages such as Powers Fort in southeastern Missouri were burned and abandoned by the early fifteenth century (Morse and Morse 1983; O'Brien 2002; O'Brien and Wood 1998; Price and Griffin 1979). The overall picture that emerges is one in which most large settlements were abandoned by the fifteenth century, with a number of smaller settlements lasting into the Historic era. During this period of reorganization and abandonment, much of the region would have still been used for hunting and travel, particularly along the Mississippi and Ohio Rivers.

In his formulation of the Vacant Quarter hypothesis, Williams (1990) suggested a number of possible causal agents for this region-wide population dispersal and abandonment, including sociopolitical change and instability, disease, climate change, earthquakes, plant disease, and warfare. Williams acknowledged the difficulties of demonstrating the presence of plant blights and diseases that do not affect bones, as well as the restricted geographic impacts of seismic events. Since the initial proposal of the Vacant Quarter hypothesis, most researchers have focused on the role of environmental change (natural and anthropogenic), political cycling, or a combination of those two factors (Cobb and Butler 2002, 2006; Dalan et al. 2003; Iseminger 2010; Milner 1998; Woods 2004).

Aside from the burned Powers phase sites in

southeast Missouri, little archaeological evidence for warfare existed when Williams proposed the Vacant Quarter, leading him to downplay the possibility of violence (Williams 1990:176). Mississippian period warfare and palisade building in the southeastern United State have been explained as a means by which political leaders legitimized authority, consolidated power, and expanded their political reach (Dye 2009; Jennings 2011; Larson 1972; Milner 1998). Warfare has similarly been linked to the evolution, expansion, and dissolution of complex societies in other parts of the world (Allen and Arkush 2006; Carneiro 1970; Earle 1997; Tainter 1988).

In terms of explaining the abandonment of the Vacant Quarter, research implicating environmental change and political cycling frequently invokes violence and warfare as effects of territorial expansion for political and economic gain. Warfare is seen as both an accretional and attritional mechanism by which lands, goods, and status are variously accumulated or lost by elites and warriors depending on success in violent encounters (Dye 2009; Jennings 2011; Larson 1972; Milner 1998). These largely positivist approaches see the causes of warfare and abandonment as outside of social processes, rooted in the external environment or in the inherent nature and instability of political organizations. But such propositions do little to explain why some (but not all) societies fight or why some regions are abandoned and other are not. Problematically, downplaying (or ignoring) historical processes can lead to models in which political systems and the environment exist as external superstructures to human actions and dispositions (Alt 2010b; Marcoux and Wilson 2010; Pauketat 2007).

Within the meshwork of war-scapes, violence enacted and experienced throughout the Mississippian Midwest would have involved entanglements between multiple groups of actors (human and nonhuman), landscapes, violent ideologies, and daily practices. Such historically contingent processes and entanglements in war-scapes would have uneven results as some communities engaged in violence, others formed alliances, the scale and intensity of violent encounters varied, tales of such encounters were spread to other regions, and some places were abandoned and others were not. Much as in the Osage war and peace ceremonies, Mississippian peoples frequently invoked the powers of objects, materials, places, and supernatural beings (Baltus and Baires 2012; Kelly and Brown 2012; Pauketat 2013; Skousen, this volume), and would have also done so in order to provide protective measures and victory in battle.

The palisaded Mississippian village of Common Field in southeastern Missouri, located in what would become the Vacant Quarter, was a community entangled in the growing hostilities of a war-scape associated with the fall of the Cahokian polity. Common Field was ultimately burned down in a catastrophic event, providing us an opportunity to explore the meshworks of people, places, materials, spirits, and events leading up to the abandonment of the Vacant Quarter.

Warfare at the Common Field Site

Common Field is located in the Mississippi River floodplain, approximately 80 km south of Cahokia (Figure 4.1c). Several contemporaneous sites are located in the floodplain as well. The Bauman site is a small hamlet/village that has been interpreted as a possible river port north of Common Field (Voigt 1985). Large caches of celt blanks and unworked galena were recovered from features. Several other sites are located along the Saline Creek, south of Common Field (Keslin 1964). The Saline Locality was a salt-producing and mortuary complex. In addition to several areas dedicated to the extraction of salt from spring water, bluff-top burial mounds (with sandstone-lined stone box graves) overlook the salt springs. Nearby a freshwater spring emerges from a cave with Mississippian petroglyphs etched on the floor (Bushnell 1914; Diaz-Granados and Duncan 2000).

Despite the archaeological practice of treating sites as bounded entities, Common Field, Bauman, and the Saline Locality formed part of a larger, interconnected landscape (King, this volume). West of Common Field, the St. Francois Mountains and the Ozarks were routinely visited by pre-Columbian peoples as part of religious practices (pilgrimages, vision quests) as well as for ritually important natural resources (basalt, galena, hematite, red cedar) (Butler 2011; Kelly and Brown 2012; Pauketat and Alt 2004). The region is marked by both mountains and caves/sinkholes,

FIGURE 4.2. Aerial photograph of the Common Field site with mounds and burned features noted (photo courtesy of F. Terry Norris, St. Louis District, U.S. Army Corps of Engineers).

forming a landscape that linked the Upper, This, and Below Worlds.

Previous work at Common Field, including aerial photography (Figure 4.2) and surface collection, points to the widescale burning and destruction of the site (O'Brien 1996; O'Brien et al. 1982). During a major Mississippi River flood in 1979–1980, a levee north of the site was breached. Floodwaters rushed across portions of Common Field, effectively scouring the plow zone from the surface of the site and exposing hundreds of Mississippian features. From the air at least three hundred structures are visible, many of them burned.

University of Missouri Columbia (UMC) conducted a surface survey following the scouring episode, documenting house basin features filled with burned debris and in situ burned posts (Ferguson 1990; O'Brien 1996; Trader 1992). The artifacts recovered during this collection point to a catastrophic demise. Many of the ceramic sherds are large, easily refitted to other sherds with old breaks, and several vessels were nearly complete despite being plowed twice before archaeologists reached the site. Michael O'Brien (1996) also reported the presence of the remains of at least twenty individuals, often still articulated, scattered across the surface of the site.

Initial analyses of the ceramics from the site were used to argue that people from Common Field practiced mixed northern (Cahokian) and southern ceramic construction and decorative traditions (Ferguson 1990; Milner 1998). Recently excavated materials and my reanalysis of the UMC ceramic collection from Common Field demonstrate that Common Field ceramics are stylistically and morphologically similar to assemblages recovered from the American Bottom (Buchanan 2009). The Common Field ceramics fit comfortably into Cahokian Moorehead (AD 1200–1275) and Sand Prairie phase (AD 1275–1350) ceramic traditions. These similarities in decorative and construction methods point to an American Bottom origin for many of the inhabitants of Common Field.

From 2010 to 2012 I conducted excavations at Common Field in order to understand the site's chronology and relationship to contemporaneous sites as well as to explore how regional violence affected people's daily lives before the destruction of the site. For the remainder of this chapter, I focus on the construction of the palisade and human remains recovered from one structure located inside the palisade wall.

Fortifying Protections

The first construction of the palisade consisted of large, upright logs set into an excavated trench. The bottoms of several of these 20-cm-diameter posts are visible as soil stains below the base of the palisade trench, indicating that the first palisade construction either was allowed to rot in place or was chopped down with the post bases left in situ.

Following the removal of the first palisade, the builders incorporated a fill mixed with crushed limestone, sandstone, polished pebbles, and galena. The second palisade construction was placed atop this mixture, and more of the mixture was used to pack around the base of posts. This mixture could have been intended as an architectural solution to settling or leaning of the palisade. However, the mixed fill is soft and loose, which would have exacerbated architectural issues rather than resolving them.

Both sandstone and limestone are readily available from the bluffs located half a kilometer from Common Field. The polished pebbles, on the other hand, come from an unknown source. Pebbles have been recovered from other features on site, but never in the quantity found in the palisade.

The pebble fill includes highly polished, subangular local chert cobbles, quartz pebbles, and siltstone. In addition to these locally available stones, there are polished fragments of rhyolite (with hematite flecks), basalt, and granite, all of which come from nonlocal parent source materials, likely the St. Francois Mountains. The high degree of polishing, the subangular shape of the stones, and the presence of nonlocal materials are characteristic of fill from a low-velocity creek or stream with a source at a higher elevation (Richmond and Weide 1993). The Springfield and Salem Plateaus that make up the Ozark Uplift region and the St. Francois Mountains are composed of igneous bedrock and bands of chert, and contain several hematite and galena sources (Ray 2007; Weller and St. Clair 1928). This uplift area west of Common Field is intercut with numerous creeks and streams, many lined with the kinds of waterworn, polished pebbles found in the palisade fill.

Several pieces of galena were also incorporated in the fill. Source locations for galena include four counties (Crawford, Washington, Iron, and Reynolds) that encircle the St. Francois Mountains and the eastern portion of the Ozarks. Galena has been recognized as a prestige and sacred item at Cahokia, where it was ground into white pigment, turned into other objects (such as beads), or left unmodified (Betzenhauser 2007; Emerson 1997; Pauketat 2004). As noted previously, the St. Francois Mountains and the surrounding Ozark region were part of a sacred landscape (Butler 2011; Kelly and Brown 2012; Pauketat and Alt 2004). Caves, sinkholes, and other unusual natural features in the region were visited by Mississippians and earlier peoples (Diaz-Granados and Duncan 2000). Many of these caves, including the Bushnell Ceremonial cave in the Saline Locality, are marked with cross-in-circle (axis mundi) and avian motifs. Caves are permeable places where the boundaries between This World, the World Above, and the World Below are fluid and transgressable by humans, animals, and spirits. Materials brought back from the Ozark/St. Francois Mountain region no doubt had their own associated essences and powers. It is unknown at this point whether the pebbles recovered from the palisade fill came from the Saline Locality or whether they were collected and transported from other streambeds in the region.

Much like the Osage belief that certain substances were animate (imbued with the power of *wa-kon-da*), the inclusion of a sacred material into the foundations of the primary defensive feature on site would create a protected space that people experienced daily. Since these materials are not naturally occurring in the floodplain where Common Field is located, their removal from a sacred landscape and incorporation into the palisade construction indicates an intentional deposition. Structured deposits of specially prepared alternating mantles of light and dark soils in mounds have similarly been argued as evidence for the gathering of dispersed agentic forces at Mississippian sites in the American Bottom and uplands (Pauketat 2008). The deposition of materials from the Ozarks and their association with the palisade at Common Field suggest a bundling (sensu Pauketat 2013) or gathering of agentic powers (physical and spiritual) around the village for defensive purposes.

Casualties of War

Human remains encountered on the surface of the site following the flood in 1979 were found in still-articulated positions, which led University of Missouri researchers to conclude that they were burials (O'Brien et al. 1982; O'Brien 1996). Burials recorded at the nearby Saline Locality were all found in formal graves lined with limestone slabs or large fragments of salt pan (Bushnell 1914; Keslin 1964). Stone box graves are found throughout the Mississippi and Ohio River valleys and are the predominant burial method during the Moorehead phase at Cahokia and the American Bottom (Brown 1981; Emerson and Hargrave 2000).

The accounts of human remains recovered from the Common Field surface survey make no mention of limestone slabs. One individual was recovered by UMC in the fill of a house basin, unaccompanied by funerary goods or stone slabs for a grave. The presence of this individual in basin fill (rather than a subfloor feature) indicates that he or she was left, not buried, in the abandoned structure. Articulated human remains, a lack of formal burial features, the presence of one individual in house basin fill from the 1980 project, and numerous burned structures suggest a catastrophic death event in which individuals were not afforded proper burial.

Another individual was recovered from house basin fill during excavations in 2011. Portions of a left and right femur as well as a tibia, patella, radius, and multiple phalanges were encountered during the excavation of a house structure located just inside the palisade wall. As with the human remains noted by UMC, there was no burial feature.

Carnivore gnawing and puncture marks are present on long-bone elements. The distal condyles and part of the distal shaft of the left femur were completely destroyed by carnivore gnawing. The greater and lesser trochanters were gnawed, although the femur head and neck were largely intact. In addition, carnivore damage was noted along the major muscle attachments of the femur shaft. The only portions of the right femur that remained intact were the distal condyles, also marked with puncture and scour marks from canine teeth. The proximal and distal articular portions of the right tibia were destroyed via carnivore damage, and as with the shaft of the femur, scour marks are present along major muscle attachments.

These remains appear to come from a single individual who was left exposed to carnivores while flesh was still adhering to the bone. The presence of carnivore gnawing demonstrates that this individual was left exposed for an indeterminate amount of time (Milner et al. 1991). It is unlikely that a deceased individual would have been left exposed and available to carnivores if the structure or nearby structures were still inhabited by the living; contemporaneous American Bottom cemeteries are located some distance from habitation sites and areas.

Several patches of burned and oxidized soil on the floor of the house, as well as postholes with evidence of burning, indicate that the individual was left in the structure at approximately the same time it was burned. After the cessation of the conflagration, the deceased individual was left in or near the structure, exposed, and was eventually destroyed by carnivores before natural processes filled in the remainder of the basin.

Similar patterns of extreme carnivore gnawing have been recorded at the Norris Farms #36 cemetery in the Illinois River valley and the Crow Creek massacre site in South Dakota (Milner 1999; Milner et al. 1991; Willey and Emerson 1993; Zimmerman 1997; Zimmerman and Bradley 1993). Both Norris Farms #36 and Crow Creek were the sites of violent attacks. At Crow Creek at least 486 individuals were killed and mutilated in a surprise attack (Wiley and Emerson 1993; Zimmerman 1997). Survivors of the attack returned to the village and buried the deceased, but not before the dead were set upon by carnivores. Victims of attacks at Norris Farms #36 were similarly mutilated, left exposed, and gnawed by carnivores before being buried by returning survivors.

In contrast to Norris Farms #36 and Crow Creek, at Common Field the recovery of human remains in house basins rather than burial features (the deceased from Crow Creek were interred in the palisade trench) and the extreme carnivore gnawing on at least one individual point to a different scenario of violence. As the village was attacked and homes burned, some people were killed and left exposed. During that period of exposure, carnivores consumed the deceased and chewed their bones. If survivors returned to bury the dead, not all were found and afforded burial. More likely, survivors did not return to bury the dead as they did at Norris Farms #36 and Crow Creek.

Discussion

As the Pax Cahokiana ended, palisades were constructed across the Midwest, large numbers of people left major political centers, and the town of Common Field was established by immigrants from the American Bottom region. Once settled in the floodplain, they constructed a palisade, enclosing their earthen platform mounds and habitation area. Structures located outside the palisade were dismantled and filled with soil. In the second construction of the palisade the builders incorporated a prepared fill that included highly polished pebbles and galena.

In his account of Osage war ceremonies, Francis La Flesche (1939:228) noted that the Osage preferred to avoid war for fear of reprisal, often engaging in defensive practices for long periods of time before going on the offensive. The Osage avoided offensive warfare because the only way to defeat one's enemies was to completely destroy them (Bailey 1995). Although La Flesche does not provide details about what is entailed in Osage defensive practices, his descriptions of war ceremonies and preparations give clues about the nature of human and supernatural interactions during war times. Members of the war party pray, cry, and sing to *wa-kon-da* for aid and success in battle. Sacred materials and animals, themselves considered to be part of or imbued with *wa-kon-da*, were brought together and assembled for marches, dances, prayer, guidance, and worship.

After the return of war parties, members of the community gathered to mourn any losses. Throughout the Eastern Woodlands and Plains, Native American tribes' mourning ceremonies for deceased warriors or community members killed in attacks often involved the bundling of souls (in the form of bones and hair) for extended periods before releasing their spirits to the next world (Hall 1997; La Flesche 1939). The Osage believe that souls sleep until someone on earth is able to avenge their death and dispatch them to the realm of spirits. Hunters would report hearing the voices of restless dead after visiting areas where violence had taken place. La Flesche (1939: 87) also reports that the journey the spirits make to the afterlife is lonely. Thus war parties were sometimes formed to kill an enemy to accompany their deceased friend to the spirit realm. In parts of the Eastern Woodlands, captives were frequently taken, tortured, and adopted to take the place of deceased individuals (DeBoer 2008; Hall 1997; Peregrine 2008).

Pauketat (2013) draws on the metaphor of the bundle in order to interrogate the connections between agency and religion. Bundles may refer to a physical, wrapped group of things, but the term may be extended to refer to the association of distinct sets of things. According to Pauketat (2013:27), bundles are "nodes in a larger field or web of relationships where material and metaphorical relations and associations articulate with one another." Bundles, then, have the power to bring together some relationships, the power to mediate others, and the ability to effect change (cf. Zedeño 2008). At Common Field the placement of galena and polished pebbles in the palisade was not simply a dedicatory offering or a symbol of power; it was the bundling of distinct materials and associated powers (from the permeable realm of the Ozarks) with felled logs in order to create a larger meshwork of physical and spiritual protections (sensu Ingold 2011; Brown Vega, this volume).

As in the accounts of Osage war preparations, the use of sacred materials was a defensive strategy. But despite the efforts of the people at Common Field to bundle physical and spiritual protections around the perimeter of their town, the palisade was eventually burned and breached, leading to the burning of homes, the desecration of sacred spaces, and the killing of numerous people. The penetration and destruction of the fortification wall imbued with protective powers would have been a signal to the people of Common Field that their attempts at supernatural and physical defense were unheard, disregarded, or denied. Just as materials were brought together, woven, entangled, enmeshed, and bundled with each other, they were rent apart and unmade (see also Baltus, this volume).

People who were killed after the penetration of the palisade were left unburied, their bodies consumed by carnivores. Survivors of the attack may have scattered to other places; some were likely taken captive. The lack of burial treatment and exposure to carnivores indicate that the deceased were not properly mourned after their death; their spirits not dispatched to the other realm because survivors were unable to create physical bundles and burials. Like the restless victims heard by hunters, the unmourned dead at Common Field would have had a lingering human presence, even after the living were gone. The movements of the dead continued to animate the region after the living dispersed.

The bundling of physical and spiritual protection, the burning of the town and its fortification, and the presence of victims of the attack were all actors involved in the abandonment of the Vacant Quarter. At the time of Common Field's destruction and abandonment, large numbers of people were leaving the American Bottom, and towns throughout the region constructed palisades. Multiple groups of actors interacted in novel ways in this changing social and political landscape. The Midwestern war-scape involved rapidly changing entanglements between people, spirits, landscapes, and places. Part of these entanglements involved the acquisition and use of materials from spiritually charged places, meshworks of human and supernatural forces, death, and in some cases, destruction.

In this respect, the Vacant Quarter was not vacant at all, as the unsettled spirits of the deceased continued to inhabit places like Common Field. When archaeologists speak of abandonment, they typically mean that sites are no longer occupied by living humans. However, "abandoned" regions and sites are frequently still inhabited by spirits and visited by the living (Bell 1997; Colwell-Chanthaphonh and Ferguson 2006; Gardner 1987). Such "abandonments" may have created the ideal conditions for nonhuman agents to inhabit spaces. In 1673 Père Marquette and Illiniwek guides encountered such an inhabited space in the same general region as Common Field. As they traveled down the Mississippi River, they first encountered a pictograph on a river bluff depicting two creatures with antlers, scales, and fish tails, similar to a creature depicted in Picture Cave, located along the periphery of the Ozarks. As their journey progressed south, Marquette recounted that they "passed by a place that is dreaded by the savages, because they believe that a Manitou is there—that is to say, a demon—that devours travelers; and the savages, who wished to divert us from our undertaking, warned us against it" (Thwaite 1900:143–145). Approximately three hundred years after the burning of Common Field and two hundred years after the abandonment of the Vacant Quarter, certain parts of the Mississippi River valley were still inhabited by supernatural beings.

Sites of violence may be contested, memorialized, and manipulated (Logan and Reeves 2009). After people dispersed from the Vacant Quarter, recognizable archaeological signatures become difficult to trace. The kinds of events that resulted in the destruction of Common Field would have necessitated a reconfiguration of material culture, symbolism and iconography, and daily life for survivors. Following the abandonment of the Vacant Quarter, knowledge of Cahokia and other Mississippian towns and cities was forgotten. With the evidence of the violent conflict that took place at Common Field, it is increasingly clear that the reverberations of violence shook social, political, and spiritual worlds.

When we attempt to understand the causal factors behind the abandonment of the Vacant Quarter, materialist and behavioralist approaches that implicate political cycling or environmental change fall short in explaining all the hows and whys behind the particular processes that led to violence and abandonment. In an animated, entangled, transformational war-scape, the events of violent encounters are not predetermined, nor are their outcomes. This world-in-formation, where both aggression and defense in times of war involved the supernatural, also transgresses permeable boundaries between the living and the dead. The consequences of violent actions had lasting impacts that echoed beyond battles and sites of violence. At the Common Field site, Mississippian inhabitants quickly built their palisade and fortified it with spiritual protection. Yet they were attacked—their homes burned, kith and kin killed, many of their bodies left behind and eaten by carnivores. No one returned. As survivors dispersed, the dead lingered. The attack resulted in displaced refugees, fear of reprisal and further attacks, rumors of war spread to other peoples, and entire regions devoid of the living but animated with the spirits of the dead. The Vacant Quarter was far from abandoned.

Acknowledgments

I am grateful to the people and funding sources that made this research possible. Susan M. Alt has generously provided equipment, training, and encouragement over the years. Excavations at Common Field were funded by a Wenner-Gren Dissertation Field Work Grant (Gr. 8366), a Foundation for Restoration of Ste. Genevieve Research Grant, and the Indiana University Department of Anthropology David C. Skomp Summer Research Fund. Additionally, I thank the Roth family, F. Terry Norris, and the many people who have aided my excavations at Common Field. Elizabeth L. Watts, Dawn M. Rutecki, B. Jacob Skousen, and two reviewers all provided valuable comments and feedback on earlier drafts.

Note

1. I rely primarily on ethnohistoric accounts of Prairie-Plains peoples, particularly the Osage, for two reasons. First, it has become increasingly clear that Dhegiha Siouan peoples (such as the Osage) are some of the descendants of the Mississippian societies from the Midwest (see, for example, Kelly and Brown 2012; Pauketat 2008). Second, the rich corpus of historic and ethnographic accounts relating to the peoples of Prairie-Plains written by both Euro-American and Native American authors allows for the examination of broad patterns in oral and material traditions across space and time.

References Cited

Allen, Mark W., and Elizabeth N. Arkush
2006   Introduction: Archaeology and the Study of War. In *The Archaeology of Warfare: Prehistories of Raiding and Conquest*, edited by Elizabeth N. Arkush and Mark W. Allen, pp. 1–19. University Press of Florida, Gainesville.

Alt, Susan M.
2001   Cahokian Change and the Authority of Tradition. In *The Archaeology of Traditions: Agency and History Before and After Columbus*, edited by Timothy R. Pauketat, pp. 141–156. University Press of Florida, Gainesville.
2006   The Power of Diversity: The Roles of Migration and Hybridity in Culture Change. In *Leadership and Polity in Mississippian Society*, edited by Brian M. Butler and Paul D. Welch, pp. 289–308. Occasional Paper No. 33. Center for Archaeological Investigation, Southern Illinois University, Carbondale.
2008   Unwilling Immigrants: Culture, Change and the "Other." In *Invisible Citizens: Captives, Slaves, and Cultural Transmission in Middle Range Societies*, edited by Catherine M. Cameron, pp. 205–222. University of Utah Press, Salt Lake City.
2010a   Complexity in Action(s): Retelling the Cahokia Story. In *Ancient Complexities: New Perspectives in Pre-Columbian North America*, edited by Susan M. Alt, pp. 119–137. University of Utah Press, Salt Lake City.
2010b   Considering Complexity: Confounding Categories with Practices. In *Ancient Complexities: New Perspectives in Pre-Columbian North America*, edited by Susan M. Alt, pp. 1–7. University of Utah Press, Salt Lake City.

Anderson, David G.
1994   *The Savannah River Chiefdoms: Political Change in the Late Pre-historic Southeast*. University of Alabama Press, Tuscaloosa.

Bailey, Garrick A.
1995   *The Osage and the Invisible World: From the Works of Francis La Flesche*. University of Oklahoma Press, Norman.

Baltus, Melissa R., and Sarah E. Baires
2012   Elements of Ancient Power in the Cahokian World. *Journal of Social Archaeology* 12:167–192.

Bell, Michael Mayerfeld
1997   The Ghosts of Place. *Theory and Society* 26:813–836.

Benden, Danielle M., Timothy R. Pauketat, and Robert F. Boszhardt
2010   Early Mississippian Colonists in the Upper Mississippi Valley: 2009 Investigations at the Fisher Mounds Site Complex. *Wisconsin Archeologist* 91:131–132.
2011   The Mississippian Initiative: Year Two at Trempealeau. *Wisconsin Archeologist* 92:73–75.

Benson, Larry V., Timothy R. Pauketat, and Edward R. Cook
2009   Cahokia's Boom and Bust in the Context of

Climate Change. *American Antiquity* 74:467–483.

Betzenhauser, Allen
2007 Greater Cahokian Farmsteads: A Quantitative and Qualitative Analysis. Unpublished Master's thesis, Department of Anthropology, University of Illinois, Urbana.

Bhabha, Homi K.
1994 *The Location of Culture*. Routledge, New York.

Brown, Ian
1981 A Study of Stone Box Grave in Eastern North America. *Tennessee Anthropologist* 6:1–26.

Brown, James A.
2003 The Cahokia Mound 72-Sub1 Burials as Collective Representation. *Wisconsin Archeologist* 84:81–97.

Buchanan, Meghan E.
2009 Materiality and Personhood at a Mississippian Village: Ceramics from the Common Field Site. Paper presented at the 66th Annual Southeastern Archaeology Conference, Mobile, Alabama.

Bushnell, David I., Jr.
1914 Archaeological Investigations in Ste. Genevieve County, Missouri. *United States National Museum, Proceedings* 46:641–668.

Butler, Amanda J.
2011 Playing Detective with Mississippian Period Axe-Heads: Detailing the Results of a Provenance Study Using Portable X-Ray Fluorescence. Paper presented at the 57th Midwest Archaeological Conference, La Crosse, Wisconsin.

Butler, Brian M., and Charles R. Cobb
2012 Paired Mississippian Communities in the Lower Ohio Hinterland of Southern Illinois. *Midcontinental Journal of Archaeology* 37:45–72.

Carneiro, Robert L.
1970 A Theory of the Origin of the State. *Science* 169:733–738.

Cave, Alfred A.
2006 *Prophets of the Great Spirit: Native American Revitalization Movements in Eastern North America*. University of Nebraska Press, Lincoln.

Cobb, Charles R., and Brian M. Butler
2002 The Vacant Quarter Revisited: Late Mississippian Abandonment of the Lower Ohio Valley. *American Antiquity* 67:625–641.
2006 Mississippian Migration and Emplacement in the Lower Ohio Valley. In *Leadership and Polity in Mississippian Society*, edited by Brian M. Butler and Paul D. Welch. Occasional Paper No. 33. Center for Archaeological Investigation, Southern Illinois University, Carbondale.

Cobb, Charles R., and Bretton Giles
2009 War Is Shell: The Ideology and Embodiment of Mississippian Conflict. In *Warfare in Cultural Conflict: Practice, Agency, and the Archaeology of Violence*, edited by Axel E. Nielsen and William H. Walker, pp. 84–108. University of Arizona Press, Tucson.

Colwell-Chanthaphonh, Chip, and T. J. Ferguson
2006 Memory Pieces and Footprints: Multivocality and Meanings of Ancient Times and Ancestral Places among the Zuni and Hopi. *American Anthropologist* 108:148–162.

Conrad, Lawrence
1991 The Middle Mississippian Cultures of the Central Illinois River Valley. In *Cahokia and the Hinterlands: Middle Mississippian Cultures of the Midwest*, edited by Thomas E. Emerson and R. B. Lewis, pp. 119–156. University of Illinois Press, Urbana.

Dalan, Rinita A., George R. Holley, William I. Woods, Harold W. Watters Jr., and John A. Koepke
2003 *Envisioning Cahokia: A Landscape Perspective*. Northern Illinois University Press, DeKalb.

DeBoer, Warren R.
2008 Wrenched Bodies. In *Invisible Citizens: Captives and Their Consequences*, edited by Catherine M. Cameron, pp. 233–261. University of Utah Press, Salt Lake City.

Diaz-Granados, Carol, and James R. Duncan
2000 *The Petroglyphs and Pictographs of Missouri*. University of Alabama Press, Tuscaloosa.

Dorsey, James O.
1885 *Omaha Sociology*. 3rd Annual Report of the Bureau of American Ethnology. Smithsonian Institution, Washington, D.C.

Dye, David H.
2009 *War Paths, Peace Paths: An Archaeology of Cooperation and Conflict in Native Eastern North America*. AltaMira Press, Lanham, Maryland.

Earle, Timothy
1997 *How Chiefs Come to Power: The Political Economy in Prehistory*. Stanford University Press, Stanford, California.

Emerson, Thomas E.
1997 *Cahokia and the Archaeology of Power*. University of Alabama Press, Tuscaloosa.
2007 Cahokia and the Evidence for Late Pre-Columbian War in the North American Midcontinent. In *North American Indigenous Warfare and Ritual Violence*, edited by Richard J. Chacon and Rubén G. Mendoza, pp. 129–148. University of Arizona Press, Tucson.

Emerson, Thomas E., and Eve Hargrave
2000 Strangers in Paradise? Recognizing Ethic Mor-

tuary Diversity on the Fringes of Cahokia. *Southeastern Archaeology* 19:1–23.

Ferguson, Jacqueline C.
1990   Pottery Classification, Site Patterns, and Mississippian Interaction at the Common Field Site (23SG100), Eastern Missouri. Unpublished Master's thesis, Department of Anthropology, University of Missouri, Columbia.

Fortier, Andrew C. (editor)
2007   *The Archaeology of the East St. Louis Mound Center, Part II: The Northside Excavations*. Illinois Transportation Archaeological Research Program Reports No. 22. University of Illinois, Urbana.

Gardner, D. S.
1987   Spirits and Conceptions of Agency among the Mianmin of Papua New Guinea. *Oceania* 57:161–177.

Green, William, and Roland L. Rodell
1994   The Mississippian Presence and Cahokian Interaction at Trempealeau, Wisconsin. *American Antiquity* 59:334–359.

Hall, Robert L.
1997   *An Archaeology of the Soul: North American Indian Belief and Ritual*. University of Illinois Press, Urbana.

Heidegger, Martin
1971   *Poetry, Language, Thought*. Translated by Albert Hofstadter. Harper and Row, New York.

Ingold, Tim
2006   Rethinking the Animate, Re-animating Thought. *Ethnos* 71:9–20.
2008   Bindings against Boundaries: Entanglements of Life in an Open World. *Environment and Planning* 40:1796–1810.
2011   *Being Alive: Essays on Movement, Knowledge and Description*. Routledge, New York.

Iseminger, William R.
2010   *Cahokia Mounds: America's First City*. History Press, Charleston, South Carolina.

Jennings, Matthew
2011   *New Worlds of Violence: Cultures and Consequences in the Early American Southeast*. University of Tennessee Press, Knoxville.

Kelly, John E., and James A. Brown
2012   In Search of Cosmic Power: Contextualizing Spiritual Journeys between Cahokia and the St. Francois Mountains. In *Archaeology of Spiritualities*, edited by Kathryn Rountree, Christine Morris, and Alan A. D. Peatfield, pp. 107–129. Springer, New York.

Keslin, Richard O.
1964   Archaeological Implications on the Role of Salt as an Element of Cultural Diffusion. Special issue, *Missouri Archaeologist* 26:1–181.

La Flesche, Francis
1939   *War Ceremony and Peace Ceremony of the Osage Indians*. Bulletin No. 101. Bureau of American Ethnology, Washington, D.C.

Larson, Lewis H., Jr.
1972   Functional Considerations of Warfare in the Southeast during the Mississippi Period. *American Antiquity* 37:383–392.

Logan, William, and Keir Reeves
2009   Introduction: Remembering Places of Pain and Shame. In *Places of Pain and Shame: Dealing with "Difficult Heritage,"* edited by William Logan and Keir Reeves, pp. 1–14. Routledge, New York.

Long, Colin, and Keir Reeves
2009   "Dig a Hole and Bury the Past in It": Reconciliation and the Heritage of Genocide in Cambodia. In *Places of Pain and Shame: Dealing with "Difficult Heritage,"* edited by William Logan and Keir Reeves, pp. 68–81. Routledge, New York.

Marcoux, Jon Bernard, and Gregory D. Wilson
2010   Categories of Complexity and the Preclusion of Practice. In *Ancient Complexities: New Perspectives in Pre-Columbian North America*, edited by Susan M. Alt, pp. 138–152. University of Utah Press, Salt Lake City.

Milner, George
1998   *The Cahokia Chiefdom: The Archaeology of a Mississippian Society*. Smithsonian Institution Press, Washington, D.C.
1999   Warfare in Prehistoric and Early Historic Eastern North America. *Journal of Archaeological Research* 7:105–151.

Milner, George R., Eve Anderson, and Virginia G. Smith
1991   Warfare in Late Prehistoric West-Central Illinois. *American Antiquity* 56:581–603.

Monaghan, G. William, and Christopher S. Peebles
2010   The Construction, Use, and Abandonment of Angel Site Mound A: Tracing the History of a Middle Mississippian Town through Its Earthworks. *American Antiquity* 75:935–953.

Morse, Dan F., and Phyllis A. Morse
1983   *Archaeology of the Central Mississippi Valley*. University of Alabama Press, Tuscaloosa.

Nielsen, Axel E., and William H. Walker
2009   Introduction: The Archaeology of War in Practice. In *Warfare in Cultural Context: Practice, Agency, and the Archaeology of Violence*, edited by Axel E. Nielsen and William H. Walker, pp. 1–14. University of Arizona Press, Tucson.

Nordstrom, Carolyn
1997   *A Different Kind of War Story*. University of Pennsylvania Press, Philadelphia.

O'Brien, Michael J.
1996 *Paradigms of the Past: The Story of Missouri Archaeology*. University of Missouri Press, Columbia.
2002 *Mississippian Community Organization: The Powers Phase in Southeastern Missouri*. Kluwer Academic, New York.

O'Brien, Michael J., John L. Beets, Robert E. Warren, Tachpong Hotrabhavananda, Terry W. Barney, and Eric E. Voigt
1982 Digital Enhancement and Grey-Level Slicing of Aerial Photographs: Techniques for Archaeological Analysis of Intrasite Variability. *World Archaeology* 14:173–190.

O'Brien, Michael J., and W. Raymond Wood
1998 *The Prehistory of Missouri*. University of Missouri Press, Columbia.

Pauketat, Timothy R.
2001 Practice and History in Archaeology: An Emerging Paradigm. *Anthropological Theory* 1:73–98.
2004 *Ancient Cahokia and the Mississippians*. Cambridge University Press, Cambridge.
2007 *Chiefdoms and Other Archaeological Delusions*. AltaMira Press, Lanham, Maryland.
2008 Founders' Cults and the Archaeology of Wa-kan-da. In *Memory Work: Archaeologies of Material Practices*, edited by Barbara J. Mills and William H. Walker, pp. 61–79. School for Advanced Research Press, Santa Fe, New Mexico.
2009 Wars, Rumors of Wars, and the Production of Violence. In *Warfare in Cultural Conflict: Practice, Agency, and the Archaeology of Violence*, edited by Axel E. Nielsen and William H. Walker, pp. 244–261. University of Arizona Press, Tucson.
2010 The Missing Persons in Mississippian Mortuaries. In *Mississippian Mortuary Practices: Beyond Hierarchy and the Representationist Perspective*, edited by Lynne P. Sullivan and Robert C. Mainfort Jr., pp. 14–29. University Press of Florida, Gainesville.
2013 *An Archaeology of the Cosmos: Rethinking Agency and Religion in Ancient America*. Routledge, New York.

Pauketat, Timothy R. (editor)
2005 *The Archaeology of the East St. Louis Mound Center, Part I: The Southside Excavations*. Transportation Archaeological Research Reports No. 21. Illinois Transportation Archaeological Research Program, University of Illinois, Urbana.

Pauketat, Timothy R., and Susan M. Alt
2004 The Making and Meaning of a Mississippian Axe-Head Cache. *Antiquity* 78:779–797.

Pauketat, Timothy R., Andrew C. Fortier, Susan M. Alt, and Thomas E. Emerson
2013 A Mississippian Conflagration at East St. Louis and Its Political-Historical Implications. *Journal of Field Archaeology* 38:210–226.

Pauketat, Timothy R., and Neil Lopinot
1997 Cahokian Population Dynamics. In *Cahokia: Domination and Ideology in the Mississippian World*, edited by Timothy R. Pauketat and Thomas E. Emerson, pp. 103–123. University of Nebraska Press, Lincoln.

Peregrine, Peter
2008 Social Death and Resurrection in the Western Great Lakes. In *Invisible Citizens: Captives and Their Consequences*, edited by Catherine M. Cameron, pp. 223–232. University of Utah Press, Salt Lake City.

Pollack, David
2004 *Caborn-Welborn: Constructing a New Society after the Angel Chiefdom Collapse*. University of Alabama Press, Tuscaloosa.

Price, James E., and James B. Griffin
1979 *The Snodgrass Site of the Powers Phase of Southeast Missouri*. Anthropological Papers No. 66. Museum of Anthropology, University of Michigan, Ann Arbor.

Ray, Jack H.
2007 *Ozarks Chipped-Stone Resources: A Guide to the Identification, Distribution, and Prehistoric Use of Cherts and Other Siliceous Raw Materials*. Special Publications No. 8. Missouri Archaeological Society, Springfield.

Richmond, Gerald M., and David L. Weide
1993 *Quaternary Geologic Map of the Ozark Plateau Quadrangle*. Miscellaneous Investigations Series 1420(NJ-15). U.S. Geological Survey, Reston, Virginia.

Steadman, Dawnie Wolfe
2008 Warfare Related Trauma at Orendorf, a Middle Mississippian Site in West-Central Illinois. *American Journal of Physical Anthropology* 136:51–64.

Tainter, Joseph A.
1988 *The Collapse of Complex Societies*. Cambridge University Press, New York.

Thwaite, Reuben Gold (editor)
1900 *The Jesuit Relations and Allied Documents: Volume LIX, Lower Canada, Illinois, Ottawas, 1673–1677*. Burrows Brothers, Cleveland, Ohio.

Trader, Patrick D.
1992 Spatial Analysis of Lithic Artifacts from the Common Field Site (23STG100), a Mississippian Community in Ste. Genevieve County, MO. Unpublished Master's thesis, University of Missouri, Columbia.

Voigt, Eric E.
1985 *Archaeological Testing of the Bauman Site (23STG158), Ste. Genevieve County, Missouri.* St. Louis District Cultural Resource Management Report No. 23. United States Army Corps of Engineers, St. Louis, Missouri.

Walker, William H.
1998 Where Are the Witches of Prehistory? *Journal of Archaeological Method and Theory* 5:245–308.
2009 Warfare and the Practice of Supernatural Agents. In *Warfare in Cultural Conflict: Practice, Agency, and the Archaeology of Violence*, edited by Axel E. Nielsen and William H. Walker, pp. 109–135. University of Arizona Press, Tucson.

Weller, Stuart, and Stuart St. Clair
1928 *Geology of Ste. Genevieve County, Missouri.* Reports, 2nd Series, Vol. 22. Missouri Bureau of Geology and Mines, Rolla.

Willey, Patrick S., and Thomas E. Emerson
1993 The Osteology and Archaeology of the Crow Creek Massacre. *Plains Anthropologist* 38:227–269.

Williams, Stephen
1990 The Vacant Quarter and Other Late Events in the Lower Valley. In *Towns and Temples along the Mississippi*, edited by David H. Dye and Cheryl Anne Cox, pp. 170–180. University of Alabama Press, Tuscaloosa.

Woods, William I.
2004 Population Nucleation, Intensive Agriculture, and Environmental Degradation: The Cahokia Example. *Agriculture and Human Values* 21: 255–261.

Zedeño, María Nieves
2008 Bundled Worlds: The Roles and Interactions of Complex Objects from the North American Plains. *Journal of Archaeological Method and Theory* 15:362–378.

Zimmerman, Larry J.
1997 The Crow Creek Massacre, Archaeology, and Prehistoric Plains Warfare in Contemporary Perspective. In *Material Harm: Archaeological Studies in War and Violence*, edited by John Carman, pp. 75–94. Cruithne Press, Glasgow.

Zimmerman, Larry J., and Lawrence E. Bradley
1993 The Crow Creek Massacre: Initial Coalescent Warfare and Speculations about the Genesis of Extended Coalescent. *Plains Anthropologist* 38:215–226.

5

Weaving Together Evil Airs, Sacred Mountaintops, and War

Margaret Brown Vega

Until recently in the Andes, relatively few intensive excavations targeted fortifications (see next set of references and Connell et al. 2003; Earle et al. 1987). At some of the more well documented fortified sites, evidence for ritual activities, as well as "nondefensive" practices, is present (Arkush 2005, 2011; Brown Vega 2008, 2009; Ghezzi 2006, 2007; Lau 2010a, 2010b; Lippi and Gudiño 2008; Mantha 2009; Swenson 2007, 2012; Vogel 2012). Detailed analysis of surface features has also proven to be very informative regarding defensive and other (including ceremonial) activities that took places at these sites (Brown Vega et al. 2011; Mantha 2006, 2009; Topic 1989; Topic and Topic 1978; Topic 1990; Topic and Topic 2009).

It is this kind of "mixed" evidence that has led some scholars to minimize the role that conflict or war may have played at these sites. Some interpretations of fortified sites lack consideration of conflict or reject outright the possibility of conflict. Sites located on remote hilltops that have perimeter walls and slingstones have been unquestioningly called ceremonial sites or temples (*adoratorios*) (Van Dalen Luna 2009:272). In other instances, defensible location, perimeter walls, or even ditches are overlooked without mention of fortification. In still other instances, the concept of *tinku* (ritual battles) is invoked, and cosmological motivations for building forts are favored over "practical" defensive strategies (Topic and Topic 1997; Topic and Topic 2009). This tendency pervades many interpretations of sites in the Andes that have some defensive characteristics (Arkush and Stanish 2005:3–4).

Yet foregrounding the defensive functions of these kinds of sites to remedy this situation perhaps tends to minimize evidence for ceremonial activities. In response to recent survey work on walled hilltop sites (Brown Vega et al. 2011), some colleagues have taken issue with my apparent overemphasis on fortification, arguing that these sites are not fortresses but mountaintop shrines. However, when one reviews the ethnographic and ethnohistoric literature for the region, there is ample support for more complex interpretations that recognize these sites as multifunctional. Archaeologists are increasingly critical of interpretations that separate ritual, economic, and other dimensions of past settlements and structures (e.g., Bradley 2005). While discussions still tend toward polarization, some archaeologists working in the Andean region, including myself, strive to draw attention to more nuanced interpretations that negate neither conflict nor ceremony (e.g., Swenson 2012). In this chapter I use Tim Ingold's (2010, 2013) concept of meshwork to talk about war, healing ceremonies, and sacred landscapes as entangled threads that form a fabric of culture change. I use a specific case study from the Huaura Valley, central coast of Perú (Figure 5.1), where survey and excavation data identified evidence of both ritual and defensive activities at fortified sites. As key evidence for war, and for people's negotiation of

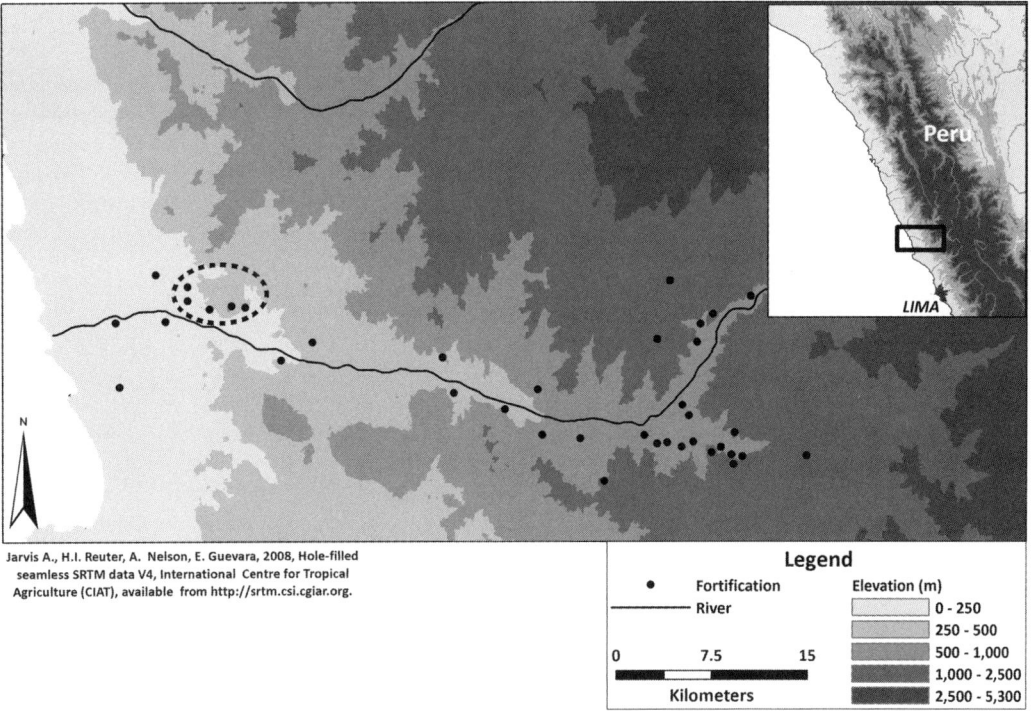

FIGURE 5.1. Map of the Huaura Valley. Cerros San Cristóbal is circled.

war, fortifications are better understood when evidence for ceremonies and concepts of the sacred are taken into account (see also Nielsen 2009). Activities aimed at both physical and spiritual defense should be expected at fortifications. To situate my use of the concept of meshwork, and my overall discussion, I provide some background on ritual battles (*tinku*) and sacred places (*huacas*).

Tinku and Huacas

Whether fortified or enclosed sites are *either* defensive or symbolic/ceremonial is not a new discussion, nor is it one specific to the Andes (Golitko and Keeley 2007; Keeley 1996; Parkinson and Duffy 2007). In the Andes, however, there has been a lengthy discussion of tinku (ritual battles) and the interpretation of fortifications (see a detailed treatment in Arkush and Stanish 2005). The word *tinku* means the coming together of two parts (*la junta de dos cosas* [Sp.]) (Holguín 2007 [1608]:224), but different aspects of tinku and closely related words can refer to violent encounters (Allen 1988:205–207). Ethnographically documented tinku are arranged affairs with spectators, associated festivities, and expected outcomes (Bastien 1985a; Orlove 1994). Tinku are viewed as highly ritualized, and analogies made between them and prehispanic conflict tend to characterize the latter as highly ritualized as well. Prehispanic warfare thus may be viewed as more about ritual and less about "real war" (Arkush and Stanish 2005). The dichotomy is a hindrance to our understanding of prehispanic conflict and how it was experienced in the region.

The tendency to characterize prehispanic warfare in the Andes as ritual is related to the documented belief in huacas as part of a sacred, or animated, geography (Curatola Petrocchi and Ziółkowski 2008). Huacas are sacred spots on the landscape that include both human-made constructions and "natural" features such as mountains. Fortifications built by people on potent features such as mountains, then, may be considered first and foremost to be huacas. While I agree that both tinku and huacas are important concepts, I think there is more to consider when we are dealing with evidence for conflict in the Andes. I now turn to a fuller picture of mountains and war.

Meshworks

Ingold cautions us that isolating things as objects further distances us from understanding life (Ingold 2010:96). This is a matter not just of reanimating objects as if they were akin to people but of recognizing the world as flows of materials. One way to conceptualize these flows is to view them as a mesh, or meshwork. As Ingold defines them, meshworks are relational fields of interwoven lines (Ingold 2006:13). Significantly, these lines do not connect but rather entangle with each other (Ingold 2013:132). Rather than conceive of worldly relationships as links between points (say, people), and nodes (say, objects or features), meshworks emphasize movement. That is, people and things are constantly in the process of becoming in the world *with* each other, and all are attached to their trails (or lines) of history. Beings "[thread] their own paths through the meshwork" (Ingold 2006:14).

To operationalize this concept, I treat winds and mountain summits as separate threads. In doing so, I intend to show how winds and mountains intertwine with each other, and I weave in treatments of illness, aspects of worship, and geography. I then discuss fortifications and offerings, and how they thread through all of these things. That treatment adds an additional consideration of time to examine how the changing relationships between these various worldly components shifted over a couple of millennia.

Winds, Evil Airs, and Sickness/Illness

Abundant ethnographic literature on the Andean region links the landscape in general to bodies and health (Bastien 1985b; Greenway 1998). Two important relationships are pointed out that describe contemporary Andean communities: first, "the body cannot be separated from the landscape," and second, "an individual's health [cannot] be disassociated from that of the household or community" (Greenway 1998:993). Individual health, community health, and the physical landscape are linked, or better said, entangled.

Many illnesses that have been characterized as psychosomatic or folk illnesses in the Andes are caused by aspects of the landscape and weather conditions, such as wind or air. *Wayra* (wind) is generally "conceptualized as a localized circulatory agent of subterranean energy" (Allen 1988:53). Wind is a tangible manifestation of *sami*, an animating essence found in many things. Sami is in constant flow, and its direction can be guided through ritual (Allen 1988:49–54). Wind and other forces, such as water and light, are animated currents that circulate in the world in which people act and live (Allen 1988:226).

There are different kinds of winds. Evil airs, or *males aires*, enter a person's body when he or she is vulnerable. Males aires infect individuals from the inside and require removal through healing ceremonies. *Machu wayra* (bad winds [Quechua]), an affliction reported by Andean peoples, is caused by exposure to different kinds of winds (Carey 1993:284). Wind-related illnesses can vary, and there are variations regarding where they come from and what they do. Generally, however, they are caused by not making the appropriate offerings to spirits, deities, or ancestors in the landscape (Rotondo 1980; Simmons 1955:62–63). The winds literally attack people (Allen 1988:56). Healing ceremonies to correct these imbalances involve the use of a variety of items, including plants, minerals, and miniature items. The ceremonies also enlist the help of a ritual specialist well versed in the use of these cures.

Winds, however, can also heal and be called on for protection. In contemporary healing ceremonies the presence of wind can be a demonstration of a healer's power (Glass-Coffin 2010:71–75). Powerful forces, such as deities called on during healing ceremonies, arrive "in the form of wind to receive offerings" (Ramirez 2005:145). One way to call the wind is to whistle (Glass-Coffin 2010:75). Whistling and musical accompaniment to healing ceremonies is well documented in the Andes and adjacent areas. As Fred Katz and Marlene Dobkin de Rios put it in their analysis of Ayahuasca healing sessions, "whistling is the way in which the spiritual forces of nature and the guardian spirit of the vine, itself, can be evoked by the healer" (Katz and Dobkin de Rios 1971:324).

What do airs and illness have to do with mountaintops? As I detail below, mountains are a source of tremendous power, both benevolent and maleficent.

Spirited Peaks

Studies of ethnohistoric literature and early colonial documents support the idea that a living landscape was prevalent in the Andes in prehispanic times (Besom 2009; Curatola Petrocchi and Ziółkowski 2008; MacCormack 1991:148; Salomon et al. 1991). Among the features that make up the "living landscape" are mountaintops and peaks, referred to as huacas and considered to be deities/sacred beings (Salomon et al. 1991:1). In the Central Andes, home of a large section of the Andean mountain range, there are abundant stories, myths, and histories linked to mountains, peaks, and even lower hills. Generally, mountains and people are in a reciprocal relationship. Appeals to mountains can result in benefits for individuals and communities, but people may also upset the mountains, with negative results (Sillar 2009:369). The highest snowcapped peaks on the landscape are *apus*, a special kind of mountain deity (Mishkin 1940:237). The lower peaks are in a hierarchical relationship with the apus and are less senior. Any illnesses caused among humans by lower peaks must be remedied through appeals to the apu (Mishkin 1940:237).

Bernard Mishkin (1940) relates a story from the Cuzco area in the highlands that specifically links mountains to deities that cause illness. Mountain divinities, known as *aukis*, owned the lands of the area in the "earliest of times." When a battle between the sun and the local inhabitants ensued, all perished, including those who had sought refuge and built their houses on the mountain peaks. Those vengeful entities who perished atop the mountains descend from the hills and cause illnesses among modern-day inhabitants (Mishkin 1940:235).

A key practice linked to mountains entails payments, or *pagos*, in the form of offerings. When payments cease to be made, spirits or enchantments of the mountains retaliate (Polia Meconi 1996:215–222). Hungry spirits that have not been placated with regular offerings attack passersby, causing illness such as *susto* (fright). Walking too close to or visiting a huaca might cause someone to suffer from evil airs (Glass-Coffin 1998:117; Platt 1997:216).

What I have attempted to illustrate are strands of health and danger that move in the Andean world. These flows are linked to individual bodies, ancestors, and sacred beings. Ancestors and sacred beings are mountain peaks. Thus, winds and mountains are part of a living environment in which humans also exist. Peaks in particular become additionally charged when people occupy them, becoming further enmeshed in other flows that include ancestors. The relationships between these various inhabitants of the world are negotiated through ritual practices, including the assemblage and offering of pagos. As Mario Polia Meconi observes, "In the Andes, enchantment is the 'normal' result of the interaction of the forces that animate nature and that humans can direct in their favor by means of ritual action" (Polia Meconi 1996:210; my translation).

While elevated mountainous peaks and ridges are viewed as sacred, they are also spaces used for defense. Mountaintop fortifications, then, would seem to be enmeshed along with other aspects of the environment in a greater conceptualization of existence. I now discuss the evidence for the fortification of some peaks and summits.

Ritual Spaces of Defense: The Huaura Valley

Recent investigations have identified numerous fortifications in the Huaura Valley of the central coast of Perú (Brown Vega et al. 2011). The earliest ones date to the Early Horizon (ca. 900–200 BC), but fortifications appear to be reused throughout subsequent periods up to the time of contact (ca. AD 1532) and even into the present. These sites have a long history, in most cases extending beyond two thousand years.

In the Huaura Valley one prominent set of hills, known as Cerros San Cristóbal, is my focus (Figure 5.2). Cerros San Cristóbal are located at the neck of the Huaura Valley (Figure 5.3). Five fortifications have been documented on these hills, all within 5 km of each other. Each of the five fortifications was initially built in the Early Horizon. The highest peak, known by the name Cerro San Cristóbal, has occupations on its summit and flanks that span all time periods up until the Late Horizon (ca. AD 1475). The surrounding four fortifications vary in terms of when they were in use. Three of the five forts on Cerros San Cristóbal were likely permanent settlements,

FIGURE 5.2. Cerros San Cristóbal (photo by Nathan Craig).

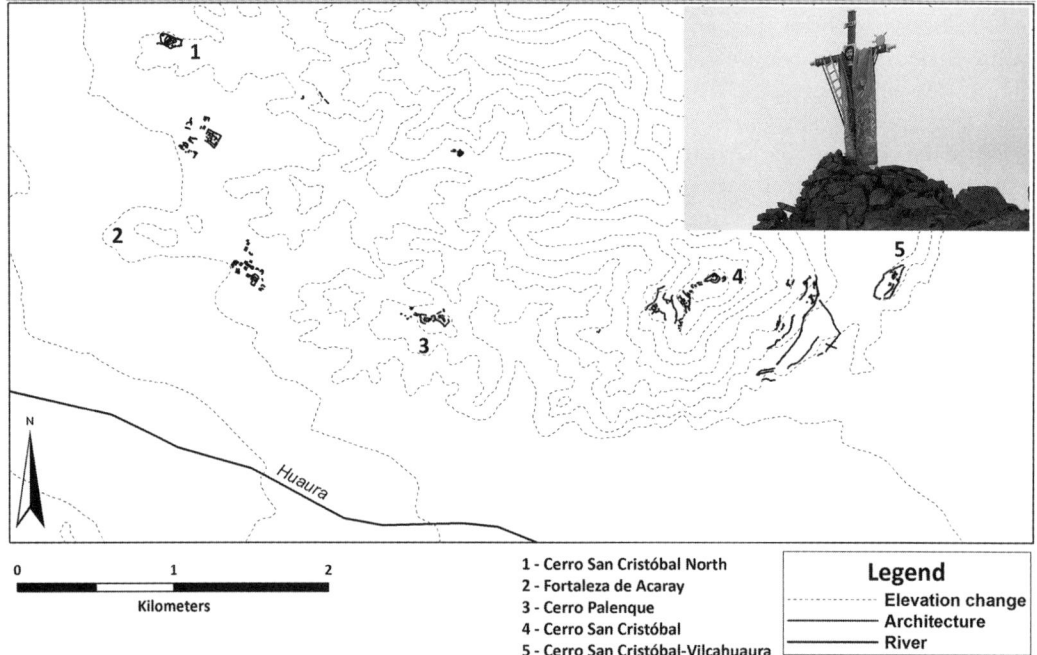

FIGURE 5.3. Detail of Cerros San Cristóbal fortifications. *Inset:* The Christian cross that tops the highest peak today.

while the other two do not appear to have been intensively used.

In this valley, and elsewhere along the neighboring coastal valleys, present evidence indicates that people do not start building on summits until the Early Horizon (Brown Vega 2010; Ghezzi 2006, 2007). When they start, however, what they build, by and large, are fortifications. Despite a long tradition of building very large architecture, such as massive mounds, in these areas before this time, the efforts that predated the Early Horizon focused on valley bottom areas (Haas and Creamer 2006; Stanish 2001:45–46, 48–49). Before the Early Horizon, summits do not appear to be perceived as spaces on which to build large settlements or other kinds of monumental structures. But in the Early Horizon people ascended their neighboring hills, such as Cerros San Cristóbal, to build concentric or perimeter defensive walls on summits. Many of these walled spaces also have parapets, bastions, and baffled entryways that give strategic advantage to those who would seek safety behind the walls. On their ascents people hauled large quantities of carefully selected river cobbles to be used as slingstones. Many of these were assembled in piles along the defensive walls. Early Horizon people used panpipes (*antaras*), which are ubiquitous at Early Horizon fortified sites. Antaras are wind instruments, consisting of a series of tubes, and fragments indicate they were made of fired clay.

According to one early native chronicler, in an earlier age (*Auca Pacha Runa*, Age of Warlike People [Quechua]), long before the Inca Empire came to power, people went to war with weapons that included antaras (Guaman Poma de Ayala 2001 [ca. 1615]). Judging by ethnohistoric and ethnographic examples, musical instruments were and are integral to rituals in the Andes. The sounds of antaras and trumpets were like the wind, and would be used to call nonhuman agents to intervene in battle on behalf of humans (Nielsen 2009:230).

After a first thrust of fort building in the Early Horizon, these sites rarely lay in ruin. They were reused in various ways and in some cases augmented extensively. They remain important points on the landscape to the present day. In the early part of the Early Intermediate Period (ca. 200 BC–AD 500) two of the forts around Cerro San Cristóbal continued to be used. Two forts were in use during the subsequent Middle Horizon (ca. AD 500–1000), and three were used during the Late Intermediate Period (ca. AD 1000–1475). There are indications that one fort, the Fortress of Acaray, was used in the Late Horizon (ca. AD 1475–1532). The very name of the hills—after Saint Christopher—suggests that the extirpators of idolatry in the early Colonial period (post–AD 1532 to the mid-1600s) took an interest in this location. A Christian cross now marks the highest peak, Cerro San Cristóbal, and it is the focus of yearly pilgrimages. From the Early Horizon to the Late Horizon, this geographical feature is one of a few areas where we see a high density of fortifications in the valley. These hills are the focal point of fort construction, rebuilding, and visitation for more than 2,500 years. The prehispanic use of these hills and ancient structures, and their potency and influence, might have something to do with colonial Spanish interest in appropriating them.

Detailed information on changes in the relationship between people and their landscape through time comes from excavation data at Acaray, one of the Cerro San Cristóbal forts. Acaray was built in the Early Horizon as a permanent walled settlement. People built terraces and used the hillslopes of Acaray as early as ca. 800 BC. However, radiocarbon dates from the defensive walls indicate that these perimeter walls were not constructed until the end of the Early Horizon, ca. 200 BC–AD 0 (Brown Vega et al. 2013). Destruction episodes detected in excavated architecture indicate that the site was likely attacked and partially destroyed. Early Horizon architecture on the summit of Acaray was dismantled; stairs, benches, and pillars of a plastered stepped platform were removed. Unlike the case in ritual closing events, which have been documented elsewhere in the Andes and at one other Early Horizon fortified temple (Ghezzi 2006), the destroyed architecture at Acaray was left unburied.

Although previously I argued that the site lay in ruin for the next millennium (Brown Vega 2009), recent radiocarbon dates and a few fragments of Early Intermediate Period pottery suggest that Early Horizon conflict extended into the early part of that period and that people may have used the fort. Some Middle Horizon pottery on the site's surface also suggests people may have at least passed through the site (Brown Vega 2008). Current evidence, however, does not indicate the building of new architecture or regular intensive use of the fort between AD 0 and 1100.

By the Late Intermediate Period there is abundant evidence for a massive remodeling of the Early Horizon fortification. Partially standing walls were "filled in" where collapsed, and entirely new defensive walls were built. Radiocarbon dates indicate that these rebuilding efforts occurred no earlier than AD 1100 (Brown Vega 2009). Little evidence was recovered from excavations to indicate that people were living within the walls of the fort for long periods. Despite a large rebuilding effort, it appears the site was used sporadically. Excavations also revealed evidence that around this time people reconfigured one of the principal summit structures. There are indications that people engaged in periodic visits to this building and carried out rituals within it. These rituals are of special interest because of the items used.

The Early Horizon structure had numerous benches and steps and at least one column. When reconfigured in the Late Intermediate Period, however, the space was divided into smaller rooms built of crudely quarried stone, most likely reused stone. Small pits were dug into the ancient floors of the structure, which had been finely plastered in its interior (Figure 5.4). These pits, filled with a variety of remains, were associated with small, one-time burning events. Additionally, new benches were constructed that were dedicated with offerings.

FIGURE 5.4. Excavation of pit features from the summit structure.

Pits and Burned Features

Food remains of peanut, friar's plum, squash, beans, maize, and *lúcuma* and *pacay* fruits were deposited in the pits. These food remains were found along with plants that tend to be characterized as weeds or processing waste: *cola de caballo* (horse tail), cotton, *capulí* (cape gooseberry), *molle*, and *pájaro bobo* (river alder). Seeds from the *coca* plant were also recovered. Coca seeds are usually accepted as a sign of chewing the leaves, which has potent social and ritual connotations. But it is interesting to explore the ethnographically documented use of many of the weeds and seemingly mundane foods and plants as ritual and medicinal items.

As I have noted elsewhere, a number of these plants are known to have other significance or to be used in magical and healing rituals (Brown Vega 2015a). Beans of various kinds, maize, lúcuma (fruits and leaves) and pacay are found in a variety of caches and offering contexts along the coast of Perú, sometimes in association with burials (Towle 1961). The association with "weeds" that are used to treat ailments of various kinds in contemporary healing contexts (Bussmann et al. 2010; Bussmann and Sharon 2006) suggests that the pits were not merely wastebins. A mineral, probably alum (*alumbre*), was deposited in one pit along with these plant remains. Alum is a common item used in healing ceremonies in the Andes.

The pit features are associated with the remains of what I have characterized as ephemeral (or one-time) burning events (Brown Vega 2008: 267–276). These features are consistent with the kinds of residues left behind from "crematory basins" (Kuznar 2001:59). Ethnographically, these shallow features have been linked to altars used at sacred places by contemporary Andean peoples (Kuznar 2001:50). The burned items, sometimes referred to as *despachos* (burned offerings), accompany pagos.

Buried Offerings

Offerings were excavated from within two different benches, in two separate rooms, inside the summit structure. A vessel filled with maize and beans, with a handstone placed on the jar's opening, was placed inside a bench during construction. The offering of these items, especially a still

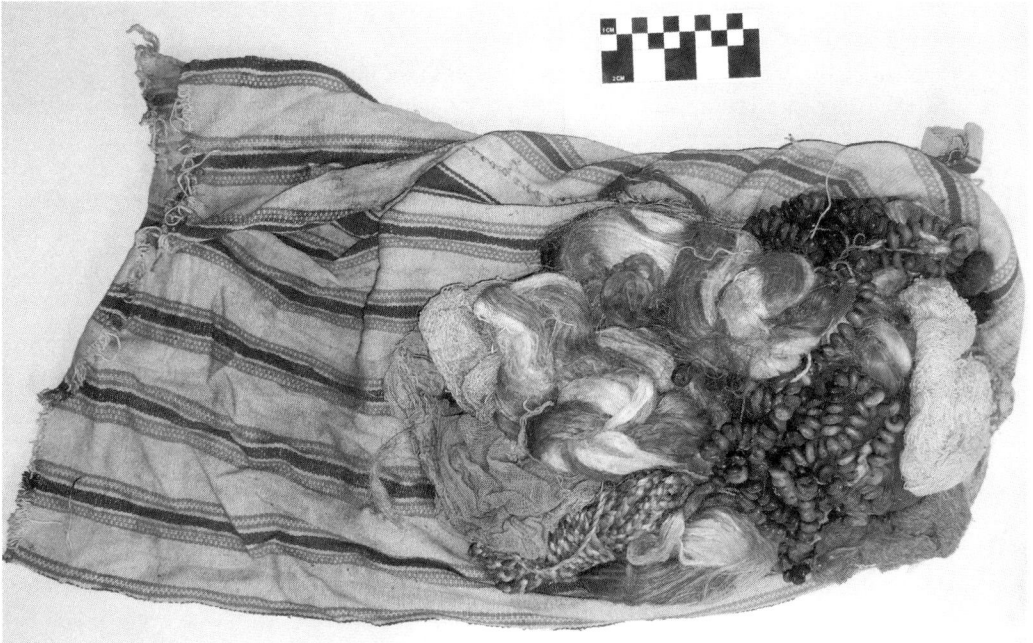

FIGURE 5.5. Textile bundle containing seed necklaces.

useful piece of groundstone, suggests they were deposited for sacrificial purposes, interred perhaps to harness their power (Walker 1995, 1998).

Inside another bench in an adjacent room, people deposited a dedicatory offering that is similar to ethnographically documented *mesas*, or altars, used in healing (Bolton and Bolton 1976; Tschopik 1951). The offering (Figure 5.5), consisting of two textile bundles that contain a series of smaller bundles and items, is an assemblage of various items that I discuss in greater detail elsewhere (Brown Vega 2015b). Here I highlight some of the more significant inclusions.

One item in the offering, a bag of bundled tips from the plant *cóndor*, is used today by healers to cure various maladies, including mal aire, as well as to ensure luck (Bussmann et al. 2010:615). A necklace contained in another bag inside the offering is made of *ishpingo* seeds. *Ishpingo* is used to cure mal aire, susto, and enchantment (Bussmann et al. 2010:614). At the center of each textile bundle was a bag containing a white mineral similar to comestible earths known to be used for medicinal purposes (Browman and Gunderson 1993). Another bag holds miniature items, including miniature seed necklaces and small pieces of the white mineral just mentioned, reminiscent of miniature items found in numerous ethnographically documented pagos (Lorente Fernández 2010).

Discussion

The pits, the remains from the burning events, and the offerings contain items that could have been used as payment to earthly deities. These remains and offerings, pagos, might also have been used in healing ceremonies. Based on ethnographic information, the two are not mutually exclusive (Bolton and Bolton 1976). It is problematic, however, to project contemporary ethnography and more recent history to the Late Intermediate Period. That is not my intention here. What I would like to consider, however, is that animism and the belief in a lively world full of human and nonhuman beings has deep roots among the peoples of ancient Perú. The relationships between human and nonhuman agents would have changed over time, however.

For the Early Horizon, it is difficult to characterize the nature of the relationship between people and mountains. Nevertheless, I think it is reasonable to say that people viewed mountains not solely as natural, static features but rather as forces that also inhabited the world. In seeking to build structures for safety atop these animated spaces, people would have had to contend with, and perhaps draw on, the forces that inhabited these summits. They may have appealed to them for aid. Music from antaras, like whistling, could have been used at Acaray, and probably at other Early Horizon fortifications, to call other forces via winds and sounds for spiritual protection. This transformation of the relationship between people and mountains would have been brokered through rituals to pay or appease mountain spirits. The plastered summit structure might have been a place where human and other forces negotiated this relationship.

Once people began to construct on and inhabit the summits of Cerro San Cristóbal, additional strands of history become further entangled in this animated landscape. After the Early Horizon, in addition to being a social or cosmological force, the summits at Acaray are now built on, becoming the focal point for memories associated with old wars, ancestors, and living in fear. Those strands further intertwine over time as people continued to relate to Acaray and Cerros San Cristóbal as part of their world, if in less frequent ways. In the Early Intermediate Period and Middle Horizon the forts show signs of less use. At Acaray specifically, periodic visits and offerings were carried out less often. There is no material evidence for the same kinds of ritual activities taking place on top of the fortified mountaintops at these times. The relationship between people, mountains, and other forces changed.

In the Late Intermediate Period a number of worldly and social forces converge in such a way that the fortified summits become the site of community rituals. This is manifest in the rebuilding of Acaray, where efforts were also afoot to cure illness through healing ceremonies. Memories, histories, and sacred beings were either harnessed or appeased for protection (see also Buchanan, this volume). It is possible that such beings began to create problems for those living in the valley bottom below, in part because of histories and memories. People suffered as war loomed, but they may also have endured the ire of angry mountain spirits and ancestors. The threat of war was heightened as people prepared to defend themselves with weapons and walls against outsiders. They also defended themselves by making appeals, through ritual, to powerful and possibly angry forces. The social balance between those beings that inhabited the world (people, mountains, winds, and their animating forces) broke down and had to be repaired. The pits and offerings discussed above were assemblages that forged new relationships between various materials, landscapes, and people. Intertwined with these new relationships were memories and histories that bound people and landscape into reciprocal relationships.

Given the links between illness and imbalance as well as the landscape and community that have been documented ethnographically, we might consider what happens during times of conflict and war in the late prehispanic period. Cosmological imbalances resulting from strained or broken relationships between landscape spirits and people translate into social imbalances. Social imbalances manifest themselves in individual and social ills. During times of war there would certainly seem to be a breakdown of social relationships. Those eroded social relationships would be not only between people but tied to hungry spirits upset by the social imbalance. Ritual neglect, community fissioning, and intra- or even intercommunity conflict might elicit the wrath of the living landscape. The spirits and animated flows of that landscape would unleash illness on their human counterparts.

Efforts aimed at healing illnesses may be prompted by outside threats to the community, and may relate to a struggle for continuity and resistance to unwelcome culture change (Greenway 1998:1002). Because healing imbalance is important for community health and survival, it is expected that conflict would go hand in hand with efforts to heal not only physical injury but social imbalances. Geography and cosmology would be intimately linked. Prior suggestions that Andean fortifications would have little to do with defense of territories or populations (Topic and Topic 1997:585) are thus problematic. I contend that fortifications were locales at which people would seek physical and spiritual defense against harm, even if the peaks themselves were in part responsible for the harm. Fortifications were strategic for community health and safety, as well as for maintaining community lands. Huacas, such as mountains and the structures people built on them, "represented the history and concerns of the community" (MacCormack 1991:147). Thus mountaintop fortifications are enmeshed in the multiple threads that make up the world, carried through from ancient times. Given the flows of people, materials, and landscapes that exist in the world, we should not treat fortifications as mere objects of defense. By drawing on ethnohistoric and ethnographic data to specify the entangled nature of ritual and war, archaeologists are better equipped to analyze culture change and conflict.

Conclusion

Fortifications like the ones documented at Cerros San Cristóbal are enmeshed in flows of airs, animating forces, and spiritual beings that inhabit the world with humans. Within the meshwork of being, these lines converge, entangle, and become knotted. In a recent treatment of meshworks, Ingold expands on the concept. Specifically, he argues that places might be knots in the meshwork, where many threads or lines are drawn together (Ingold 2013:132–133). In some ways, what I have tried to discuss are two contexts of knotting at Acaray: the bundling together of various loose strands that continue on beyond their knots to entangle with more threads to make more knots.

Because of this meshwork, and this knotting, discussing fortifications solely in terms of war presents an incomplete picture of the social world and culture change. On the other hand, characterizing mountaintop walled sites as only ceremonial sites obscures an appreciation of the dangers people faced as they sought to defend themselves. Threats and attacks by human enemies and other worldly forces motivated people to arm themselves and invest in physical structures for defense. That this occurred at different moments in time and in different ways speaks to the changing relationship between human communities and nonhuman entities as they moved forth, sometimes entangling, in an animated world in flux.

Acknowledgments

I am grateful to Meghan Buchanan and Jacob Skousen for inviting me to participate in the Society for American Archaeology session they organized, in which I presented the paper that became this chapter. I thank both of them for their feedback on the chapter as it further developed and their hard work in seeing this book through to publication. I also thank the anonymous reviewers, who encouraged incorporation of some more recent literature that has further shaped my thinking of Acaray, and being in the world more generally. That new thinking is only hinted at in this chapter and will have to await a future opportunity for further elaboration.

References Cited

Allen, Catherine J.
1988 *The Hold Life Has: Coca and Cultural Identity in an Andean Community*. Smithsonian Institution Press, Washington, D.C.

Arkush, Elizabeth N.
2005 Colla Fortified Sites: Warfare and Regional Power in the Late Prehispanic Titicaca Basin, Peru. Unpublished Ph.D. dissertation, Department of Anthropology, University of California, Los Angeles.
2011 *Hillforts of the Ancient Andes: Colla Warfare, Society, and Landscape*. University Press of Florida, Gainesville.

Arkush, Elizabeth N., and Charles Stanish
2005 Interpreting Conflict in the Ancient Andes. *Current Anthropology* 46:3–28.

Bastien, Joseph W.
1985a *Mountain of the Condor: Metaphor and Ritual in an Andean Ayllu*. Waveland Press, Prospect Heights, Illinois.
1985b Qollahuaya-Andean Body Concepts: A Topographical-Hydraulic Model of Physiology. *American Anthropologist* 87:595–611.

Besom, Thomas
2009 *Of Summits and Sacrifice: An Ethnohistoric Study of Inka Religious Practices*. University of Texas Press, Austin.

Bolton, Charlene, and Ralph Bolton
1976 Rites of Retribution and Restoration in Canchis. *Journal of Latin American Lore* 2:97–114.

Bradley, Richard
2005 *Ritual and Domestic Life in Prehistoric Europe*. Routledge, London.

Browman, David L., and James N. Gunderson
1993 Altiplano Comestible Earths: Prehistoric and Historic Geophagy of Highland Peru and Bolivia. *Geoarchaeology* 8:416–425.

Brown Vega, Margaret
2008 War and Social Life in Prehispanic Perú: Ritual, Defense, and Communities at the Fortress of Acaray, Huaura Valley. Unpublished

Ph.D. dissertation, Department of Anthropology, University of Illinois, Urbana.

2009 Conflict in the Early Horizon and Late Intermediate Period: New Dates from the Fortress of Acaray, Huaura Valley, Perú. *Current Anthropology* 50:255–266.

2010 Regional Patterns of Fortification and Single Forts: Evaluating the Articulation of Regional Sociopolitical Dynamics with Localized Phenomena. In *Comparative Perspectives on the Archaeology of Coastal South America*, edited by R. Cutright, E. López Hurtado, and A. Martin, pp. 169–189. Center for Comparative Archaeology, University of Pittsburgh, Pittsburgh; Fondo Editorial, Pontificia Universidad Católica del Perú, Lima; Ministerio de Cultura del Ecuador, Quito.

2015a Ritualized Coping during War: Congregation and Conflictat the Late Prehispanic Fortress of Acaray. In *Fear and Anxiety: Emotive States Materialized*, edited by J. Fleisher and N. Norman. Springer, New York, forthcomings.

2015b Ritual Practices and Wrapped Objects: Unpacking Sacred Bundles. *Journal of Material Culture* (forthcoming).

Brown Vega, Margaret, Nathan McDonald Craig, Brendan J. Culleton, Douglas J. Kennett, and Gerbert Asencios Lindo

2013 AMS Radiocarbon Dates from Prehispanic Fortifications in the Huaura Valley, Central Coast of Perú. *Radiocarbon* 55 (1): 1–12.

Brown Vega, Margaret, Nathan Craig, and Gerbert Asencios Lindo

2011 Ground Truthing of Remotely Identified Fortifications on the Central Coast of Perú. *Journal of Archaeological Science* 38:1680–1689.

Bussmann, Rainer W., Ashley Glenn, and Douglas Sharon

2010 Healing the Body and Soul: Traditional Remedies for "Magical" Ailments, Nervous System and Psychosomatic Disorders in Northern Peru. *African Journal of Pharmacy and Pharmacology* 4:580–629.

Bussmann, Rainer W., and Douglas Sharon

2006 Traditional Medicinal Plant Use in Northern Peru: Tracking Two Thousand Years of Healing Culture, with Supplementary File 1. *Journal of Ethnobiology and Ethnomedicine* 2:47. http://www.ethnobiomed.com/content/2/1/47. doi:10.1186/1746-4269-2-47.

Carey, James W.

1993 Distribution of Culture-Bound Illnesses in the Southern Peruvian Andes. *Medical Anthropology Quarterly, New Series* 7:281–300.

Connell, Samuel V., Chad Gifford, Ana Lucía González, and Maureen Carpenter

2003 Hard Times in Ecuador: Inka Troubles at Pambamarca. *Antiquity Bulletin* 77 (295). http://antiquity.ac.uk/projgall/connell295/.

Curatola Petrocchi, Marco, and Mariusz S. Ziółkowski (editors)

2008 *Adivinación y oráculos en el mundo andino antiguo*. Pontificia Universidad Católica del Perú Fondo Editorial, Lima.

Earle, Timothy K., Terence N. D'Altroy, Christine Hastorf, Catherine Scott, Cathy Costin, Glen Russell, and Elsie Sandefur

1987 *Archaeological Field Research in the Upper Mantaro, Peru, 1982–1983: Investigations of Inka Expansion and Exchange*. Institute of Archaeology, University of California, Los Angeles.

Ghezzi, Ivan

2006 Religious Warfare at Chankillo. In *Andean Archaeology III: North and South*, edited by W. Isbell and H. Silverman, pp. 67–84. Springer, New York.

2007 La naturaleza de la guerra prehispánica temprana: La perspective desde Chankillo. *Revista Andina* 44:199–226.

Glass-Coffin, Bonnie

1998 *The Gift of Life: Female Spirituality and Healing in Northern Peru*. University of New Mexico Press, Albuquerque.

2010 Shamanism and San Pedro through Time: Some Notes on the Archaeology, History and Continued Use of an Entheogen in Northern Peru. *Anthropology of Consciousness* 21:58–82.

Golitko, Mark, and Lawrence H. Keeley

2007 Beating Ploughshares Back into Swords: Warfare in the *Linearbandkeramik*. *Antiquity* 81:332–342.

Greenway, Christine

1998 Hungry Earth and Vengeful Stars: Soul Loss and Identity in the Peruvian Andes. *Social Science and Medicine* 47:993–1004.

Guaman Poma de Ayala, Felipe

2001 [ca. 1615] *El primer nueva corónica y buen gobierno (GkS 2232)*. Royal Library, Copenhagen.

Haas, Jonathan, and Winifred Creamer

2006 Crucible of Andean Civilization: The Peruvian Coast from 3000–1800 BC. *Current Anthropology* 47:745–775.

Holguín, Diego González

2007 [1608] Vocabulario de la lengva general de todo el Perv llamada lengua Qquichua, o del Inca. Edited by www.runasimipi.org. http://

www.illa-a.org/cd/diccionarios/Vocabvlario QqichuaDeHolguin.pdf.

Ingold, Tim
2006 Rethinking the Animate, Re-animating Thought. *Ethnos* 71:9–20.
2010 The Textility of Making. *Cambridge Journal of Economics* 34:91–102.
2013 *Making: Anthropology, Archaeology, Art and Architecture*. Routledge, London.

Katz, Fred, and Marlene Dobkin de Rios
1971 Hallucinogenic Music: An Analysis of the Role of Whistling in Peruvian Ayahuasca Healing Sessions. *Journal of American Folklore* 84 (333): 320–327.

Keeley, Lawrence H.
1996 *War before Civilization*. Oxford University Press, New York.

Kuznar, Lawrence A. (editor)
2001 *Ethnoarchaeology of Andean South America*. International Monographs in Prehistory, Ann Arbor, Michigan.

Lau, George F.
2010a Fortifications as Warfare Culture: The Hilltop Centre of Yayno (Ancash, Peru), AD 400–800. *Cambridge Archaeological Journal* 20:419–448.
2010b House Forms and Recuay Culture: Residential Compounds at Yayno (Ancash, Peru), a Fortified Hilltop Town, AD 400–800. *Journal of Anthropological Archaeology* 29:327–351.

Lippi, Ronald D., and Alejandra M. Gudiño
2008 Inkas and Yumbos at Palmitopamba in Northwestern Ecuador. In *Distant Provinces in the Inka Empire: Toward a Deeper Understanding of Inka Imperialism*, edited by M. A. Malpass and S. Alconini, pp. 260–278. University of Iowa Press, Iowa City.

Lorente Fernández, David
2010 3-cerro y 4-mundo: Los números del banquete en las ofrendas quechuas. *Anthropogógica* Año XXVIII (28): 163–190.

MacCormack, Sabine
1991 *Religion in the Andes: Vision and Imagination in Early Colonial Peru*. Princeton University Press, Princeton, New Jersey.

Mantha, Alexis
2006 Late Prehispanic Social Complexity in the Rapayán Valley, Upper Marañón Drainage, Central Andes of Peru. In *La complejidad social en la Sierra de Ancash: Ensayos sobre paisaje, economía y continuidades culturales*, edited by A. Herrera, C. Orsini, and K. Lane, pp. 35–61. Civiche Raccolte d'Arte applicata del Castello Sforzesco—Raccolte Extraeuropee, Milan.
2009 Territoriality, Social Boundaries and Ancestor Veneration in the Central Andes of Peru. *Journal of Anthropological Archaeology* 28 (2): 158–176.

Mishkin, Bernard
1940 Cosmological Ideas among the Indians of the Southern Andes. *Journal of American Folklore* 53 (210): 225–241.

Nielsen, Axel E.
2009 Ancestors as War: Meaningful Conflict and Social Process in the South Andes. In *Warfare in Cultural Context: Practice, Agency, and the Archaeology of Violence*, edited by A. E. Nielsen and W. H. Walker, pp. 218–243. University of Arizona Press, Tucson.

Orlove, Benjamin
1994 Sticks and Stones: Ritual Battles and Play in the Southern Peruvian Andes. In *Unruly Order: Violence, Power, and Cultural Identity in the High Provinces of Southern Peru*, edited by D. Poole, pp. 133–164. Westview Press, Boulder, Colorado.

Parkinson, William A., and Paul R. Duffy
2007 Fortifications and Enclosures in European Prehistory: A Cross-Cultural Perspective. *Journal of Archaeological Research* 15:97–141.

Platt, Tristan
1997 The Sound of Light: Emergent Communication through Quechua Shamanic Dialogue. In *Creating Context in Andean Cultures*, edited by R. Howard-Malverde, pp. 196–226. Oxford University Press, New York.

Polia Meconi, Mario
1996 *"Despierta, remedio, cuenta…": Adivinos y médicos del Ande*. 2 vols. Pontificia Universidad Católica del Perú Fondo Editorial, Lima.

Ramirez, Susan E.
2005 *To Feed and Be Fed: The Cosmological Basis of Authority and Identity in the Andes*. Stanford University Press, Stanford, California.

Rotondo, Humberto
1980 Creencias culturales relativas a la enfermedad en migrantes procedentes de la sierra. In *El hombre y la cultura andina: Actas y trabajos, segunda seria tomo IV*, edited by R. Matos Mendieta, pp. 718–744. III Congreso Peruano del Hombre y la Cultura Andina, Lima.

Salomon, F., J. Urioste, and F. de Avila
1991 *The Huarochirí Manuscript: A Testament of Ancient and Colonial Andean Religion*. University of Texas Press, Austin.

Sillar, Bill
2009 The Social Agency of Things? Animism and Materiality in the Andes. *Cambridge Archaeological Journal* 19:367–377.

Simmons, Ozzie G.
1955 Popular and Modern Medicine in Mestizo Communities of Coastal Peru and Chile. *Journal of American Folklore* 68 (267): 57–71.

Stanish, Charles
2001 The Origin of State Societies in South America. *Annual Review of Anthropology* 30:41–64.

Swenson, Edward R.
2007 Local Ideological Strategies and the Politics of Ritual Space in the Chimú Empire. *Archaeological Dialogues* 14 (01): 61–90.
2012 Warfare, Gender, and Sacrifice in Jequetepeque, Peru. *Latin American Antiquity* 23:167–193.

Topic, John R.
1989 The Ostra Site: The Earliest Fortified Site in the New World? In *Cultures in Conflict: Current Archaeological Perspectives*, edited by D. C. Tkaczuk and B. C. Vivian. Archaeological Association of the University of Calgary, Calgary, Alberta.

Topic, John R., and Theresa L. Topic
1978 Prehistoric Fortification Systems of Northern Peru. *Current Anthropology* 19:618–619.
1997 Hacia una comprensión conceptual de la guerra andina. In *Arqueología, antropología e historia en los Andes: Homenaje a María Rostworowski*, edited by R. Varón Gabai and J. Flores Espinoza, pp. 567–590. IEP Ediciones, Lima, Peru.

Topic, Theresa L.
1990 Territorial Expansion and the Kingdom of Chimor. In *The Northern Dynasties: Kingship and Statecraft in Chimor*, edited by M. E. Moseley and A. Cordy-Collins, pp. 177–194. Dumbarton Oaks Research Library and Collection, Washington, D.C.

Topic, Theresa L., and John R. Topic
2009 Variation in the Practice of Prehispanic Warfare on the North Coast of Peru. In *Warfare in Cultural Practice: Practice, Agency, and the Archaeology of Violence*, edited by A. E. Nielsen and W. H. Walker, pp. 17–55. University of Arizona Press, Tucson.

Towle, Margaret A.
1961 *The Ethnobotany of Pre-Columbian Peru.* Viking Fund Publications in Anthropology No. 30. Aldine Press, Chicago.

Tschopik, Harry, Jr.
1951 *The Aymara of Chucuito, Peru: 1, Magic.* American Museum of Natural History, New York.

Van Dalen Luna, Pieter
2009 Sistemas de asentamiento tardíos en el valle medio del río Chancay-Huaural y la quebrada de Orcón-Quilca. *Kullpi: Revista de Investigaciones Culturales en la Provincia de Huaural y el Norte Chico* 4:217–294.

Vogel, Melissa A.
2012 *Frontier Life in Ancient Peru: The Archaeology of Cerro la Cruz.* University Press of Florida, Gainesville.

Walker, William H.
1995 Ceremonial Trash? In *Expanding Archaeology*, edited by J. M. Skibo, W. H. Walker, and A. E. Nielsen, pp. 67–79. University of Utah Press, Salt Lake City.
1998 Where Are the Witches of Prehistory? *Journal of Archaeological Method and Theory* 5:245–308.

6

Maya Religion and Gods

Relevance and Relatedness in the Animic Cosmos

Eleanor Harrison-Buck

Any discussion of ancient Mesoamerican "religion" and "gods" should probably begin by questioning the relevance of these two Western analytical categories. As general concepts, neither actually seems to have existed in the past (Graham et al. 2013; Wright 2011:223). No direct translations of either term can be found in any of the indigenous languages of Mesoamerica (Pharo 2007; Houston and Stuart 1996). Lars Pharo (2007) notes that the Yucatec Maya translation of the word "religion" offered in the earliest Spanish-Maya dictionaries was *okol k'uh,* which "can mean 'to enter god' [and] can refer to phenomena of mysticism where the believer becomes a part of the divine" (Pharo 2007:44). Here and in more recent definitions, *k'uh* or *ch'u* often is glossed as "god," but Stephen Houston and David Stuart (1989:291) suggest that a more accurate translation is "sacred entity" (see also Stuart 2005:275). I believe that this translation is still somewhat problematic in that it offers a static view of what may be better understood as a *relational* act centered on a conscious awareness of one's positioning and activity in the world. This way of knowing the world emphasizes one's relationship with it—what Nurit Bird-David (1999) has described as a two-way conversation of "responsive relatedness" in the world and what is sometimes referred to as a *relational ontology* (as discussed throughout the chapters of this book). Severin Fowles (2013:157) describes this as a complex *interdependency* rather than a simple "cause-and-effect" relationship—"a nonmodern cosmology…in which human doings and the cosmos are consistently read in light of one another."

In this chapter I explore the nature of a Maya relational ontology and the vital forces that constitute what Tim Ingold (2006) refers to as the "meshwork" of entangled relationships within an animic cosmos. Here I examine aspects of an entity the Maya referred to as "Itzamnaaj," who is often described by scholars as a "paramount god" of Maya religion from Classic through Postclassic times (Taube 1989, 1992a; Thompson 1970). As a dual-sexed composite of earth and sky, Itzamnaaj is a generative life force who not only created everything in the world but also maintains the cycles of time and the regeneration of life. In this way, the different aspects of Itzamnaaj exemplify the entangled relationships of daily human and other-than-human experience and existence in the world. In an effort to make sense of this complex "meshwork" of the animic cosmos, Mesoamerican scholars tend to examine it as a collection of related systems or "animic centers" comprising a series of "animic entities" (López Austin 1988) or "deity complexes" (Gillespie and Joyce 1998). Most current studies have focused on isolated aspects of Maya cosmology and provide only a limited understanding of the total system (Vail 2000:128), effectively obscuring the two fundamental components of an animic cosmos, *movement* and a *relational constitution of being* (Ingold 2006:12). I show how these two distinctive features of an animic cosmos are expressed in Maya iconography and epigraphy. As the heart of the Maya animic cosmos and central generative life force, Itzamnaaj—conflated with other human and nonhuman entities—highlights this relational ontology and the ongoing growth and movement of this cosmic force through (not across) the earth-sky.

The Maya "Pantheon" as Relational Ontology

In *Maya History and Religion* J. Eric S. Thompson (1970) suggested that a "pantheon" of gods was represented in ancient Maya religion but that Itzamnaaj was the preeminent deity, whose worship approached something close to a form of Maya "monotheism" (Thompson 1970:233). This interpretation was subsequently criticized for its colonialist thinking, which implied that a shift toward monotheistic religion signaled an increasing evolutionary complexity (Farriss 1984; Freidel et al. 1993:46–50). Due in part to this negative critique, alongside a virtual explosion of hieroglyphic decipherment in the 1980s and 1990s, scholars have since emphasized the polytheistic nature of Maya religion and its multiple gods (Freidel et al. 1993; Schele and Miller 1986; Taube 1992a; but see Sachse 2004:11).

Despite the rejection of Thompson's earlier notion of a monotheistic religion, most scholars today still generally agree that Itzamnaaj represents a "paramount god" in the so-called Maya pantheon (Bassie-Sweet 2008:140; Farriss 1984; Freidel et al. 1993:47; Hellmuth 1987; Houston et al. 2006:234; Stuart 2005; Taube 1992a:31). To his credit, Thompson (1970) noted that the Old World parallels implicit in the term "pantheon" are problematic in the context of ancient Maya religion. Current discussions of ancient Mesoamerican cosmology, however, still commonly describe the different personified forces of the underworld, earthly, and celestial realms as a "pantheon of gods" (Bassie-Sweet 2008:235; Clark and Colman 2012:44; Houston et al. 2006:270). Western preconceptions of a "god" who is all-powerful, infallible, and generally beneficent to humankind continue to be indiscriminately applied to the ancient Maya and other cultures of Mesoamerica but are inaccurate portrayals of these deified essences, who are born and can die and have "human-like" vulnerabilities (Houston and Stuart 1996:291). Based on their epigraphic decipherments, Houston and Stuart (1996:289, 291) conclude that the term "god" is inherently problematic because it "distorts nuances of indigenous belief." Yet the vast majority of archaeological literature today presents Maya "theology" as similar to other world religions, centered on "systematized doctrine" and the worship of almighty gods.

Here I argue that the Maya "pantheon" may be more productively understood in the context of a relational ontology, centered on the conscious awareness of one's positioning and activity in the world, rather than a systematized theology characteristic of most normative religious traditions (see also Romain, this volume). This relational ontology is described by contemporary Maya not as a set of beliefs but as "ways of living their beliefs" (Molesky-Poz 2006:45). As a "bodily felt process" (sensu Skora 2007), this animic ontology is heavily reliant on human physiology and bodily sensation (Furst 1997; Harrison-Buck 2012a; Houston et al. 2006; López Austin 1988). These groups "turned, not to theological pronouncements and speculations to verify their ideas, but to experience—to what can be seen, touched, heard, and in some cases, even smelled" (Furst 1997:2–3). This "theology of experience" (Molesky-Poz 2006:154–168) contradicts most normative religious traditions but best characterizes the physical aspects of Maya spirituality and ritual practice documented in ethnographic and epigraphic studies (Houston and Taube 2000; Houston et al. 2006; Molesky-Poz 2006; Stross 1998; Tedlock 1982). Among the contemporary K'iche' Maya in highland Guatemala, Jean Molesky-Poz (2006:154–168) describes this as a distinct way of knowing that reflects "the profound sense of relatedness rooted in the perception of a shared spiritual reality in all creation" (Molesky-Poz 2006:156).

Elsewhere, Bird-David (1999:68–69) describes the relational ontology of the Nayaka in South India as "responsive relatedness," a different way of knowing the world that emphasizes one's relationship with it, which is perceived as "mutually responsive changes in things in-the-world and at the same time in themselves" (e.g., Alberti and Bray 2009; Fowles 2013; Harvey 2006; Ingold 2006; and chapters throughout this volume). In many ways, Bird-David's responsive relatedness is analogous to Fowles's (2013) notion of *sympathy*, which he discusses in his study of Pueblo religion. "Sympathy is where ecology and morality meet, where one walks gently on the earth because the earth is the mother" (Fowles 2013:158). This kind of empathetic concern for another sentient being (human or otherwise) aligns well with what we know from both contemporary and ancient contexts about the Maya relational ontology, which is centered on bodily feelings and a conscious awareness of one's positioning and activity in the world as a reciprocal and relational being (Brown and Emery 2008; Harrison-Buck 2012a; Molesky-Poz 2006; Vogt 1969, 1976; Watanabe 1992). Among the contemporary Maya, the relational self is described as a "dialogical interaction" that defeats selfish individuality by spawning personal transformation through continuous interaction with others and, in this way, is "a process of seeking personal responsibility and accountability" in life (Arias 1996:6; for further discussion, see Molesky-Poz 2006:57–90).

In our quest to understand the relational self, Marilyn Strathern's (1988) identification of the "dividual" in her ethnographic study of personhood in Papua New Guinea has been highly influential. As a result of her work, anthropologists have become increasingly aware that conceptions of the self as a unique and autonomous individual, often attributed to "Modernist" society, are not universal categories. Other conceptions of the individual, often attributed to "non-Western" societies, are defined in terms of a relational self, that is, a shared sense of personhood based on one's role(s) and relationship(s) within a larger social collective (Gillespie 2001). While many chapters in this book, including my own, critique the use and relevance of certain "Western" categories, it would be naive to suggest that any group (Western or non-Western) is internally consistent and without contradiction (Fowler 2004; Fowles 2010; Harris and Robb 2012). Julia Hendon (2010:150) points out that "to contrast Western individuals with non-Western dividuals is really to contrast an ideology to a set of practices; the self is more relational even in the West than philosophy has allowed historically." The point here is that it is critical that we avoid homogenization when taking on board the ontological project. If we aim to elevate the status of indigenous theory, then we must contextualize the relational self as it pertains to the local context on a case-by-case basis. The generalization of "indigenous ontology" will only further the false divide that exists between the "West and the rest," which postcolonial scholars have been working so hard to dismantle (see Harrison-Buck 2012a:65 for further discussion).

According to my understanding of ethnographic and epigraphic accounts, the Maya relational self undergoes a dualistic process of change in both form and location (Stross 1998:38). As Stuart (1996:164) observes, this involves a life cycle of transformation and renewal and the "transmutation of certain 'personas' over time and space." This concept is captured in the terms *jal* and *k'ex* used by the contemporary Maya of Santiago Atitlan in highland Guatemala (Carlsen and Prechtel 1991:26–27). The dual process of change constitutes a single system of transformation and renewal manifested in both a single life cycle (from birth to death, young to old) and generational transference, which resembles a form of reincarnation (Carlsen and Prechtel 1991:26). This didactic change is manifest in the jal, meaning the change in the thing or external receptacle-body (e.g., the face as it gets old and wrinkled or the corn husk as it dries and shrivels) and in the k'ex, or "seed," that regenerates life, "a process of making the new out of the old" (Carlsen and Prechtel 1991:26–27).

The contemporary Zinacantan Maya refer to this seed or essence of life as the *ch'ulel*, which is considered a sacred coessence or life force (Vogt 1965, 1969, 1976). According to ethnographhic accounts, the ch'ulel contains multiple parts and routinely engages singly or in combination with other human and nonhuman agents in an ongoing negotiation (Gossen 1996:533; see also Monaghan 1995; Vogt 1998; Watanabe 1992). Ethnographic accounts attest to the importance of the ch'ulel in the Maya relational ontology, whereby one's coessence cannot be permanently destroyed but its divisible parts can be displaced or remain dormant (Vogt 1969:370). However, much like a seed (or k'ex), if properly nurtured the ch'ulel can regenerate and be reborn in another bodily form. For both ancient and contemporary Maya, these "bodies" are not exclusively living human bodies but can also include valued materials and important objects, such as domesticated corn, musical instruments, wooden crosses, or stone monuments, among other precious things (Harrison-Buck 2015; Stuart 1996; Vogt 1969:371).

While *ch'ulel* is a modern term, epigraphic texts suggest that the root of the word *ch'u* or *k'uh* references a similar "seed" of regeneration. This vital inner life force is not a singular entity but made up of multiple, distributed parts or coessences that "inhabit the blood and energize people and a variety of objects of ritual and everyday life" (Houston and Stuart 1996:292). One of the glyphs for *k'uh* is a monkey head (Figure 6.1a) that is consistently paired with a personified monkey image in the Maya codices (Figure 6.1b). The *k'uh* glyph often is found paired with other personified images that contain specific "god" appellatives, leading William Ringle (1988:2–5) and others to suggest that *k'uh* signified a more generic concept of "god," "sacred," or "holy" (see also Taube 1992a:30–31; Vail 2000:128–130). Houston, Stuart, and other epigraphers have offered a similar translation of *k'uh* as "sacred entity," "holy object," or "a physical manifestation of the sacred essence that occupies various spaces, people and things throughout the world" (Stuart 2005:275). Linda Schele and Mary Miller (1986:48) were among the first to suggest that the *k'uh* glyph in ancient Maya texts depicts not only a monkey head but a personified form of blood. They suggest that the circular, bead-like elements associated with the monkey head depict flowing droplets of blood and other precious substances (Stuart and Houston 1994:44; Figure 6.1a, c–e), which in some contexts may represent water (Figure 6.1f; see Bassie-Sweet 2008:84–85). Stuart (2005:275) further observes that both *yax* (green) and *k'an* (yellow) signs often are found in the flowing *k'uh* streams in ancient Maya iconography (Figure 6.1d–e). When combined, he suggests, the two signs reference "unripe-ripe" or "immature and mature maize" (Stuart 2005:275). Thus, rather than a static "sacred entity," *k'uh* may be best understood as seeds of generative life (roughly analogous to *k'ex*), brought into being through a relational act, such as a ruler who lets blood and scatters precious *k'uh* streams from his body on another human or nonhuman agent (e.g., Stuart 2005:Figure 11.5).

David Freidel and colleagues (1993:211) note that the term *k'uh* is closely related to *itz*, which constitutes vital substances of life-giving power. Itz refers specifically to sacred liquids that were thought to spawn life, such as bodily fluids like blood, milk, semen, sweat, and tears, as well as other dripping liquids, like rain, dew, sap, wax, and copal resin (Freidel et al. 1993:210n19). Karl Taube (1992a:33) notes that according to Colonial Yucatec dictionaries the word *itz* also refers to divination or witchcraft. Freidel and colleagues (1993:210n19) conclude that itz signifies "magic stuff brought forth in ritual and as secretions from all sorts of things-living and (to us but not the Maya) inanimate...and is related to ideas of knowledge, magic, occult power." The word *Itzam* has been translated as "one who does the action of itz" or one who "manipulates the magic world" (Freidel et al. 1993:210n19), which may be related to the priestly title *itz'aat*, or "wise one," known from Classic Mayan inscriptions (Graña-Behrens 2012). Itzam is closely associated with the name Itzamnaaj (Figure 6.2), who is identified as the principal "shaman-priest" and "creator" of the cosmos in both Postclassic Maya codices and Classic Maya imagery and epigraphy (Barrera Vásquez 1980:272; Freidel et al. 1993:47n19).

The Movement of Vital Forces Through (Not Over) the Animic Maya Cosmos

In this chapter I attempt to understand the role(s) of Itzamnaaj using a relational model of an *animic cosmos*, defined by Ingold (2006). In an animic cosmos the focus is on the relations of earth and sky as "indivisible fields" (Ingold 2006:18). In this "world of perpetual flux" Ingold (2006:12) observes that *movement* and a *relational constitution of being* are both accorded primacy. As he notes, "The animacy of the lifeworld, in short, is not the result of an infusion of spirit into substance, or of agency into materiality, but is rather ontologically prior to their differentiation" (Ingold 2006:10). For the Maya, the indivisible earth-sky is Itzamnaaj, also referred to as "Heart of Sky, Heart of Earth." As the heart or itz of the Maya animic cosmos, Itzamnaaj is the sacred and vital substance (rather than surface) of earth and sky that fuels the regeneration of life. Taube (1992a:34) notes that the headdress of Itzamnaaj resembles a flower (or *nik*) with an exaggerated stamen appearing as an outpouring of liquid or nectar. According to Colonial accounts, Itzamnaaj was the nectar of flowers, as well as the dew. One account

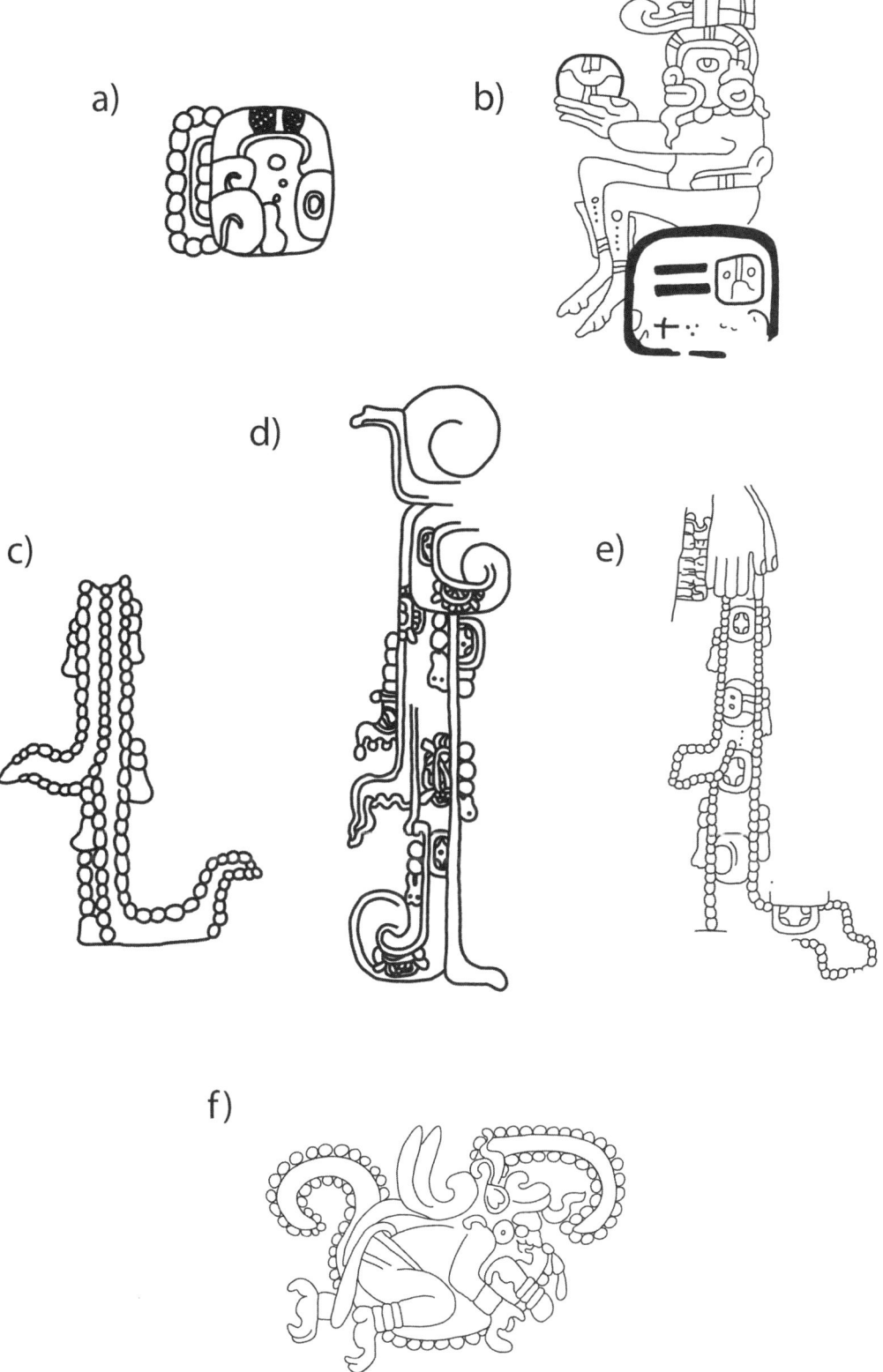

FIGURE 6.1. (*a–b*) The *k'uh* (monkey head) glyph and personified image. (*c–e*) Droplets in streams of blood and other precious substances. (*f*) Droplets as dew or water in the form of a beaded scroll representing a cloud (after Schele and Miller 1986:Figure 29b, d–e; Stuart 2005:Figure 11.5b; and Bassie-Sweet 2008:Figure 5c; redrawn by M. Brouwer Burg).

FIGURE 6.2. A personified Itzamnaaj from page 15c of the Dresden Codex (after Taube 1992a:Figure 12f; redrawn by M. Brouwer Burg).

relating to Itzamnaaj states: "I am the itz (dew or substance) of heaven, I am the itz of the clouds" (translation by Thompson 1939:152, cited in Taube 1992a:34).

The union of earth and sky is expressed at the dawn of creation, as recorded in the Quiche Maya Popol Vuh story. Initially, there is nothing existing in the world, only sky and water (Tedlock 1985). "At some point, Heart of Sky [Itzamnaaj] abandons the spiritual dimension and enters the material world as Tepew Gukumatz, or the Plumed Serpent, the egg covered in quetzal feathers that explodes giving initial life" (Cabrera 1995:86).[1] As a dual-sexed entity, Itzamnaaj as plumed serpent brings forth life in both earth and sky and sets in motion a generative life cycle for human and other-than-human forces who "continually and reciprocally bring one another into existence" (Ingold 2006:10). The serpent body of Itzamnaaj appears to serve as the material manifestation of earth-sky (Figure 6.3), where its sinuous path or trail traces the ongoing movement and growth of the animic cosmos. Ingold (2006:13) notes: "Every such trail traces a relation. But the relation is not *between* one thing and another—between the organism 'here' and the environment 'there.' It is rather a trail *along* which life is lived: one strand in a tissue of trails that together make up the texture of the lifeworld.... It is a [relational] field not of interconnected points but of interwoven lines, not a network but a *meshwork*."

Ingold's "meshwork" that constitutes an animic cosmos may best explain the imagery of Itzamnaaj as a serpent body. Maya iconography, discussed further below, shows that illustrating the serpent body's *movement* through the earth-

FIGURE 6.3. Late Classic period examples of Itzamnaaj as double-headed serpent and caiman: (*a*) framing the doorway of House E at Palenque in Chiapas, Mexico; (*b*) framing the doorway of Structure 22 at Copan in Honduras (drawings by Linda Schele, © David Schele, courtesy Foundation for the Advancement of Mesoamerican Studies, Inc., www.famsi.org).

sky was of prime importance. Equally important is illustrating the serpent's relational status with other entities (shown riding or walking on its back, emerging from its mouth, etc.). The movement of the serpent body and its association with other entities constitute the relational fields and interwoven trails or "meshwork" of the Maya animic cosmos. Typically, in Maya iconography the serpents or so-called sky bands float up above in what is often described as a celestial realm, defying gravity and invariably shown associated with one or more other beings (Figure 6.3). The body of the double-headed serpent, identified as Itzamnaaj, contains planetary glyphs that led Thompson (1970:214) to identify it as the sky aspect of Itzamnaaj (Figure 6.3a). Yet the body is not always a serpent, but sometimes an iguana or crocodile, which have been linked to Itzamnaaj's terrestrial aspect (Taube 1989). Both serpent and earth (*cauac*) imagery are associated with Itzamnaaj and emphasize this sense of an indivisible earth-sky (but see Freidel et al. 1993:46).

In some cases, this being is shown with flowing precious liquid (*itz*) pouring from its mouth, interpreted as a gushing flood of water, perhaps signaling the onset of the rainy season (Milbrath 1999:277–279; Thompson 1970:214, 281). Figure 6.3a shows a Late Classic period example of this imagery framing the doorway of House E at the Maya site of Palenque in Chiapas, Mexico. A

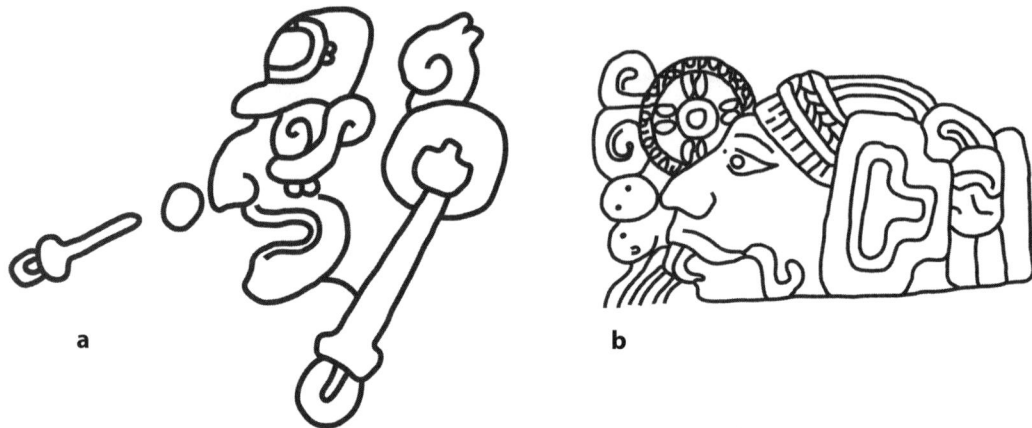

FIGURE 6.4. (*a*) Itzamnaaj with nose beads (jade or flower elements) denoting breath. (*b*) Late Classic form of *ik'* or wind showing associated beaded flower element and breath volute (after Houston et al. 2006:Figures 4.3d and 4.13; redrawn by M. Brouwer Burg).

similar image is found on page 74 of the Postclassic Dresden Codex (Milbrath 1999:Figure 6.4d). In many cases, the serpent body of Itzamnaaj is composed of S-shaped scrolls, which have been interpreted as the cloudy substance or *itz* that constitutes Itzamnaaj (Milbrath 1999:279). Additionally, I would suggest that these elements emphasize the undulation and ongoing movement of this body as a manifestation of the animic cosmos. One good example is found on Structure 22 at the Maya site of Copan in Honduras. Here a double-headed Itzamnaaj frames the doorway of this Late Classic building (Figure 6.3b). The reptilian body of the earth-sky Itzamnaaj appears to be a caiman consisting of a series of S-shaped scrolls and an assembly of seven floating personified beings who hang from these moving clouds. Susan Milbrath (1999:244, 279) suggests that the series of personified beings associated with Itzamnaaj's body may constitute the Sun, Moon, and five planets that are visible to the naked eye. Additionally, weather-related phenomena, such as wind (*ik'*) and lightning (*chac*), are commonly represented in similar scenes and are closely associated with Itzamnaaj (Milbrath 1999:245).

Ingold (2006:16–17; see also Ingold 2007 and 2010) argues that meteorological phenomena are of prime importance in the animic cosmos because it is the weather that moves and transforms the energy or *itz* in the world, from stormy to calm and from dark to light. Air is especially important not only because it enables us to breathe and gives life but also because air or wind "affords both mobility and sensory perception" in the animic cosmos (Ingold 2006:16). In the Maya codices the wind or *ik'* sign most commonly occurs with Itzamnaaj (Vail 2000:131). There is a close association between *ik'* and a series of personified glyphs, including *k'uh* and *nik*, traditionally interpreted as discrete "gods" in the Maya literature (for a full discussion, see Gods C and H in Taube 1992a). *Ik'* is wind, as well as one's breath or animacy, and is tied to the concept of *k'uh* (discussed above) in terms of life force, as well as the *nik* (flower) sign, which is frequently found on Itzamnaaj's forehead (see Figures 6.2 and 6.4). Nik references the nectar or *itz* and appears in some cases to denote a sweet smell, although in other instances it appears to reference the stench of death and decay (Houston et al. 2006:143, Figure 4.7). Together the terms *k'uh*, *ik'*, and *nik* evoke immaterial domains and share similar connections concerning the soul, breath, and smell. It is worth noting that all three of these elements are most often associated with Itzamnaaj—the giver of life—and are also frequently found in association with a personified manifestation of maize (commonly referred to as "God E"), highlighting the cycles of agriculture and human life as central components of the Maya relational ontology (e.g., the birth, death, and regeneration of maize-people).

Transformation, replacement, and regeneration are fundamental to the movement of the animic cosmos and permeate all aspects of Maya life.

"Death produces a separation of body and soul in which the former is not simply an empty and discarded vessel but one that harbors the germ and material for future reproduction" (Martin 2006:159). This partible self is relationally constituted in the cycles of birth, death, and regeneration. A frequently cited example from the Maya area is the birth, death, and resurrection (or reincarnation) of the personified Maize or "God E" (Taube 1985), delivered to the place of creation by the double-headed serpent, Itzamnaaj. This scene of creation is vividly depicted in the Preclassic murals of San Bartolo in Guatemala, where a series of seven figures are shown walking (and another one floating) along the serpent body of Itzamnaaj (Saturno et al. 2005:Figure 5). This assembly of personified characters walking along (or through) the serpent body is reminiscent of the seven celestial bodies identified by Milbrath (1999:244, 279) in later Classic period imagery (see Figure 6.3). The protagonist in the San Bartolo murals is identified as the "Maize God," who places a gourd in the birthplace of the first humans, a place of creation called "Flower Mountain" (Saturno et al. 2005:Figure 5). Five infants are born from the gourd, one in the center and the others floating in the four corners of the scene, attached to the gourd by four trails of blood (k'uh/itz) that resemble umbilical cords as well as breath volutes (ik') rising from their bodies (Saturno et al. 2005:9). Footprints along the serpent body demarcate it as a path. The breath volutes and streams of blood or umbilical cords, much like the serpent body, are trails that emphasize the movement and growth of the animic cosmos, what Ingold (2006:13) means by organisms (such as maize and newborns) being constituted within a relational field.

Inverting the normative logic, Ingold (2006:17) suggests that the paths or movement of life are in a state of becoming (rather than being). Viewed as a medium rather than a surface, the intangible domain can take many different forms, such as wind, lightning, and thunder, as well as birds (Ingold 2006:17; Pauketat 2013). The last form is particularly important in the Maya animic ontology, where birds embody swift movement and, as a *way* or spirit coessence, are oracle messengers that "pierced the membrane between different worlds, underworld and 'aboveworld,' divine and human" (Houston et al. 2006:231–232). Houston and colleagues (2006:232) note that images of birds as "embodied messengers" are a central motif in the Preclassic San Bartolo murals, discussed above. Additionally, in the Classic and Postclassic periods one of the most conspicuous "messenger" birds of a composite type is the so-called Principal Bird Deity, the birdlike avatar of Itzamnaaj (Bardawil 1976; Bassie-Sweet 2008:140–145; Houston et al. 2006:234). The images vary, but often they depict the head of Itzamnaaj with the wings and body of a bird (Figure 6.5). There is an important association between bird messengers and precious *ikatz* ("bundles" or "cargo" [Boot 2008:25; Houston et al. 2006:243]). In an unprovenienced Classic period painted cylinder vessel, known as the "God D Court Vessel," there is a depiction of a personified Itzamnaaj and his avian manifestation, behind which sits a large bundle with a glyph that Erik Boot (2008:6) reads *chanal ikatz*, or "Celestial/Of the Sky Bundle or Cargo." Boot (2008:6) notes additional bundles in the scene that are labeled *buluch k'an*, "11 yellow; ripe; precious...," with the final element of this compound undeciphered. The connection between precious bundles, bird messengers, and royal courts remains poorly understood, but it seems that Itzamnaaj in his avian aspect plays some role in bestowing rulership on a king by delivering to him a bundle of sacred power. Boot (2008:14–15, Figure 8) notes a parallel with the bundles seen in two other unprovenienced painted vessels (Kerr Nos. 2796 and 7750) that depict the royal court of an entity referred to as "God L," who also is present on the "God D Court Vessel" and who I believe represents the night-sun aspect of Itzamnaaj (see discussions of "God L" and the closely related "God M" as "travelers" in Gillespie and Joyce 1998, identified as the "Black Itzamnaaj" in Vail 2000:141–144, Figure 27).

Timothy Pauketat (2013:56) describes the bundling practices among indigenous groups of the Americas as deeply connected to travelers, whose mission seems to have involved a combination of mercantile activity, soul searching, and proselytizing in their journeys to strange lands, where bundles were transferred; then travelers "returned home with new bundle-power" (see also Baltus, this volume; Skousen, this volume). I believe the bundles associated with Itzamnaaj, along with his

FIGURE 6.5. Itzamnaaj as "Principal Bird Deity" (after Houston et al. 2006:Figure 7.12c; redrawn by M. Brouwer Burg).

"traveler" and "bird" aspects, may share similar meaning regarding the transfer of powerful objects, humans, and divine essences (k'uh, ik', nik, and itz). This bundle transfer is vividly depicted in the San Bartolo murals (Saturno et al. 2005:Figure 5) and references the original sacred journey and transfer of bundled power by the Creator, Itzamnaaj, facilitating the birth of the first humans and setting into motion the movement of the cosmos. The Tzotzil Maya word *Ch'uul Xanbal* may refer to such a spiritual journey. Although it was translated in early Spanish dictionaries as "religion," Laughlin and Haviland (1988:2:444) have suggested that it means "holy [*Ch'uul*] life or walk [*Xanbal*]." Pharo (2007:45) suggests that the term conveys "a (sacred) righteous, correct way of life," expressing a kind of moral virtue. I would argue that it likely has a more literal meaning, referencing the actual spiritual journey or walk of the ritual practitioner who carries and transfers the sacred bundle that contains power originally derived from Itzamnaaj.

Concluding Thoughts: Bundling and Unbundling the Animic Cosmos

Epigraphic studies, alongside more recent cognitive studies examining textual, historical, philosophical, and ethnographic material, have informed a more nuanced understanding of Maya spirituality as a "theology of experience" in which movement, bodily experience, and the relational self form the basis of the Maya animic ontology (Carlsen 1997; Molesky-Poz 2006; Monaghan 1995; Stross 1998; Tedlock 1982; Vogt 1969, 1976, 1998; Watanabe 1992). Maya archaeologists have been largely silent in this dialogue (for some notable exceptions, see Brown and Emery 2008; Duncan and Hofling 2011; Freidel et al. 1993; Geller 2012; Gillespie 2001; Harrison-Buck 2012a, 2012b; Harrison-Buck and Hendon 2013; Hendon 2010, 2012; Hutson 2010). This is surprising given the wealth of epigraphic and iconographic media that describe these immaterial phenomena (words like *k'uh*, *ik'*, *nik*, and *itz*), which are visually depicted in the iconography (as serpents, caimans, clouds, breath volutes, birds, and other embodied travelers). Here I argue that the epigraphy and iconography emphasize both movement and a relational constitution of being as the principal components of the Maya animic ontology. As partible beings, they fuse sky and earth and embody the relational aspects of Itzamnaaj, occupying an intangible domain that lies somewhere between *agency* and *materiality* (Ingold 2006:16). This dialectical relationship between agency and structure is what Pauketat (2013:32–33) describes as the "phenomenal relationships between things, substances, and other intangible qualities...that engage the senses—sight, sound, smell, taste, and touch—in ways that lend them agentic or transformative power."

As Ingold (2000:97) notes elsewhere, the positioning of objects in the relational field is what imbues them with power, although humans often are at the foci of this power. For contemporary Maya, this central person is the Daykeeper, or *Ajq'ij* (Ahau). Daykeepers carry the "burden of the days" (the calendar) in their bodies and maintain a tremendous energy (a "lightning in the blood") that connects them to the "Owner" of the universe and illuminates the meaning of the days, providing them with a "distinct way of knowing" the world (Molesky-Poz 2006:74, 134). The material and cosmic levels may appear as a stark dichotomy, but for the *Ajq'ijab'* and other Maya spiritual leaders it is precisely between these two planes that they stand (Molesky-Poz 2006:156). In the Maya relational ontology it is not just the sensuous qualities of the objects or substances that impart animacy but rather *dialogical activity*: the dialogue with and transfer between the sacred housed in physical phenomena. For the contemporary Maya, a dialogue is achieved with the Earth-Sky Creator by "listening to the movements in their bodies," often in the blood and breath (e.g., what can be seen, heard, smelled, tasted, touched, or felt) (Molesky-Poz 2006:158–159). In discussing an archaeology of the senses in ancient Mesoamerica, Houston and Taube (2000:263) conclude, "The sensations of the past cannot be retrieved, only their encoding in imperishable media." Yet Maya ethnography clearly demonstrates that these sensations are not buried and gone, and it suggests that they may sharply resemble the dialectical methods used by the ancient Maya, such as the breath, pulsing blood, cast seeds, aromatic censing, heat, and flames of the fire. Much more remains to be explored in terms of the ancient Maya animic ontology, especially in terms of the sights, sounds, smells, and tastes of Itzamnaaj. As this chapter illustrates, this "metasensory" understanding of the world is intimated in the glyphs and iconography showing Itzamnaaj's relatedness to breath and wind, the life-giving substances of nectar, dew, blood, and maize, and the cyclical movements and regeneration of life.

Scholars continue to reference the Maya "pantheon of gods" and rely on a Western classification system for these "gods" that was originally developed by Paul Schellhas (1904). While the use of Schellhas's deity labels provides scholars with a shared terminology, many personified images in the Maya codices that Schellhas and others have labeled discrete "gods" share clusters of attributes and appear to constitute only a small number of underlying divinities whose roles often merge (Vail 2000:123). Gabrielle Vail (2000) concludes that not all of these personified figures represent discrete "gods" (personified k'uh, whom Schellhas has labeled "God C," is a prime example) and that many of these numinous characters may best be viewed as aspects or manifestations of Itzamnaaj (e.g., Gods D, L, M, N, Z, and H). Trying to separate and label a series of "gods" as discrete entities defined by distinct traits and conceptual domains is a Westernized taxonomic approach that has proven to be an invalid representation of prehispanic Maya ideology (Gillespie and Joyce 1998; Vail 2000). By focusing on isolated, individual aspects of the Maya cosmos, we risk obscuring the fundamental components of the Maya animic ontology: movement and the relational constitution of being. Rather than compartmentalize the Maya cosmos as others have done, I have attempted to describe the fluidity and relationally constituted nature of Itzamnaaj as the heart of the Maya animic cosmos. This ontological status helps to make sense of what appears to be a disparate collection of "gods" that all seemingly overlap and have associated physical attributes. As the heart of the cosmos, Itzamnaaj brings forth life in both earth and sky, but this regenerative life cycle is reliant on the ongoing relationships among human and other-than-human forces who "continually and reciprocally bring one another into existence" (Ingold 2006:10) and help to sustain this constant state of movement and change in the world.

Note

1. Other interpretations of the Popol Vuh creation story suggest that Itzamnaaj and Gukumatz are two separate entities and that the plumed serpent becomes the First-Father when he plants the seed of life in the First-Mother, Tepew, Heart of Earth inside a cave-womb (Nielson and Brady 2006; Tedlock 1985; Thompson 1970:201).

References Cited

Alberti, Benjamin, and Tamara L. Bray (editors)
2009   Animating Archaeology: Of Subjects, Objects and Alternative Ontologies. Special Section, *Cambridge Archaeological Journal* 19:337–343.

Arias, Arturo
1996   Foreword. In *The Lived Horizon of My Being: The Substantiation of the Self and and the Discourse of Resistance in Rigoberta Menchú, M M Bakhtin, and Víctor Montejo*, by Judith Thorn. ASU Center for Latin American Studies Press, Arizona State University, Tempe.

Bardawil, Lawrence W.
1976   The Principal Bird Deity in Maya Art: An Iconographic Study of Form and Meaning. In *The Art, Iconography and Dynastic History of Palenque, Part III*, edited by Merle Greene Robertson. Pre-Columbian Art Research, Robert Louis Stevenson School, Pebble Beach, California.

Barrera Vásquez, Alfredo
1980   *Diccionario Maya Cordemex, Maya-Español, Español-Maya*. Ediciones Cordemex, Mérida, Mexico.

Bassie-Sweet, Karen
2008   *Maya Sacred Geography and the Creator Deities*. University of Oklahoma Press, Norman.

Bird-David, Nurit
1999   "Animism" Revisited: Personhood, Environment, and Relational Epistemology. *Current Anthropology* 40:S67–91.

Boot, Erik
2008   At the Court of Itzam Nah Yax Kokaj Mut: Preliminary Iconographic and Epigraphic Analysis of a Late Classic Vessel. Maya Vase Database, www.mayavase.com/God-D-Court-Vessel.pdf, accessed December 21, 2012.

Brown, Linda A., and Kitty F. Emery
2008   Negotiations with the Animate Forest: Hunting Shrines in the Guatemalan Highlands. *Journal of Archaeological Method and Theory* 15:300–337.

Cabrera, Edgar
1995   *El calendario maya: Su origen y su filosofía*. La Liga Maya, San José, Costa Rica.

Carlsen, Robert
1997   *The War for the Heart and Soul of a Highland Maya Town*. University of Texas Press, Austin.

Carlsen, Robert, and Martin Prechtel
1991   The Flowering of the Dead: An Interpretation of Highland Maya Culture. *Man* (N.S.) 26: 23–42.

Clark, John E., and Arlene Colman
2012   Structure of the Mesoamerican Universe, from Aztec to Olmec. In *Enduring Motives: The Archaeology of Tradition and Religion in Native America*, edited by Linea Sundstrom and Warren DeBoer, pp. 15–59. University of Alabama Press, Tuscaloosa.

Duncan, William N., and Charles Andrew Hofling
2011   Why the Head? Cranial Modification as Protection and Ensoulment among the Maya. *Ancient Mesoamerica* 22:199–210.

Farriss, Nancy M.
1984   *Maya Society under Colonial Rule: The Collective Enterprise of Survival*. Princeton University Press, Princeton, New Jersey.

Fowler, Chris
2004   *The Archaeology of Personhood: An Anthropological Approach*. Routledge, New York.

Fowles, Severin
2010   Animist/Analyst. Paper presented at the Annual Meeting of the Theoretical Archaeology Group, Brown University, Providence, Rhode Island, April 30–May 2.

2013 *An Archaeology of Doings: Secularism and the Study of Pueblo Religion*. School for Advanced Research Press, Santa Fe, New Mexico.

Freidel, David A., Linda Schele, and Joy Parker
1993 *Maya Cosmos: Three Thousand Years on the Shaman's Path*. HarperCollins, New York.

Furst, Jill Leslie
1997 *The Natural History of the Soul in Ancient Mexico*. Yale University Press, New Haven, Connecticut.

Geller, Pamela
2012 Parting (with) the Dead: Body Partibility as Evidence of Commoner Ancestor Veneration. *Ancient Mesoamerica* 23:115–130.

Gillespie, Susan D.
2001 Personhood, Agency, and Mortuary Ritual: A Case Study from the Ancient Maya. *Journal of Anthropological Archaeology* 20:73–112.

Gillespie, Susan D., and Rosemary A. Joyce
1998 Deity Relationships in Mesoamerican Cosmologies: The Case of the Maya God L. *Ancient Mesoamerica* 9:279–296.

Gossen, Gary H.
1996 Maya Zapatistas Move to the Ancient Future. *American Anthropologist* 98:528–538.

Graham, Elizabeth, Scott E. Simmons, and Christine D. White
2013 The Spanish Conquest and the Maya Collapse: How "Religious" Is Change? *World Archaeology* 45 (1): 161–185.

Graña-Behrens, Daniel
2012 Itz'aat and Tlamatini: The "Wise Man" as Keeper of Maya and Nahua Collective Memory. In *Mesoamerican Memory: Enduring Systems of Remembrance*, edited by Stephanie Wood and Amos Megged, pp. 15–32. University of Oklahoma Press, Norman.

Harris, Oliver J. T., and John Robb
2012 Multiple Ontologies and the Problem of the Body in History. *American Anthropologist* 114:668–679.

Harrison-Buck, Eleanor
2012a Architecture as Animate Landscape: Circular Shrines in the Ancient Maya Lowlands. *American Anthropologist* 114:64–80.
2012b Rituals of Death and Disempowerment among the Maya. In *Power and Identity in Archaeological Theory and Practice: Case Studies from Ancient Mesoamerica*, edited by Eleanor Harrison-Buck, pp. 103–115. Foundations of Archaeological Inquiry. University of Utah Press, Salt Lake City.
2015 Killing the "Kings of Stone": The Defacement of Classic Maya Monuments. In *Ritual, Violence, and the Fall of the Classic Maya Kings*, edited by Gyles Iannone, Brett Houk, and Sonja Schwake. University Press of Florida, Gainesville, forthcoming.

Harrison-Buck, Eleanor, and Julia A. Hendon
2013 Exploring Epistemologies and Ontologies of Agency and Personhood: An Introduction. Paper presented at the 78th Annual Meeting of the Society for American Archaeology, Honolulu, Hawaii.

Harvey, Graham
2006 Animals, Animists, and Academics. *Zygon* 41:9–20.

Hellmuth, Nicholas
1987 *Monster und Menschen in der Maya-Kunst*. Akademische Druck u. Verlagsanstalt, Graz, Austria.

Hendon, Julia A.
2010 *Houses in a Landscape: Memory and Everyday Life in Mesoamerica*. Duke University Press, Durham, North Carolina.
2012 Objects as Persons: Integrating Maya Beliefs and Anthropological Theory. In *Power and Identity in Archaeological Theory and Practice: Case Studies from Ancient Mesoamerica*, edited by Eleanor Harrison-Buck, pp. 82–89. Foundations of Archaeological Inquiry. University of Utah Press, Salt Lake City.

Houston, Stephen D., and David Stuart
1989 *The Way Glyph: Evidence for "Co-essences" among the Classic Maya*. Research Reports on Ancient Maya Writing No. 30. Center for Maya Research, Barnardsville, North Carolina.
1996 Of Gods, Glyphs, and Kings: Divinity and Rulership among the Classic Maya. *Antiquity* 70:289–312.

Houston, Stephen D., David Stuart, and Karl Taube
2006 *The Memory of Bones: Body, Being, and Experience among the Classic Maya*. University of Texas Press, Austin.

Houston, Stephen D., and Karl A. Taube
2000 An Archaeology of the Senses: Perception and Cultural Expression in Ancient Mesoamerica. *Cambridge Archaeological Journal* 10:261–294.

Hutson, Scott
2010 *Dwelling, Identity, and the Maya: Relational Archaeology at Chunchucmil*. AltaMira Press, Lanham, Maryland.

Ingold, Tim
2000 *The Perception of the Environment: Essays on Livelihood, Dwelling and Skill*. Routledge, New York.
2006 Rethinking the Animate, Re-animating Thought. *Ethnos* 71:9–20.

2007 Materials against Materiality. *Archaeological Dialogues* 14:1–16.
2010 Footprints through the Weather-World: Walking, Breathing, Knowing. *Journal of the Royal Anthropological Institute* N.S.: S121–S139.

Laughlin, Robert M., and John B. Haviland
1988 *The Great Tzotzil Dictionary of Santo Domingo Zinacantán: With Grammatical Analysis and Historical Commentary*. 3 vols. Smithsonian Contributions to Anthropology No. 31. Washington, D.C.

López Austin, Alfredo
1988 *The Human Body and Ideology: Concepts of the Ancient Nahuas*. Translated by Thelma Ortiz de Montellano and Bernard Ortiz de Montellano. University of Utah Press, Salt Lake City.

Martin, Simon
2006 Cacao in Ancient Maya Religion: First Fruit from the Maize Tree and Other Tales from the Underworld. In *Chocolate in Mesoamerica: A Cultural History of Cacao*, edited by Cameron L. McNeil, pp. 154–183. University Press of Florida, Gainesville.

Milbrath, Susan
1999 *Star Gods of the Maya: Astronomy in Art, Folklore, and Calendars*. University of Texas Press, Austin.

Molesky-Poz, Jean
2006 *Contemporary Maya Spirituality: The Ancient Ways Are Not Lost*. University of Texas Press, Austin.

Monaghan, John
1995 *The Covenants with Earth and Rain: Exchange, Sacrifice, and Revelation in Mixtec Sociality*. University of Oklahoma Press, Norman.

Nielson, Jesper, and James E. Brady
2006 The Couple in the Cave: Origin Iconography on a Ceramic Vessel from Los Naranjos, Honduras. *Ancient Mesoamerica* 17:203–217.

Pauketat, Timothy R.
2013 *An Archaeology of the Cosmos: Rethinking Agency and Religion in Ancient America*. Routledge, New York.

Pharo, Lars Kirkhusmo
2007 The Concept of Religion in Mesoamerican Languages. *Numen* 54:28–70.

Ringle, William M.
1988 *Of Mice and Monkeys: The Value and Meaning of T1016, the God C Hieroglyph*. Research Reports on Ancient Maya Writing No. 18. Center for Maya Research, Barnardsville, North Carolina.

Sachse, Frauke
2004 Interpreting Maya Religion: Methodological Remarks on Understanding Continuity and Change in Maya Religious Practices. In *Continuity and Change: Maya Religious Practices in Temporal Perspective*, edited by Daniel Graña-Behrens, Nikolai Grube, Christian M. Prager, Frauke Sachse, Stefanie Teufel, and Elizabeth Wagner, pp. 1–21. Anton Sauerwein, Markt Schwaben, Germany.

Saturno, William A., Karl A. Taube, David Stuart, and Heather Hurst
2005 *The Murals of San Bartolo, El Petén, Guatemala, Part 1: The North Wall*. Center for Ancient American Studies, Barnardsville, North Carolina.

Schele, Linda, and Mary Ellen Miller
1986 *The Blood of Kings: Dynasty and Ritual in Maya Art*. Kimbell Art Museum, Fort Worth, Texas.

Schellhas, Paul
1904 *Representations of Deities of the Maya Manuscripts*. Papers of the Peabody Museum of Archaeology and Ethnology, Vol. 4, No. 1. Harvard University, Cambridge, Massachusetts.

Skora, Kerry Martin
2007 The Pulsating Heart and Its Divine Sense Energies: Body and Touch in Abhinavagupta's Trika Śaivism. *Numen* 54:420–458.

Strathern, Marilyn
1988 *The Gender of the Gift: Problems with Women and Problems with Society in Melanesia*. University of California Press, Berkeley.

Stross, Brian
1998 Seven Ingredients in Mesoamerican Ensoulment: Dedication and Termination in Tenejapa. In *The Sowing and the Dawning: Termination, Dedication, and Transformation in the Archaeological Record of Mesoamerica*, edited by Shirley Boteler Mock, pp. 31–39. University of New Mexico Press, Albuquerque.

Stuart, David
1996 Kings of Stone: A Consideration of Stelae in Ancient Maya Ritual and Representation. *Res: Anthropology and Aesthetics* 29–30:148–171.
2005 Ideology and Classic Maya Kingship. In *A Catalyst for Ideas: Anthropological Archaeology and the Legacy of Douglas Schwartz*, edited by Vernon L. Scarborough, pp. 257–285. School of American Research Press, Santa Fe, New Mexico.

Stuart, David, and Stephen Houston
1994 *Classic Maya Place Names*. Dumbarton Oaks Research Library and Collection, Washington, D.C.

Taube, Karl A.
1985 The Maya Maize God: A Reappraisal. In *Fifth

Palenque Round Table, 1983, edited by Virginia M. Fields, pp. 171–181. Pre-Columbian Art Research Institute, San Francisco.

1989 Itzam Cab Ain: Caimans, Cosmology, and Calendrics in Postclassic Yucatán. www.mesoweb.com/bearc/cmr/RRAMW26.pdf, accessed December 21, 2012.

1992a *The Major Gods of Ancient Yucatan*. Studies in Pre-Columbian Art and Archaeology No. 32. Dumbarton Oaks Research Library and Collection, Washington, D.C.

1992b The Iconography of Mirrors at Teotihuacan. In *Art, Ideology, and the City of Teotihuacan*, edited by Janet C. Berlo, pp. 169–204. Dumbarton Oaks Research Library and Collection, Washington, D.C.

Tedlock, Barbara

1982 *Time and the Highland Maya*. University of New Mexico Press, Albuquerque.

Tedlock, Dennis (translator)

1985 *Popol Vuh: The Definitive Edition of the Mayan Book of the Dawn of Life and the Glories of Gods and Kings*. Simon and Schuster, New York.

Thompson, J. Eric S.

1939 *Excavations at San Jose, British Honduras*. Publication No. 506. Carnegie Institution of Washington, Washington, D.C.

1970 *Maya History and Religion*. University of Oklahoma Press, Norman.

Vail, Gabrielle

2000 Pre-Hispanic Maya Religion: Conceptions of Divinity in the Postclassic Maya Codices. *Ancient Mesoamerica* 11:123–147.

Vogt, Evon Z.

1965 Zinacanteco "Souls." *Man* 65:33–35.

1969 *Zinacantan: A Maya Community in the Highlands of Chiapas*. Harvard University Press, Cambridge, Massachusetts.

1976 *Tortillas for the Gods: A Symbolic Analysis of Zinacanteco Rituals*. University of Oklahoma Press, Norman.

1998 Zinacanteco Dedication and Termination Rituals. In *The Sowing and the Dawning: Termination, Dedication, and Transformation in the Archaeological Record of Mesoamerica*, edited by Shirley Boteler Mock, pp. 21–30. University of New Mexico Press, Albuquerque.

Watanabe, John

1992 *Maya Saints and Souls in a Changing World*. University of Texas Press, Austin.

Wright, Mark Alan

2011 A Study of Classic Maya Rulership. Unpublished Ph.D. dissertation, Department of Anthropology, University Of California, Riverside.

Part III

Temporalities

7

Entanglements of the Blackfoot

Relationships with the Spiritual and Material Worlds

Gerald A. Oetelaar

In North American archaeology, discussions of movement and entanglement are normally framed in terms of concepts familiar to those trained in the Western scientific tradition. For studies of hunter-gatherers, for example, the models and arguments presented rely on the theoretical constructs of ecology and the related field of economics. Although we may assume the presence of natural ecosystems peopled by rational actors, the day-to-day activities and interactions of First Nations communities were in fact structured by very different worldviews. The Blackfoot people, for example, live in a world inhabited by animate beings that include humans, animals, plants, rocks, and springs. Their world, like that of the ecologist, is made up of a complex web of relationships between animate and inanimate entities,[1] but these relationships are mediated by spirits who respond to the prayers and actions of the Blackfoot people. Moreover, the Blackfoot people, like their Western counterparts, seek to maintain a delicate balance in this world, but the principles underlying their strategies are radically different from those of the modern ecologist.

To understand and interpret the structured world of the Blackfoot, archaeologists must be willing to accept alternative perspectives of the ecophysical environment and its relationship to human groups (Ingold 2000; Watts 2013). They must move away from the constructed world of ecologists, where the patterned movement of human groups is predicated by the location, abundance, and seasonal availability of resources, toward the structured world of the Blackfoot, where human groups move from place to place following a network of well-defined trails. The purpose of this ritual pilgrimage, historical journey, and social odyssey is to renew the spiritual and physical relationship with the ancestral beings, the people, the land, and the resources (see Skousen, this volume). Failure to fulfill these ritual and social obligations entails serious consequences for the welfare of the living community and their descendants. The advent of the fur trade and the resultant entanglement with Western Europeans necessitated a change in itinerary, and this deviation in the patterned movement of the Blackfoot presented the first serious challenges to their structured world of social relationships and ceremonial obligations (see Baltus, this volume). Significantly, the Blackfoot people negotiated this world in transformation through the lens of their worldview and interpreted the subsequent devastating epidemics, the extinction of bison, and the unraveling of their cultural fabric as partly the consequences of their actions.

The Blackfoot Perspective on Movement

To elders, the traditional Blackfoot homeland extends from the North Saskatchewan River in the north to the Yellowstone River in the south and from the Rocky Mountains in the west to the Great Sand Hills in the east (Blackfoot Gallery Committee 2001). The boundaries of this "territory" are not rigidly defined, although the Blackfoot and their neighbors use landmarks along well-established trails to delineate the approximate margins of their respective homelands. These landmarks include distinctive peaks near mountain passes on the west (Oetelaar 2012; Oetelaar and Oetelaar 2011), important fords across rivers on the north and south, and prominent hills marking the location of trails along the eastern margin of the homeland. Pictographs, petroforms, cairns, medicine wheels, vision quest structures, and tipi rings occur on or near these named places, indicating their historical significance.

According to Blackfoot elders, the area so defined has been their traditional homeland since time immemorial, and the archaeological evidence tends to corroborate these claims of historical continuity (Vickers and Peck 2009). There is a general congruence between the extent of the Blackfoot homeland and the spatial distribution of diagnostic pottery and projectile point types (Peck and Ives 2001), of *iniskim* (Peck 2002; Reeves 1993),[2] of Napi figures (Vickers 2008),[3] of boulder monuments (Brumley 1988), and of distinctive rock art (Klassen 2003). Together the distribution of these archaeological remains and the continuity evident in the material culture suggest a patterned use of the landscape extending over a millennium or more.

To the Blackfoot, the homeland is much more than a series of resource patches for humans and migrating bison herds (Oetelaar 2004, 2006). Instead, the Blackfoot view their homeland as a series of named locales linked by paths, movements, and narratives (Oetelaar and Meyer 2006; Oetelaar and Oetelaar 2006, 2011; Zedeño et al. 2006). The places are often outstanding natural features created by the trickster Napi in the long ago whereas the paths and trails represent the accumulated imprint of countless journeys by the ancestors and the living community (sensu Ingold 1993). Myths and oral traditions explain how these landmarks were created by Napi as he traveled along the same paths and left behind songs, sacred objects, and practices to commemorate his creative acts on earth (Oetelaar and Oetelaar 2011). Throughout the year the Blackfoot retrace Napi's footsteps and those of their ancestors, stopping at the same places to perform ceremonies and activities in a prescribed order. As they travel along the paths, the physical appearance of the approaching landmark serves as a mnemonic device, eliciting the name and the appropriate narratives, thereby converting the landscape into an archive or repository of traditional knowledge. Movement across the homeland thus becomes a journey through the history of the group and a strategy designed to preserve and transmit faithfully the language, culture, and oral traditions of the group from one generation to the next.

Sanctioned by a cosmology, this movement is also a ritual pilgrimage designed to fulfill reciprocal obligations negotiated between the spirits and the Blackfoot people. In the long ago the Blackfoot established sacred alliances with the spirits who control the availability of resources and the health of living communities (Bastien 2004). During the establishment of the sacred alliances the spirits transferred medicine bundles to the Blackfoot people with explicit instructions to open these at prescribed times and at specific places on the landscape. For example, the first thunder of spring signals the return of Thunder, master of summer, who now instructs the Blackfoot people to open the Thunder Medicine Pipe Bundle and to begin the ritual cycle, including the annual pilgrimage to the sun dance grounds (Kehoe 2002). This ritual pilgrimage involves a scheduled movement from the foothills to the open prairie, and takes people by a succession of places where natural and cultural features commemorate the creative actions of ancestral beings and where portals provide more direct access to the spirits (Figure 7.1). For their part, the Blackfoot must continue to visit these places, perform the ceremonies, sing the songs, and tell the stories to ensure the continued vitality of the rocks, springs, trees, and animals and, by extension, the physical and spiritual health of the entire community, both living and dead (see Brown Vega, this volume). Failure to undertake this journey would disrupt the cosmic balance, with obvious consequences for the welfare of all living communities within the homeland.

Although the sun dance and the associated pilgrimage of renewal was the prime motivation for the annual forays onto the plains, the Blackfoot people also looked forward to renewing their ties with the ancestors. Just as the paths represent the physical imprint of countless journeys, so the places along the network of trails embody the ac-

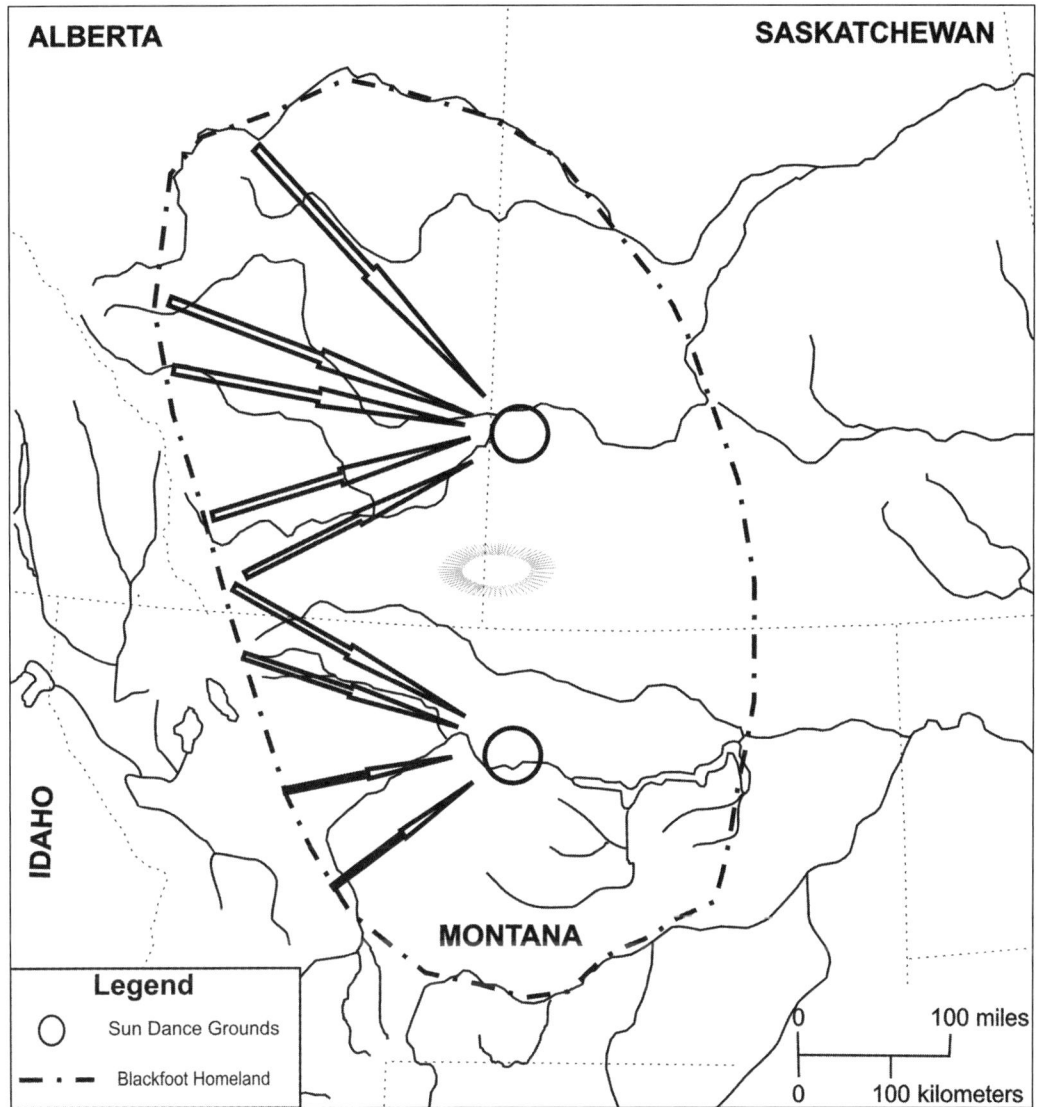

FIGURE 7.1. Map of the Northern Plains showing the Blackfoot homeland and the traditional direction of travel between the sheltered winter camps and the sun dance grounds.

tions and management activities of the people. During their successive visits the Blackfoot people intentionally and unintentionally alter the nature and the physical appearance of the place by constructing homes or monuments and by actively maintaining the living space. In the process, they introduce materials that change the biology and chemistry of the sediments at the site. At the same time, the members of the living community intentionally and unintentionally introduce new species and carefully tend the desirable resources such as cottonwood trees, berry bushes, and medicinal herbs growing in the immediate vicinity of the camp, while also systematically removing undesirable plants, animals, and debris (Oetelaar and Oetelaar 2007, 2008).

The cottonwood trees, decorated boulders, and rocky ledges are of particular interest because they serve as resting places for deceased members of the community. On arrival, the Blackfoot people first greet their dead relatives and commune with the spirits of the ancestors because, in their world, the trees, berry bushes, and herbs are there because the ancestors came to these places, told stories, sang songs, and performed appropriate rituals. Moreover, the living community must similarly engage the human and nonhuman elements of each place on the landscape to ensure the continued availability of resources for future generations. In this way, movement from grove to grove establishes a sense of continuity and spiritual attachment to place, further contributing to the vitality of the homeland (Oetelaar and Oetelaar 2011).

During this annual movement, people of all ages renew their acquaintance with members of all the Blackfoot bands whose winter encampments are scattered in the sheltered valleys of the foothills, parklands, and localized uplands distributed across the plains. In addition, groups from neighboring homelands undertake similar treks and join the Blackfoot people to celebrate the sun dance. The assembled crowd not only participates in this important ceremony but also renews its ties with real and fictive kin during the numerous social events. Trade in the form of barter, gift giving, ceremonial exchanges, and acts of reciprocity cements these bonds of friendship among neighboring groups, thereby establishing, restoring, or widening the social and political networks essential to the survival of the group (Dempsey 1993).

Travel across the landscape is therefore much more than a historical journey and a ritual pilgrimage; it is a spiritual, social, and educational odyssey. Significantly, the total landscape is necessary to tell the entire story, to complete the annual ritual cycle, to establish the social and ideological continuity of the group, and to ensure the renewal of resources. At the same time, movement across the landscape becomes a strategy designed to validate the continuity between the spirits, the ancestors, the living community, and future generations of Blackfoot. In this way, entities of the past, present, and future are actively engaged with the continued vitality of the homeland.

Although the Blackfoot people treat all nonhuman entities within their homeland as relatives, individual communities have special relationships with the spirits inhabiting their traditional winter and summer camps as well as the places located along the trails connecting these encampments. Moreover, the maintenance of reciprocal arrangements and obligations with one's human and nonhuman relatives involves a substantial investment of social capital. Given the nature and importance of these special relationships, the Blackfoot people are understandably protective of their nonhuman relatives and are therefore ready to confront any individuals who fail to follow the appropriate protocols and practices in their dealings with the human and nonhuman residents of the homeland. The arrival of Euro-Canadians in 1754 and the subsequent establishment of fur trade posts along the margins of the homeland presented the first serious challenges to the integrity and validity of these critical relationships in the Blackfoot cosmos. From this point on, the failure of humans to continue fulfilling their reciprocal obligations disrupted the cosmic balance and contributed to a series of devastating events with long-term consequences for Blackfoot communities.

The Blackfoot World in Transformation

The Blackfoot people, like all other Native Americans, were involved in extensive trade networks long before the advent of the fur trade (Dempsey 1993; Smyth 2001; Wood 1980). The exchange of goods in this precontact context, however, involved the aggregation of many groups at predetermined locations where exchange occurred in a setting with a great deal of ceremony, social interaction, and entertainment.[4] On rare occasions, groups even invited their neighbors or others to establish a trading post within their homeland. Significantly, the groups involved shared a common ideology and knew the relevant trading protocols and practices, including the consequences of inappropriate actions before, during, and after the exchange. The arrival of European traders with their different worldview and technology transformed Native American society in a matter of a few generations with obvious consequences for the structured world of the Blackfoot. Before describing the negotiations involved and the impact of this transformation, I briefly outline the nature of the interaction between the two cultures.

Sometime after establishing its first trading post on the shores of Hudson Bay in 1684, the Hudson's Bay Company (HBC) tried unsuccessfully to persuade the Blackfoot to trade at this

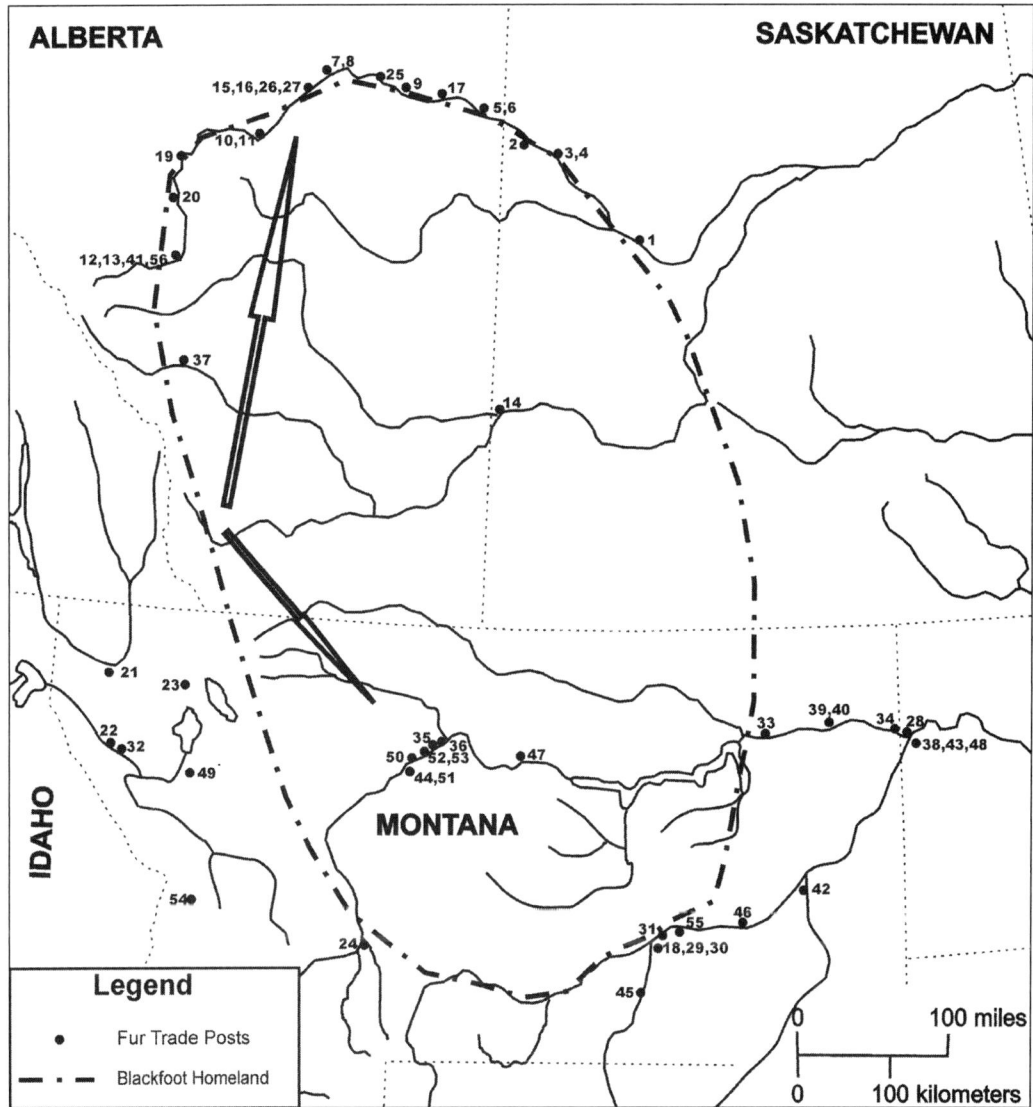

FIGURE 7.2. Map of the Northern Plains showing the Blackfoot homeland, the fur trading posts, and the direction of travel between the sheltered winter camps and the trade centers.

establishment. Shortly thereafter, in the face of stiff competition from the Northwest Company (NWC), the HBC adopted the NWC's strategy and established inland posts along the Saskatchewan drainage, usually selecting existing rendezvous centers as locations for trading posts. Anthony Henday was the first European trader to visit a Blackfoot encampment, in 1754, and although the location of the encounter remains conjectural, the camp site was located somewhere in what is today the province of Alberta (Belyea 2000). In late 1769 a group of Blackfoot set up camp near the establishment of William Pink and his Cree guides. A few days later, on January 1, 1770, the entire group moved to a nearby Blackfoot pound to kill buffalo (Smyth 2001:144–145). In April 1779 a First Nations group, variously identified as the Cree, Blackfoot, or Gros Ventre, attacked Fort Montagne d'Aigle, an independent British trading post established by Peter Pangman and John Cole on the North Saskatchewan River, close to the eastern margins of the Blackfoot homeland (Figure 7.2, Table 7.1). The murder of Cole and another Canadian during this encounter prompted the fur traders to retreat downstream to Hudson House (Binnema 2001:113). More importantly, this event was ingrained in the collective memory of the traders and encouraged them to adopt a different strategy in their dealings with the members of the Blackfoot alliance.

Presumably instigated by the maltreatment of the Indians who visited the post, the attack on Fort Montagne d'Aigle reinforced the need to observe the protocols and practices of First Nations, including greeting ceremonies, assertions of friendship, pipe smoking, and the exchange of gifts, before starting the trade (Smyth 2001:64). If the newcomers were willing to adopt the proper protocols, the Blackfoot people welcomed the establishment of trading posts within their homeland, but they also issued warnings about the consequences of trapping animals without their permission. The independent traders and trappers of the HBC and NWC probably interpreted such threats as a form of protectionism. For the Blackfoot, however, the real concern was about offending the nonhuman relatives by trapping animals without proper treatment and respect.

Five years after the Montagne d'Aigle incident, the HBC and the NWC continued to construct a succession of trading posts along the north shore of the North Saskatchewan River, but they were unable to establish a viable post within the Blackfoot homeland. Tentative forays such as Chesterfield House (1800–1802) and Peigan Post (1832–1834) were dismal failures because these inland posts failed to generate the returns expected, and the interactions between the fur traders and the members of the Blackfoot alliance were anything but congenial. Therefore, the companies encouraged the Blackfoot to visit its northern trading posts and sent traders to winter with the Blackfoot to learn their language and their culture. For the next couple of decades, then, the Blackfoot served as hosts to individuals such as Isaac Batt, James Gaddy, John Ward, David Thompson, and Peter Fidler.

South of the international border, American trappers learned similar lessons, although their initial forays into the Blackfoot homeland did not occur until 1810 (Figure 7.2, Table 7.1). In 1807 Mañuel Lisa constructed a fur trading post on the Yellowstone River near the mouth of the Bighorn River (Phillips 1961:260). Fort Mañuel was thus the first post established along the southern boundary of the Blackfoot homeland.[5] Three years later a party of thirty men left Fort Mañuel to establish a trading post (Lewis and Clark Post) at the three forks of the Missouri and to trap "beaver throughout the whole extent of the Missouri above the Great Falls" (Phillips 1961:263). They abandoned this venture after repeated attacks by the Blackfoot and the murder of eight trappers along the Jefferson (Phillips 1961:263; Smyth 2001:104). In the spring of 1823 the members of the ill-fated Immell and Jones expedition opted to harvest furs themselves near the source of the Missouri and also paid for their transgressions with their lives (Nasatir et al. 1939). Although American companies accused the HBC of inciting these attacks on their trappers, the Blackfoot chiefs had clearly warned the traders about the consequences of trapping within the homeland without their permission (Smyth 2001:128). As was the case in western Canada, these events left their imprint on the collective memory of American fur traders for almost a decade.

By 1832 several enterprising individuals and companies began constructing fur trading posts near the Blackfoot homeland, but these establishments were, for the most part, located along the south shore of the Yellowstone River within the homeland of the Crow, who were more willing to let trappers harvest furs from their land (Figure 7.2, Table 7.1). At this time the American Fur Company (AFC) established the first and only successful post within the Blackfoot homeland, just as beaver pelts were going out of style and buffalo robes were gaining popularity. The success of Fort Mckenzie has been attributed to the increasing demand for buffalo hides, the advantages of keelboats and steamers in the transport of bulky goods, and the longer season of open water on the Missouri River (Smyth 2001:429, 478). Of perhaps equal importance are the frequent requests by the Blackfoot to have a post constructed at the mouth of the Marias (Nasatir et al. 1939; Smyth 2001:432) and Mckenzie's decision to ask for permission before entering the homeland, as well as his willingness to adopt the trading protocols and practices of the Blackfoot (Smyth 2001: 421–426). The appointment of Alexander Culbertson as superintendent of the post in 1834 was also beneficial because his wife was Blackfoot and

Table 7.1. Fur Trade Posts Established on the Northern Plains in and around the Blackfoot Homeland with Dates of Use.

		Canadian Establishments			American Establishments		
No.	Fur Trade Post	Hudson's Bay Co.	Northwest Co.	XY Co.	Missouri Fur Co.	American Fur Co.	Independent traders
1	Fort Montagne d'Aigle		1778–1779				
2	Umfreville's House		1784–1787				
3	Fort de l'Isle I		1785–1794				
4	Manchester House	1786–1794					
5	Fort George		1792–1801				
6	Buckingham House	1792–1802					
7	Fort Augustus I		1795–1801				
8	Fort Edmonton I	1795–1801					
9	Fort de l'Isle II	1799–1801	1799–1801	1799–1801			
10	Upper Terre Blanche House		1799–1801				
11	Nelson House	1799–1801					
12	Rocky Mountain House I		1799–1834				
13	Acton House	1799–1834					
14	Chesterfield House	1800–1802	1800–1802	1800–1802			
15	Fort Augustus II		1801–1810				
16	Fort Edmonton II	1801–1810					
17	Fort Vermilion	1802–1810	1802–1810				
18	Fort Manuel				1807–1811		
19	Muskeg Fort		before 1808				
20	Boggy Hall		before 1808				
21	Kootenai Post		1808–1811				
22	Saleesh House		1809–1824				
23	Howse's House	1810					
24	Lewis and Clark Fort				1810		
25	Lower Terre Blanche Houses	1810–1813	1810–1813				
26	Fort Augustus III		1812–1915				
27	Fort Edmonton III	1812–1915					
28	Fort Henry						1822–1823
29	Fort Benton				1822–1823		
30	Ashley & Henry						1823–1824
31	Fort Cass					1832–1835	
32	Flathead Post	1824–1855					
33	Fort Union I					1826	
34	Fort Union II					1829–1866	
35	Fort Piegan					1831	
36	Fort Mckenzie					1832–1844	
37	Peigan Post	1832–1834					
38	Fort William (1)						1833–1834
39	Fort Jackson						1833–1834
40	Fort Assiniboine I					1834–1835	
41	Rocky Mountain House II	1835–1861					
42	Fort Van Buren					1835–1842	
43	Fort Mortimer						1842–1845
44	Fort Cotton						1842–1845
45	Fort Fox & Livingston						1842–1844
46	Fort Alexander						1842–1850
47	Fort Chardon					1844–1845	
48	Fort William (2)						1846–1858
49	Fort Connah	1846–1872					
50	Fort Campbell				1846–1860		
51	Fort Lewis (1)					1846–1847	
52	Fort Lewis (2)					1847–1850	
53	Fort Benton					1850–1864	
54	Fort Owen						1850–18??
55	Fort Sarpy					1850–1855	
56	Rocky Mountain House III	1866–1875					

Note: Numbers correspond to those in Figure 7.2.

he not only understood the Indian way of life but was respectful of their culture and lifestyle.

The primary objectives of the HBC, NWC, Missouri Fur Company (MFC), and AFC were to maximize their profit margins, but the motivations and negotiations of the Blackfoot people were influenced by very different principles and beliefs. For example, the Blackfoot were willing to exchange pemmican and the pelts of wolves, coyotes, and foxes for guns, ammunition, kettles, and beads, but they were reticent to hunt beaver because, during a severe winter in the long ago, Beaver transferred a very special medicine bundle to the people (McClintock 1968:104–112; Wissler and Duvall 1995:74–78). At the same time, the Blackfoot wanted easy access to the fur trading posts but were unwilling to let these establishments serve as supply depots for their neighbors or as bases for trappers to harvest fur-bearing animals within their homeland. The former concern pertains to their well-being whereas the latter relates directly to their perceived relationship with their nonhuman relatives. As stewards of these resources, the Blackfoot would obviously treat all animals with respect and perform the appropriate rituals to ensure the renewal of this precious resource. The trappers, especially those of European ancestry, felt no such obligations to their fur-bearing prey. Significantly, the mistreatment of the animals would have no effect on the traders but would have a direct impact on the well-being of the Blackfoot because, as stewards of the homeland and its resources, they were responsible for the welfare of the animals being trapped by foreigners.

Negotiations with the Entangled Web

From a Western scientific perspective, the Blackfoot involvement in the fur trade and the adoption of specific items represent a predictable adaptive response to a culture with a superior technology. With the advent of the fur trade, for example, the Blackfoot are assumed to have been rapidly transformed from plodding, stone-age pedestrians into mobile horsemen who were able to expand their territory through the effective adoption of the horse and gun (Binford 2001:346; Binnema 2001:86–106; Brink 1986; Ewers 1958:7; Lewis 1942; Secoy 1953; Wood 2010:272). However, the Blackfoot assessed the effectiveness and efficiency of new technologies according to very different standards. For example, they rejected metal shields in favor of their rawhide counterparts not because metal was more effective than rawhide in stopping a well-aimed musket ball but because the metal shield lacked the supernatural power to protect the warrior. To the Blackfoot, the protective designs painted on the shields and the medicines attached to these instruments of war protected the warrior, not the physical properties of the shields (Ewers 1972). Similar criteria were used for making decisions about the most desirable trade items, such as "firearms, alcohol, and tobacco" (Smyth 2001:197).

To understand Blackfoot decisions about the nature and desirability of European goods, it is necessary to adopt their worldview and their interpretations of these new items. For example, the Blackfoot word for the horse is *ponokamita*, which can be literally translated as elk-dog (Baldwin 1994; Uhlenbeck and van Gulik 1930:109). To the Blackfoot, then, the horse was adopted first and foremost as a companion to the dog, the normal beast of burden in Blackfoot society. Only later did these animals become the well-known buffalo runners, valuable commodities in their own right (Lewis 1942). Later still this animal became a status symbol and the basis for innumerable raids on the camps of neighboring groups and fur trade posts. In short, the tales of David Thompson notwithstanding, the desirability and initial adoption of the horse was based on its fit into an existing social context. Even there, the adoption of the horse influenced the patterned movement of the Blackfoot people in important ways, including the choice of destination during their travels (Ewers 2001; Landals 2003; Wissler 1914).

The adoption of the gun can be interpreted in a similar light. One of the important spirit beings in the Blackfoot cosmology is Thunder, the master of summer, whose home is Chief Mountain, perhaps the most sacred landmark in the Blackfoot homeland (Reeves 1994). Thunder transferred the Thunder Medicine Pipe Bundle to the Blackfoot people after the outcome of a battle with Raven, master of the winter (Blackfoot Gallery Committee 2001:16–17; Oetelaar 2012). Although Thunder's lightning bolts were effective at harming the Blackfoot occupants of a tipi, they were somewhat less effective against the cold winds emanating from the wings of Raven. To this day, the Blackfoot people open the Thunder Medicine Pipe Bundle when they hear the first thunder in spring. This sound announces the return of Thunder and the beginning of the annual ritual cycle, which in the past included the pilgrimage toward the sun dance ground. The first thunder also reminds people of the hazards of moving across a prairie landscape in the summer (Oetelaar 2012), particularly the risk that lightning will strike the protruding poles of tipis erected along the valley margins (Oetelaar and Olson 2000), killing or incapacitating the occupants of the lodges. Given this perception of lightning, one can easily imagine the amazement of the first Blackfoot warrior to witness the power of a gun during a visit to the post, in the heat of battle, or during the chase. This individual would have seen the flash of lightning, heard the roar of thunder, and then watched in absolute dismay as a distant human or bison fell dead to the ground. The warrior's interpretation of this event would have been that the traders must somehow have managed to harness and control the power of Thunder.

Although there is no documented account of this encounter, Peter Fidler's description of a similar event on Wednesday, December 12, 1792, serves to illustrate the impact of first encounters with the perceived power of European technology.[6] On this clear day, Fidler used a "burning glass" fixed to the top of his tobacco box to light a pipe, much to the amazement of a visiting Snake Indian, who immediately jumped up and withdrew in fear of someone who could light a pipe without fire. To this individual, Fidler somehow brought down the Sun to light the contents of the pipe. The Blackfoot, who were accompanying Fidler and Ward, seized this opportunity to extol the special powers of their European guests and to impress on their Snake visitor the benefits of having access to the fur trade posts and their bounty.

Encounters such as these gave the Blackfoot people the impression that Europeans somehow were able to harness the power of Thunder and Sun, two of their most powerful deities. By extension, the Europeans must somehow have more direct or better access to the powerful spirit beings of the Blackfoot people. Objects with such power were obviously desirable and would command a great deal of respect in the community. The Blackfoot people also soon realized the practicality and desirability of the weapon and the burning glass as intimidation factors in their negotiations with their traditional neighbors and enemies. In the process, however, they became more and more reliant on the fur trading posts, the only place to acquire such powerful items as well as the necessary gunpowder and lead balls.

As European fur traders adopted the protocols and practices of their hosts, alcohol and Brazilian tobacco soon became important constituents in the greeting ceremonies, assertions of friendship, pipe smoking, and gift exchanges. Again, the desirability of these products must be understood in light of the Blackfoot worldview. In the world of the Blackfoot, dreams and trances are viewed as communications from the spirits and are carefully interpreted and used to guide the actions of individuals (Lee 1994). Although dreams are not treated lightly, the most important event in the life of a young Blackfoot male is the vision quest. During this four-day ordeal the young man retreats to a secluded location and deprives his body of food until he obtains a vision (Dormaar 2001, 2003; Dormaar and Reeves 1993). The animate being, usually an animal, which appears to the young warrior in the vision will serve as his guide and protector for the rest of his life.

One can imagine the wonder of such a Blackfoot warrior who arrives at a fur trading post and is offered a glass of very strong alcohol. After only a couple of drinks, this individual would experience the same sensations as he felt on perhaps the fourth day of his vision quest. Moreover, he would interpret the evidence as yet another indication that the Europeans were granted special powers and more direct access to the spirit beings. Such beliefs would prompt this young warrior to revisit the post for additional experiences with the special elixir until the return visits were motivated more by addiction to the substance than by the desire to communicate with the spirits.

The desirability of European tobacco can be explained along similar lines regardless of the supposed differences in taste. Tobacco was domesticated in the Americas and played a key role in Native American rituals and ceremonies. In the Blackfoot homeland, tobacco was planted in places specifically designated for this purpose

(Grinnell 1962:268–269; McClintock 1968:108, 528). Even the planting and harvesting of this crop involved a great deal of ritual because the effectiveness of the substance depended on the nature of its treatment from seed to smoke. During household rituals the smoke from the pipe carried the prayer or message of the smoker up along the tipi poles and through the opening to the spirits (Oetelaar 2000). The reaction of the spirit to the pleas of the smoker depended on the qualities of the person, the message, and the medium. To the Blackfoot traders who witnessed the power of the gun, the alcohol, and the burning glass, European tobacco must have been viewed as a superior medium and a more direct link to the powerful spirits of the newcomers. Thus, the acceptance and eventual desirability of European tobacco should be attributed to its perceived spiritual potential rather than its supposed superior taste, although taste ultimately came into play as different trading posts tried to entice Native Americans to trade at their respective establishments with offers of the best-tasting tobacco (Smyth 2001:181, 197–198).

The lure of these and other desirable products soon prompted a change in the nature and scheduling of the patterned movement across the homeland. As noted earlier, the traditional movement involved a journey from the winter camps scattered along the foothills and parkland to one or more of the favored sun dance grounds at the confluence of the Red Deer and South Saskatchewan Rivers, in the Cypress Hills, or at the confluence of the Judith and Missouri Rivers (Figure 7.1). At the first sound of thunder, the Blackfoot people initiated preparations for the journey, beginning with the opening of the Thunder Medicine Pipe Bundle and ending with the sun dance at the summer solstice. This schedule conflicted with the annual cycle of the fur trade, which involved the collection of furs during the winter months when the pelts were in their prime and the delivery of these goods to the trading post in time for the trading season in June and July. Moreover, travel to and from the trading posts involved movement away from the sun dance grounds (compare Figure 7.1 and Figure 7.2).

The resulting conflicts in the scheduling and direction of movement no doubt instigated intense discussions about the relative merits of each route, the young warriors arguing in favor of travel to the trading posts and the elders stressing the importance of the traditional ritual pilgrimage and historical journey. The proposed resolution to this problem appears to have been a division of responsibilities: most of the people traveled to the sun dance ground, and a small contingent visited fur trading posts located within or just beyond the traditional homeland. This strategy was probably justified by the traditional practice of leaving a small number of individuals in the winter camps to provide for those who were unable to make the journey and to safeguard the nearby sacred tobacco patch. To support their counterargument, the elders no doubt issued warnings about the potential consequences of the group's failure to meet its ritual and social obligations.

The consequences of the young warriors' actions became obvious shortly after the initial encounters with fur traders. In the spring of 1781, after intermittent contact with the traders for a decade or more, a terrible smallpox epidemic spread through the homelands of the Blackfoot and their neighbors, forever changing the human landscape of the Northwest (Binnema 2001:108; Ewers 1972; Smyth 2001:160). To Western researchers, the rapid decimation of the Blackfoot population was due to a lack of immunological experience with introduced diseases, combined with healing practices such as sweat bathing or immersion in cold water, which simply aggravated an already precarious situation and resulted in the loss of even more lives (Lux 2001). To the Blackfoot, the epidemic was a message from the spirits condemning the living community for its failure to observe the ceremonial and social obligations to the land, the resources, and the people (cf. Buchanan, this volume). To make matters worse, the smallpox epidemic selectively killed the elderly and very young members of the community while the survivors were mostly the younger adults, who had a taste for the commodities available at the fur trading posts. As a result, interest and participation in the fur trade did not decline after the population recovered from the epidemic; if anything, Blackfoot involvement in the fur trade increased whereas the commitment to the traditional pilgrimages and historical journeys abated despite the pleas of the few surviving traditionalists.

As the human population was being decimated by epidemics, missionaries were introduced into Blackfoot communities, and their proselytizing presented further challenges to the traditional belief systems (Byrne 1973; De Smet 1847; Rundle 1977). The missionaries presented their god as benevolent and all powerful while denouncing all Blackfoot deities as malevolent and condemning their ceremonies as pagan rituals honoring the devil. They were particularly critical of the sun dance, the single most important ritual of the year, and recommended the abandonment of the ritual pilgrimage in favor of a more sedentary lifestyle centered on the House of God. Even though the Blackfoot were suspicious of the new religious practitioners and their teachings, they had to acknowledge the evidence in support of the missionaries' claims about the superiority of their god. In addition to the power of the guns, alcohol, and tobacco, the cures recommended by the missionaries appeared to be more effective than the medicines offered by traditional healers. Since ailments and their cures were attributed to spiritual forces, the spirits of the missionaries must be more powerful than those of the Blackfoot people. In fact, some Blackfoot leaders such as Rainy Chief embraced Christianity primarily to obtain some of the supernatural power of the newcomers (Dempsey 1982:101). Moreover, the Blackfoot believed that the missionaries themselves must have been very strong individuals to control the evil spirits that were decimating the native communities. Once again, the Blackfoot people were faced with a difficult decision, the outcome of which could have devastating consequences.

Although the missionaries brought some relief, new diseases and epidemics continued to inflict pain, suffering, and death within the living community (Ewers 1972; Smyth 2001:273). At the same time, the size of the bison herds decreased and their movements became far less predictable (Ray 1984). The unusual behavior of the bison was one more line of evidence that the spirits were displeased with the failure of the Blackfoot people to engage in the annual ritual pilgrimage and ceremony of renewal. Since the bison no longer responded to the buffalo calling ceremony, the movement of the Blackfoot became somewhat more erratic as they relied more and more on their horses to locate the small migrant herds and used their guns to dispatch the animals at a greater distance. To address this impersonal affront to the spirit of reciprocity and the total lack of respect for the nonhuman relatives, the bison refused to offer themselves to the hunter. Although the majority of the Blackfoot felt a certain responsibility for the disappearance of the buffalo, others assumed that the powerful spirits of the white man had somehow trapped the animals in a cave just as Crow-Arrow had managed to do before the bison were liberated by Beaver and Little-Dog (Wissler and Duvall 1995:50–53).

As the bison herds continued to dwindle and the fur trade waned, the governments of the United States and Canada began treaty negotiations to prepare the West for settlement. Faced with a dwindling food supply and the imminent threat of starvation, Native Americans agreed to the terms of the negotiations and signed treaties with the U.S. government in 1855 and the Canadian government in 1877. The governments in each country designated large parcels of land as reserves for the now decimated populations. Although Native Americans acknowledged the designation and role of the reservations, they also assumed that they had retained the right to harvest resources from beyond the boundaries of the reserves. By contrast, the agents of the respective governments saw the reservations as training grounds where Native Americans would be encouraged to work the land and raise animals to produce the food needed for survival. At the same time, the missionaries established schools and churches on the reserves to educate and convert the Blackfoot people. As more and more settlers established claims on sections of land beyond the reserves, the movement of the Blackfoot people was increasingly confined to smaller and smaller reservations. Unable to visit the places, retell the stories, sing the songs, and perform the rituals, the Blackfoot people watched helplessly as they lost part of their culture, their language, and their landscape archive. As they longed for their glorious past, the Blackfoot also felt a degree of responsibility for the events that had unfolded in such a short interval of time.

Conclusion

Before the arrival of Europeans, the Blackfoot people moved across their homeland following an established network of trails that connected a series of named places. The places were outstanding natural features created by Napi in the long ago and landmarks serving as mnemonic pegs for the narratives, songs, and rituals stored in the landscape archive. The paths and trails connecting these places represented the accumulated imprint of countless journeys by the ancestors and the living community. Movement from the wintering to the summering grounds was thus (1) a historical journey designed to preserve and transmit faithfully the language, culture, and oral traditions of the group; (2) an annual pilgrimage to the sun dance grounds to fulfill ritual and reciprocal obligations toward the land, the resources, and the people; and (3) a social odyssey during which the people renewed their ties with the ancestors, the members of other Blackfoot bands, and the people from neighboring homelands. This annual journey preserved the vitality of the homeland. To the Blackfoot, then, the rocks, springs, trees, berry bushes, and animals are there because the ancestors visited the places, told the stories, sang the songs, and performed the rituals. The living community, in turn, must conduct the same ritual pilgrimage, historical journey, and social odyssey to ensure the continuity of the homeland for future generations. Failure to fulfill these reciprocal obligations would entail consequences for the health of the land, the resources, and the people. The arrival of Europeans and their trade goods presented the first serious challenges to this structured world and managed to disrupt the patterned movement of the people, including their interactions with the spirit beings in the homeland.

Although the Blackfoot were involved in extensive trade networks before the arrival of Europeans, the previous exchange systems generally involved interactions with people who shared a similar worldview. Negotiations with Euro-Canadian traders who introduced new technologies and a different worldview presented new opportunities and new challenges. During the initial encounters with these European traders the Blackfoot employed aggressive tactics to impress upon the newcomers the importance of appropriate protocols and practices in the maintenance of the intricate relationships between the people and their nonhuman relatives. Although Western researchers explain the outcome of these negotiations as a result of basic economic imperatives and a superior technology, the Blackfoot assessed the benefits and effectiveness of the new technologies according to very different standards. More specifically, they interpreted the superiority of this new technology in terms of the European ability to harness the power of spirit beings in their cosmos. The lure of the objects and their associated powers introduced scheduling conflicts that gradually transformed the traditional itineraries and practices of the Blackfoot with unexpected consequences for their livelihood.

The entanglement in the fur trade and the introduction of new technologies created the illusion of access to powerful forces, attracting the young warriors to the posts and eventually disrupting the traditional patterned movement across the landscape. The failure of the people to fulfill their reciprocal obligations with nonhuman beings had devastating consequences for the Blackfoot communities, including a succession of epidemics, the disappearance of the bison herds, the replacement of their cosmological beliefs, and the restricted access to their historical archive (see also Buchanan, this volume). Confined to small parcels of their once immense homeland, the Blackfoot people witnessed the gradual erosion of their culture, language, and traditions. To some, these were the expected consequences of their failure to fulfill the ritual obligations negotiated in the long ago between the spirits and the Blackfoot people.

Acknowledgments

This chapter began as a paper presented at the 77th Annual Meeting of the Society for American Archaeology. I thank Meghan Buchanan and Jacob Skousen for inviting me to participate in the session titled "Theories of Entanglement: Movement, Agents, and Worlds in Transformation" and for their initiative in organizing the contributions to this book. I thank D. Joy Oetelaar for her thorough review of historical documents and her help in compiling the data in Table 8.1. I also thank the University of Calgary for financial support during the preparation of this chapter. Finally, I owe a debt of gratitude to several members of the Blackfoot Nation who have tried to help me understand and appreciate an alternative worldview. However, I alone am responsible for any errors of interpretation.

Notes

1. In the Blackfoot language the gender of words is listed as animate or inanimate. Moreover, the animate entities in the Blackfoot world do not correspond to livings things in the Western world, nor do their inanimate entities correspond to the non-living components of our world.
2. The iniskim, or sacred buffalo stone, is a fossil ammonite in the form of a bison. Although such fossils occur at many places on the plains, only the special ones are included in medicine bundles and used in the buffalo calling ceremony.
3. Napi is the personification of the trickster among the Blackfoot. He created many of the important landmarks in the Blackfoot homeland and commemorated his actions by creating outlines of his body with stones.
4. Although these locations were originally used for ritual celebrations such as the sun dance, they became known to the traders as rendezvous centers.
5. Originally named Fort Raymond, this post was generally known as Mañuel's Fort or Lisa's Fort, hence the name Fort Mañuel.
6. This incident is described in "Journal of a Journey over Land from Buckingham House to the Rocky Mountains in 1792 &3," Hudson's Bay Company Archives, E.3-2, folios 11d–11.

References Cited

Baldwin, Stuart J.
1994 Blackfoot Neologisms. *International Journal of American Linguistics* 60 (1): 69–72.
Bastien, Betty
2004 *Blackfoot Ways of Knowing: The Worldview of the Siksikaitsitapi*. University of Calgary Press, Calgary, Alberta.
Belyea, Barbara (editor)
2000 *A Year Inland: The Journal of a Hudson's Bay Company Winterer*. Wilfrid Laurier University Press, Waterloo, Ontario.
Binford, Lewis R.
2001 *Constructing Frames of Reference: An Analytical Method for Archaeological Theory Building Using Ethnographic and Environmental Data Sets*. University of California Press, Los Angeles.
Binnema, Theodore
2001 *Common and Contested Ground: A Human and Environmental History of the Northwestern Plains*. University of Oklahoma Press, Norman.
Blackfoot Gallery Committee (editor)
2001 *Nitsitapiisinni: The Story of the Blackfoot People*. Glenbow Museum, Calgary, Alberta.
Brink, Jack W.
1986 *Dog Days in Southern Alberta*. Archaeological Survey of Alberta Occasional Papers No. 28. Alberta Culture, Edmonton.
Brumley, John
1988 *Medicine Wheels on the Northern Plains: A Summary and Appraisal*. Archaeological Survey of Alberta, Manuscript Series No. 12. Alberta Culture and Multiculturalism, Edmonton.
Byrne, M. B. Vernini
1973 *From the Buffalo to the Cross: A History of the Roman Catholic Diocese of Calgary*. Calgary Archives and Historical Publishers, Calgary, Alberta.
Dempsey, Hugh A.
1982 History and Identification of Blood Bands. In *Plains Indian Studies: A Collection of Essays in Honor of John C. Ewers and Waldo R. Wedel*, edited by Douglas H. Ubelaker and Herman J. Viola, pp. 94–104. Smithsonian Institution Press, Washington, D.C.
Dempsey, James
1993 Effects on Aboriginal Cultures Due to Contact with Henry Kelsey. In *Three Hundred Prairie Years: Henry Kelsey's "Inland Country of Good Report,"* edited by Henry Epp, pp. 131–135. Canadian Plains Research Center, Regina, Saskatchewan.
De Smet, Pierre J.
1847 *Oregon Missions and Travels over the Rocky Mountains in 1845-46*. Edward Dunigan, New York.
Dormaar, Johan F.
2001 *Sweetgrass Hills: A Natural and Cultural History*. Archaeological Society of Alberta, Calgary.
2003 Archaeology and Geography of Vision Quests. In *Archaeology in Alberta: A View from the New Millennium*, edited by Jack W. Brink and John F. Dormaar, pp. 188–207. Archaeological Society of Alberta, Medicine Hat.
Dormaar, John F., and Brian O. K. Reeves
1993 Vision Quest Sites in Southern Alberta and Northern Montana. In *Kunaitupii—Coming Together on Native Sacred Sites: Their Sacredness, Conservation, and Interpretation*, edited by Brian O. K. Reeves and Margaret A. Kennedy, pp. 162–178. Archaeological Society of Alberta, Calgary.

Ewers, John C.
1958 *The Blackfeet: Raiders on the Northwestern Plains.* University of Oklahoma Press, Norman.
1972 The Influence of the Fur Trade upon the Indians of the Northern Plains. In *People and Pelts: Selected Papers of the Second North American Fur Trade Conference*, edited by Malvina Bolus, pp. 1–26. Peguis Publishers, Winnipeg.
2001 *The Horse in Blackfoot Indian Culture with Comparative Material from Other Western Tribes.* Reprint, University Press of the Pacific, Honolulu. Originally published in 1955 by the Smithsonian Institution, Washington, D.C.

Grinnell, George B.
1962 *Blackfoot Lodge Tales: The Story of a Prairie People.* Reprint, University of Nebraska Press, Lincoln. Originally published in 1892 by Charles Scribner's Sons, New York.

Ingold, Tim
1993 The Temporality of the Landscape. *World Archaeology* 25 (2): 152–174.
2000 *The Perception of the Environment: Essays on Livelihood, Dwelling and Skill.* Routledge, London.

Kehoe, Alice Beck
2002 Thunder's Pipe: The Blackfoot Ritual Year. *Cosmos* 18:19–33.

Klassen, Michael A.
2003 Spirit Images, Medicine Rocks: The Rock Art of Alberta. In *Archaeology in Alberta: A View from the New Millennium*, edited by Jack W. Brink and Johan F. Dormaar, pp. 154–186. Archaeological Society of Alberta, Medicine Hat.

Landals, Alison
2003 Horse Heaven: Change in Late Precontact to Contact Period Landscape Use in Southern Alberta. In *Archaeology on the Edge: New Perspectives from the Northern Plains*, edited by Brian Kooyman and Jane Kelley, pp. 211–262. University of Calgary Press, Calgary, Alberta.

Lee, Irwin
1994 Dreams, Theory, and Culture: The Plains Vision Quest Paradigm. *American Indian Quarterly* 18 (2): 229–245.

Lewis, Oscar
1942 *The Effects of White Contact upon Blackfoot Culture, with Special Reference to the Role of the Fur Trade.* Monographs of the American Ethnological Society No. 6. J. J. Augustin, New York.

Lux, Maureen K.
2001 *Medicine That Walks: Disease, Medicine, and Canadian Plains Native People, 1880–1940.* University of Toronto Press, Toronto.

McClintock, Walter
1968 *The Old North Trail: Life, Legends and Religion of the Blackfeet Indians.* Reprint, University of Nebraska Press, Lincoln. Originally published in 1910 by Macmillan, London.

Nasatir, A. P., E. P. Gaines, Fort Vanderburgh, William Gordon, and Joshua Pilcher
1939 The International Significance of the Jones and Immell Massacre and of the Aricara Outbreak in 1823. *Pacific Northwest Quarterly* 30 (1): 77–108.

Oetelaar, Gerald A.
2000 Beyond Activity Areas: Structure and Symbolism in the Organization and Use of Space inside Tipis. *Plains Anthropologist* 45 (171): 35–61.
2004 Stone Circles, Social Organization and Special Places: Forbis' Skepticism Revisited. In *Archaeology on the Edge: New Perspectives from the Northern Plains*, edited by Brian Kooyman and Jane Kelley, pp. 125–155. University of Calgary Press, Calgary, Alberta.
2006 Mobility and Territoriality on the Northwestern Plains of Alberta, Canada: A Phenomenological Approach. In *Notions de territoire et de mobilité: Exemples de L'Europe et des Premières Nations en Amérique du Nord avant le contact européen*, edited by Céline Bressy, Ariane Burke, Pierre Chalard, and Hélène Martin, pp. 137–141. Études et Recherches Archéologiques No. 116. University of Liège, Liège.
2012 The Archaeological Imprint of Oral Traditions on the Landscape of Northern Plains Hunter-Gatherers. In *The Oxford Handbook of North American Archaeology*, edited by Timothy R. Pauketat, pp. 336–346. Oxford University Press, Oxford.

Oetelaar, Gerald A., and David Meyer
2006 Movement and Native American Landscapes: A Comparative Approach. *Plains Anthropologist* 51 (199): 355–374.

Oetelaar Gerald A., and D. Joy Oetelaar
2006 People, Places and Paths: The Cypress Hills and the *Nitsitapii* Landscape of Southern Alberta. *Plains Anthropologist* 51 (199): 375–398.
2007 The New Ecology and Landscape Archaeology: Incorporating the Anthropogenic Factor. *Canadian Journal of Archaeology* 31 (3): 65–92.
2008 Indigenous Stewardship: Lessons from Yesterday for the Parks of Tomorrow. Paper presented at Canadian Parks for Tomorrow: 40th Anniversary Conference, May 8–11, University of Calgary, Calgary, Alberta. http://dspace.ucalgary.ca/handle/1880/46905.
2011 The Structured World of the *Niitsitapi*: The

Landscape as Historical Archive among Hunter-Gatherers of the Northern Plains. In *Structured Worlds: The Archaeology of Hunter-Gatherer Thought and Action*, edited by Aubrey Cannon, pp. 69–94. Cambridge University Press, Cambridge.

Oetelaar, Gerald A., and Carmen Olson
2000 Historic Trails and Precontact Landscapes: A Study of Land Use in the Calgary Area. In *The Entangled Past: Integrating History and Archaeology*, edited by Matthew Boyd, John C. Erwin, and Mitchell Hendrickson, pp. 312–18. Archaeological Association of the University of Calgary, Calgary, Alberta.

Peck, Trevor R.
2002 Archaeologically Recovered Ammonites: Evidence for Long-Term Continuity in Nitsitapii Ritual. *Plains Anthropologist* 47 (181): 147–164.

Peck, Trevor R., and John W. Ives
2001 Late Side-Notched Projectile Points in the Northern Plains. *Plains Anthropologist* 46 (176): 163–193.

Phillips, Paul C.
1961 *The Fur Trade*. Vol. 2. University of Oklahoma Press, Norman.

Ray, Arthur J.
1984 The Northern Great Plains: Pantry of the Northwest Fur Trade, 1774–1885. *Prairie Forum* 9 (2): 263–280.

Reeves, Brian O. K.
1993 Iniskim: A Sacred Nitsitapii Religious Tradition. In *Kunaitupii—Coming Together on Native Sacred Sites: Their Sacredness, Conservation, and Interpretation*, edited by Brian O. K. Reeves and Margaret A. Kennedy, pp. 194–247. Archaeological Society of Alberta, Calgary.
1994 Ninaistakis—The Nitsitapii's Sacred Mountain: Traditional Native Religious Activities and Land Use Tourism Conflicts. In *Sacred Sites, Sacred Places*, edited by David L. Carmichael, Jane Hubert, Brian O. K. Reeves, and Audhild Schanche, pp. 265–296. Routledge, London.

Rundle, Robert T.
1977 *The Rundle Journals, 1840–1848*. Edited by Hugh A. Dempsey. Historical Society of Alberta, Calgary.

Secoy, Frank R.
1953 *Changing Military Patterns on the Great Plains (17th Century through Early 19th Century)*. Monographs of the American Ethnological Society, Vol. 21. J. J. Augustin, Locust Valley, New York.

Smyth, David
2001 The Niitsitapi Trade: Euroamericans and the Blackfoot-Speaking Peoples to the mid-1830s. Unpublished Ph.D. dissertation, Department of History, Carleton University, Ottawa, Ontario.

Uhlenbeck, Christianus C., and Robert H. van Gulik
1930 *An English-Blackfoot Vocabulary Based on Material from the Southern Peigans*. Koninklijke Akademie van Wetenschappen, Amsterdam.

Vickers, J. Roderick
2008 Anthropomorphic Effigies of the Plains. *Plains Anthropologist* 53 (206): 199–221.

Vickers, J. Roderick, and Trevor R. Peck
2009 Identifying the Prehistoric Blackfoot: Approaches to Nitsitapii (Blackfoot) Culture History. In *Painting the Past with a Broad Brush: Papers in Honour of James Valliere Wright*, edited by David L. Keenlyside and Jean-Luc Pilon, pp. 473–497. Mercury Series, Archaeology Paper No. 170. Canadian Museum of Civilization, Ottawa, Ontario.

Watts, Christopher (editor)
2013 *Relational Archaeologies: Humans, Animals, Things*. Routledge, London.

Wissler, Clark
1914 The Influence of the Horse in the Development of Plains Culture. *American Anthropologist* 16 (1): 1–25.

Wissler, Clark, and D. C. Duvall
1995 *Mythology of the Blackfoot Indians*. Edited by Alice Beck Kehoe. Reprint, University of Nebraska Press, Lincoln. Originally published in 1908, Anthropological Papers of the American Museum of Natural History, Vol. 2, No. 1, New York.

Wood, W. Raymond
1980 Plains Trade in Prehistoric and Protohistoric Intertribal Relations. In *Anthropology on the Great Plains*, edited by W. Raymond Wood and Margot Liberty, pp. 98–109. University of Nebraska Press, Lincoln.
2010 The Earliest Map of the Mandan Heartland: Notes on the Jarvis and Mackay 1791 Map. *Plains Anthropologist* 55 (216): 255–276.

Zedeño, María Nieves, Kacy Hollenback, and Calvin Grinnell
2006 From Path to Myth: Journeys and the Naturalization of Territorial Identity along the Missouri River. In *Landscapes of Movement: Trails, Paths, and Roads in Anthropological Perspective*, edited by James E. Snead, Clark L. Erickson, and J. Andrew Darling, pp. 106–132. University of Pennsylvania Museum of Archaeology and Anthropology, Philadelphia.

8

Unraveling Entanglements

Reverberations of Cahokia's Big Bang

Melissa R. Baltus

The spatio-temporal phrase "Middle Mississippian" references the culmination of a series of large-scale events, broad trends (though with local interpretations), and intertwined histories of the late pre-Columbian period (circa AD 1000–1500) in the Southeastern and Midwestern regions of the United States. Initially defined by William Holmes (1903) as a ceramic complex, it was refined by Thorne Deuel (1935) to refer to all or some particular traits, including, but not limited to, shell-tempered pottery, pyramidal mound construction, mound and plaza town organization, "complex" hierarchical social organization, and maize agriculture (e.g., Muller and Stephens 1991; Smith 1978). However, variations in the combination of Mississippian traits has become a perplexing conundrum for archaeologists in the business of identifying and defining "Mississippian" in the wild because it is a shifting and slippery concept (Cook 2007; Esarey and Conrad 1998). Previous research often focused on typologizing Mississippian sites (e.g., ritual vs. economic centers, simple vs. complex chiefdoms or chiefdom vs. state, corporate vs. network leadership strategies) (Anderson 1994; Beck 2003; Milner 1998; Muller 1995; Porter 1969; Trubitt 2000) rather than investigating the historical processes that resulted in those archaeological deposits.

Rather than reify "Mississippian" by attempting to nail down its definition, I feel it is more fruitful to consider this period of history as constantly changing and becoming (Ingold 1993). The pre-Columbian world, like the world today, is one in which communities are fluid and relational ties are created and re-created daily. Following Robert Hall (1991), it seems more useful to understand *how* people participated in the processes of becoming relationally entangled in the Mississippian world.

Theories of entanglement or relational engagements differ somewhat in their scope. For example, Tim Ingold's (2006) conception of entanglements premises a world woven together through material practices and movement through an ever-changing social universe. Ian Hodder (2012:17–18) considers these entangled relationships in terms of human-thing and thing-thing "dependence" and "dependency" that develop over time through use. Both of these approaches to entanglement seem to imply it is a nondiscursive process. Rather, I suggest here that people are aware of these material entanglements and may intentionally manipulate, negotiate, or transform them via the material objects actively engaged within those relationships.

In addressing the material entanglements of the Middle Mississippian world, I engage two uses of the word "movement": one meaning the physical transfer of a being, object, or idea; and the second in reference to a series of choices made to intentionally instigate social, political, or religious change (a.k.a. "revitalization" movements [Wallace 1956] or "prophetic" movements [Spier 1935]). In particular, in the context of the eleventh-century pre-Columbian North American city of Cahokia, I aim to explore how the movement of persons (human and nonhuman), practices, ideas, and objects integral to the spread of a political-religious movement created entangled relationships among objects, people, and places, and how people negotiated those relationships, especially during moments of political and social tension.

Movement in Movements

Movement is an inherent quality of an inhabited world; according to Ingold (2006:15), "wherever there is life, there is movement." Beings do not simply inhabit the world through movement but rather weave the world into existence; movement is an animating process of becoming, including place-making, as well as thing-making and person-making. I argue here that movement in the first sense (that of the physical) is necessary to generate social, political, and religious movements in the second sense.

The creation and growth of social-political-religious movements are predicated on the gathering together of like-minded people with similar goals and, sometimes, shared histories—the creation of relational entanglements, if you will. Shared, perhaps invented, traditions provide a means of binding people together through practice (Pauketat and Alt 2003), while physical movements (large scale as well as small) not only help *create* relationships, memories, and histories but are integral to the requisite interaction for sustaining them. Therefore, movements in the large-scale social-political sense need movement in the physical sense: "the movement of people for food gathering; for conquest, war or plunder; for indoctrination; for friendship and curiosity—or for whatever reason—leads to new ideas, new inventions, new problems, new institutions" (Stewart 1987:51).

The relationships that constitute the world around us are continually changing and changeable through a combination of choice and chance. Therefore, in addition to exploring the processes by which people's lives become entangled with things and with each other, we need to explore the ways in which entanglements are transformed. In a world in "perpetual flux" (Ingold 2006:17), incessantly moving, changing, and becoming, it is impossible to understand a given moment in history without considering the prior choices, actions, movements, and relationships that brought that moment into being.

I use the mid-eleventh-to-fourteenth-century Native American city of Cahokia to illustrate the processes by which people's identities and biographies became entangled with ideas, practices, places, objects, and persons (human and other-than-human) to create what archaeologists term the "Mississippian" tradition. During the mid-eleventh century a cultural confluence in the American Bottom, the wide area of the Mississippi River floodplain near the physical confluences of the Missouri and Illinois Rivers, resulted in a suite of seemingly sudden social, religious, and political changes. These changes transpired within and along the meshwork of existing personal relationships and everyday experiences, creating new relationships among people, places, and material objects. In Bjornar Olsen's sense (Olsen 2010), the material objects engaged in these relationships are significant as co-creators of what we consider to be "the social" or "the political." These new relationships resulted in the city of Cahokia and the spread of Cahokian objects, ideas, and practices.

The movements of life compel change, resulting in a continual ebb and flow of relationships. The relational entanglements that helped bring Cahokia into being were no different; a series of additional large- and small-scale social changes during the late twelfth to early thirteenth centuries have been suggested to signal political disintegration due to warfare, environmental failure, or the rise of factionalism. In contrast to theories that suggest passive reactions to exterior forces, I propose that these twelfth-to-thirteenth-century changes were deliberate; the relational entanglements of the mid-eleventh to mid-twelfth centuries were intentionally unraveled and re-entwined in new ways. Choices were made to break with particular traditions, transform certain practices, disengage with past social identities, and engage in new social relationships.

The Cahokian Meshwork

Cahokia's florescence, circa AD 1050, involved the movement of interrelated people, powers, ideas, and material objects into and out of the city, located near modern-day East St. Louis, Illinois

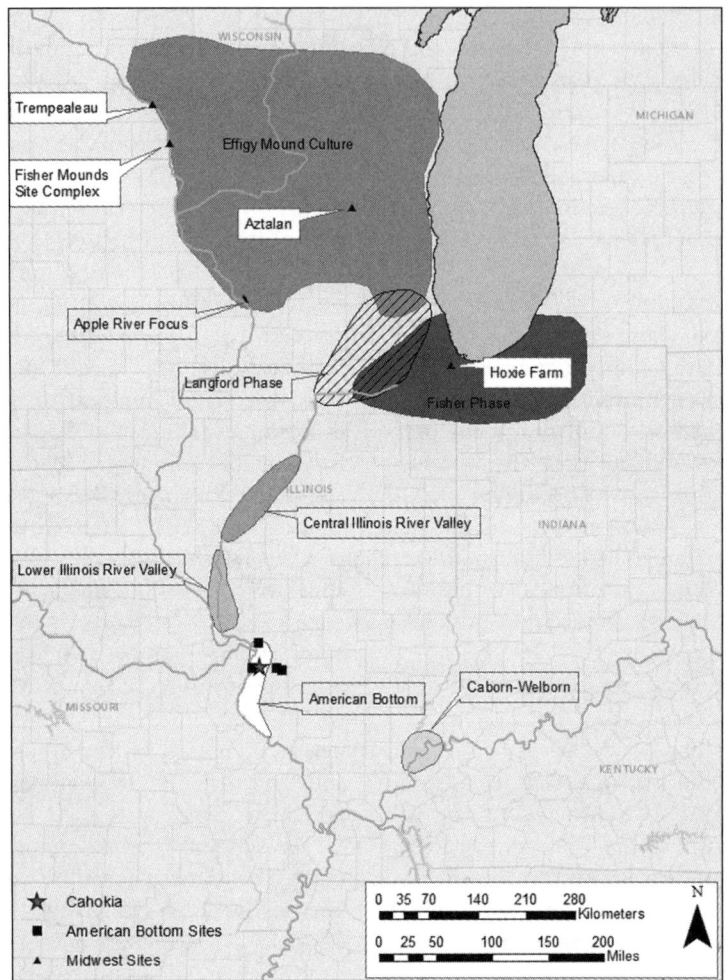

FIGURE 8.1. Midwestern social-political entanglements during the twelfth to fourteenth centuries.

(Figure 8.1). Once a sizeable village of perhaps 2,000 people around the beginning of the eleventh century, Cahokia grew suddenly to a population of 10,000 to 15,000 (Pauketat and Lopinot 1997), augmented by large-scale immigration from southeast Missouri and southern Indiana as well as smaller-scale movements within the American Bottom (Alt 2006a; Emerson 2013). People began building houses using wall trenches rather than single post construction, effectively transforming social relationships even within family groups (Pauketat and Alt 2005). Large-scale earthen pyramid and plaza construction projects began in earnest (Dalan et al. 2003), all oriented to a near-cardinal "Cahokia Grid" (Fowler 1969).

As populations coalesced in the city, the rural areas were likewise reconfigured into small farmsteads, hamlets, and "nodal sites" (Emerson 1997b, 1997c); entire villages of immigrant populations settled in the Richland complex in the uplands to the southeast of Cahokia (Alt 2006b; Pauketat 2003). In addition to changes in building construction and community configuration, a significant number of material changes occurred, specifically involving pottery; agricultural tools; valuation of and access to certain pigments, minerals, or raw materials; and the spread of particular objects imbued with religious imagery or significance (e.g., long-nosed god maskettes, flint-clay figurines, chunkey stones) (Emerson 1997b; Hall 1991; Pauketat 2004).

The processes of weaving Cahokia into being appear to have been in motion before the so-called Big Bang that signaled the ascendance of Cahokia (Hall 1991; Pauketat 1997). Recent archaeological investigations at the Fisher Mounds site complex and the Trempealeau site in southwest Wisconsin (Benden et al. 2010, 2011) have identified evidence for sustained interaction between the Upper Mississippi Valley and the American Bottom just before, or on the cusp of, Cahokia's florescence. Around the time that Cahokia began transitioning from village to city, people carrying American Bottom pottery, southern Illinois chert nodules, and the practice of wall-trench building construction appear to have arrived in southwest Wisconsin, perhaps in multiple visits (Benden et al. 2010). Evidence from Trempealeau suggests a short-term Mississippian occupation in the early Lohmann phase, during which people sculpted a series of platform mounds out of a natural bluff and built wall-trench structures atop those mounds, where a series of politico-religious practices appear to have taken place (Benden et al. 2011; Pauketat, personal communication 2010).

Similarly, a unique building type—the keyhole structure, so called due to an elongated ramp with pit extending from the square building (e.g., Kelly et al. 1987)—has been found at Terminal Late Woodland (AD 900–1050) sites in the American Bottom near Cahokia (e.g., Range, Fish Lake) as well as at roughly contemporaneous sites in southeastern Wisconsin (e.g., Statz site) (Fortier et al. 1984; Kelly et al. 1987; Meinholz et al. 1997). The unique form of this structure seemingly suggests a certain degree of interaction between the regions. Pauketat (personal communication, 2010) has suggested that perhaps these early movements, and the existing personal relationships cultivated through them, were part of the entanglement process that helped weave Cahokia into being.

The sudden social, political, and religious changes that signaled the beginning of something new at Cahokia have been described as something akin to a revitalization movement (Harkin 2004; Pauketat 2004, 2010), described by Anthony Wallace (1956) as a deliberate push for change made using a social or religious agenda. The religious, political, and social realms of daily life are highly interdigitated among many Native North American groups (Adair 2005 [1775]; Bailey 1995; Fletcher and La Flesche 1992 [1911]; Radin 1970 [1923]; Swanton 2001 [1931]; Warren 2009 [1885]). Therefore, such social-religious movements were inevitably political and thus able to reconfigure the political landscape as well as the physical.

Ethnohistorically documented political-religious movements among Native North American groups (e.g., Ghost Dance, Prophet Dance, Peyotism) demonstrate the ways in which these movements are historically contingent and socially negotiated processes, involving choices and changes (Daro et al. 2008; Smoak 2006). Leslie Spier (1935) argued that preexisting cosmologies and ideologies provided reference for the mid-nineteenth-century Prophet Dance in the far West. Likewise, Gregory Smoak (2006) demonstrated how personal and group identities and histories, as well as individual perceptions of circumstances, had great bearing on whether people chose to participate in the late-nineteenth-century Ghost Dance. The practices and messages of these prophetic movements were spread systematically by intentional prophets and proselytizers and inconsistently and unevenly by witnesses and participants (Smoak 2006). These choices and negotiations led to an uneven expansion of varying permutations of the movements.

Revitalizations and other social-religious movements spread through the physical movement of practices and experiences that are inherently material. Rhetoric, written propaganda, performance, dance, prayer, cult objects, and the like become the material co-creators of these social-religious movements, simultaneously carrying and constituting the movement. The construction of these material messages is itself a process of entanglement, tying material objects, spaces, ideologies, and identities through practices, performances, and experiences. Material meanings are created through the production, use, consumption, and destruction of objects, substances, places, and spaces as part of social relationships (Meskell 2004, 2005; Mintz 1985).

As part of the eleventh-century Cahokian Movement, people reinterpreted traditional practices and reinvented cosmologies, using new materials and negotiating new social relationships (Emerson 1997a, 1997b; Pauketat 2004).

The city itself was cosmologically engineered—neighborhoods, mounds, and plazas were constructed to reference a local grid (Fowler 1969). Previous practices of termination (i.e., the burning of domiciles) were integrated with new practices of renewal via mound additions, perhaps as a gathering together of powerful elements of fire and earth (Baltus and Baires 2012). The living engaged with the ancestors in and through this new landscape, as the deceased were gathered together in charnel structures and mound interments (Baires 2012). The newly transformed Cahokian religion—centered on world renewal and maintaining the cosmic balances between life and death, fertility and ancestors, light and dark, upper world and underworld, innovation and tradition—was lived daily (Emerson 1997b; Pauketat and Emerson 1991). The novel addition of shell-tempering in pots combined an underworld material with the "present-world" element of clay, transformed through fire to be consumed by people. Agricultural implements were increasingly made from nonlocal materials, and traditional tools and materials were given new meanings as people gathered them together in caches, mounds, and even house floors and walls (e.g., projectile points, groundstone celts, hoes, chunkey stones) (Pauketat and Alt 2004). The preference for nonlocal materials actively bound material to person to place (Butler 2011). People even reorganized their domestic structures to reference significant cardinal or astrological points rather than kin-group relationships, reconfiguring community relations (Kelly 1990; Pauketat 2003, 2013).

It seems that the spread of Cahokian practices, people, ideas, and objects was likewise a social negotiation, contingent on existing relationships, practices, beliefs, and needs. Proselytizers, prophets, and missionaries (intentionally or not) helped spread the Mississippian message embedded within daily and religious practices and associated material objects across the landscape. Certain objects appear to have been intentionally designed for "carrying" the message to distant places; Ramey Incised pots, chunkey stones, flint-clay figurines, and long-nosed-god maskettes are especially clear markers of Cahokian interaction in the hinterlands, and some of these items may have been more than objects, acting in social relationships as other-than-human persons (Hall 1991, 1997; Hallowell 1975). Given the dispersed and seemingly disconnected nature of early Cahokian connections, the initial spread of the Cahokian Movement may have followed lines of already existing relations of kinship, marriage, and/or trade, especially as these early forays appear to have been invited or welcomed (Green 1997).

During the early twelfth century this movement simultaneously became more widespread and more politicized. This politicization may be evident in the formalized L-, T-, and circular-shaped political-religious buildings (i.e., Emerson's [1997a] "architecture of power"); in spaces such as Cahokia's woodhenge—a means by which religious specialists could mark time or even demonstrate control over time, seasons, and cosmological phenomena (Baltus 2010b); and through the material objects of the Cahokian Movement (e.g., Ramey Incised pottery, chunkey stones, flint-clay figurines). As practices and spaces became increasingly political, it is likely that associated identities were likewise politicized. What may have begun as communal practices and spaces became constructed as elite. Spaces, structures, and objects were imbued with power through use in religious events; at the same time, religious practitioners were constructed as politically powerful (Baltus and Baires 2012).

It was also during this period that more intensive Cahokian connections were made with Late Woodland populations in northern Illinois (Central Illinois River Valley [CIRV]), eastern Illinois, southeast Minnesota, and southern Wisconsin (Barrett 1933; Conrad 1991; Douglas 1976; Gibbon 1991; Goldstein and Richards 1991) (see Figure 8.1). Seemingly, the comings and goings of people, carrying material messages and practiced ideas, into and out of the American Bottom were part of what continually created the city of Cahokia as a place of importance (sensu Ingold 2008; see also Skousen, this volume).

Of course, these twelfth-century entanglements were not limited to direct interaction between Cahokians and local Late Woodland populations. As the Mississippian message spread outward from Cahokia, ideas, practices, and traits were variably adopted, transformed, localized, or rejected according to local needs, histories, and beliefs. Therefore, new relationships of the twelfth century included connections among and between "Mississippianized" locals—persons who to varying degrees had witnessed, performed, and incorporated various aspects of Mississippian material practices—as well as with people who chose to eschew Mississippian ways (Emerson 1991; Pauketat 2004; Smoak 2006). The result, archaeologically, is an ill-defined series of Upper Mississippian ceramic "traditions"—likely representing a multiplicity of social groups—across the upper Midwest that have been broadly typologized as Langford, Fisher, Huber, Oneota, or Fort Ancient (Brown 1961; Cook 2007; Esarey and Conrad 1998; Griffin 1943; Faulkner 1972). Currently, a number of researchers are working on the problem of refining the histories and interactions of Upper Mississippian groups, with the promise of intriguing results (e.g., Cook 2007; Emerson 2013; Schneider 2013).

Difficulties arise, of course, when we attempt to understand these archaeological "types" without addressing the various, and variable, tangled human relationships that gave rise to them. Thomas Emerson (2012:405) suggests, given the "coincidental timing" of cultural patterns and material markers in the American Bottom and among the Upper Mississippian groups of the upper Midwest, that the "mutual histories" of people in these areas were "inescapably linked." Emerson (2013:4) has also recently suggested that interactions between Middle Mississippian peoples and the Late Woodland groups of northern Illinois resulted in the "creation of a new society" (i.e., Langford), while Fisher (another possibly intrusive population from the east) and Langford peoples were "clearly interdigitated."

Cahokian Unravelings

It is important to keep the variability of these intertwined relationships in mind when we attempt to understand the later years of Cahokian influence throughout the Midwest. Around AD 1150, just about a generation after the newly politicized Mississippian Movement seems to have taken root in portions of the northern Midwest, violence erupts. Fortifications appear at Aztalan, in the Central Illinois River Valley, at Cahokia, and at a handful of sites in the American Bottom. Entire villages in the CIRV were burned to the ground, and human fatalities became more frequent across northern Illinois (Conrad 1991; Steadman 2008). Although many archaeologists presume the palisade at Aztalan was constructed during the initial founding of the site in the late eleventh or early twelfth century (Goldstein and Richards 1991), the nondefensible location of the site and evidence for multigroup community integration events (Zych 2013) conversely suggests that the concern for defense was not immediate or necessary. Likewise, regional evidence for violence is not apparent before AD 1150 (Pauketat 2004); multiple palisades were present at Aztalan (Barrett 1933; Richards 1992), suggesting that the area encompassed by the palisade was perhaps expanded or contracted at least once.

While the same evidence for widespread conflict was not found in the American Bottom, significant changes took place in this period of regional violence. People abandoned the upland farming villages of the Richland complex (Pauketat 2003, 2004). Fortifications were built at Cahokia, East St. Louis, and the upland site of Olin (Baltus 2007; Fortier 2007; Iseminger et al. 1990; Pauketat 2005). The construction of these walls around civic-ceremonial spaces, rather than around domestic village spaces, suggests that the threat of violence was felt to be directed against the civic-ceremonial spaces, or more accurately, at the practices and identities enmeshed with these spaces and the objects maintained there (Baltus 2007; Fortier 2007; Iseminger et al. 1990; Pauketat 2005).

Perhaps violence did occur, but not in the traditional sense. Some structures were burned, along with a fortification wall at East St. Louis (Fortier 2007; Pauketat 2005). But evidence suggests these episodes of burning were isolated, directed, and may not have been associated with typical raiding practices. The wall at East St. Louis, for instance, surrounded a series of storage structures containing objects that were seemingly nondomestic (i.e., intended for politico-religious offerings or feasting) in nature (Fortier 2007; Pauketat 2005; Pauketat et al. 2013). Likewise, specific isolated structures were burned around the same time elsewhere at East St. Louis, Cahokia, and the nearby Sponemann site (Boles and Benson 2010; Collins 1990; Pauketat 1987). Each of these structures contained similar contents, including what appear to have been complete vessel assemblages and household tools, as well as pigments, crystals, and pipes. Had the burning of these structures resulted from a raid or external attack, we would expect surrounding structures to have similar evidence for burning (Wilson and Baltus 2014). Rather, it appears that these structures were burned—possibly in related episodes, as suggested by Pauketat (2005)—as a means of physically, politically, and spiritually terminating these spaces, the objects contained within, and even the practices and identities associated with them (Baltus and Baires 2012; Wilson and Baltus 2014).

Unlike in the Central Illinois River Valley, evidence for human trauma is not prevalent in the American Bottom; however, a number of female figurines—objects that not only could have *represented* ancestor-deities but may have been related to *as* social persons themselves (Baltus 2009)—have been found fragmented, burned, and buried. Significantly, these burned, broken, and buried figurines were often found in relation to many of the above-mentioned specially burned structures (Barrett 1933; Boles and Benson 2010; Emerson and Jackson 1984; Jackson et al. 1992). Conversely, male figurines, also produced at Cahokia during the twelfth century, were dispersed to the south sometime during the early thirteenth century and often converted into smoking pipes (Birmingham and Emerson 2011; Emerson et al. 2003), providing a clear example of reentanglement between places, persons, materials, engagement, and meaning.

Cahokian Reentanglements

Archaeologists often point to the succeeding Moorehead phase (AD 1200–1275/1300) as the "beginning of the end" for Cahokia (Hall 1991; Pauketat 2004). Warfare, environmental degradation, and social unrest are among the proximal causes offered for the depopulation of the region and the eventual abandonment of Cahokia itself by the late fourteenth century (Lopinot and Woods 1993; Milner 1998). Others (Kelly 1997; Trubitt 2000) have pointed to a Moorehead phase resurgence centered on the Grand Plaza and East Plaza at Cahokia, with a denouement during the latter part of the Moorehead phase. Using extant regional data, together with evidence drawn from my work with two upland villages that span the late twelfth to early thirteenth century (Baltus 2014), I argue for an intentional break with "classic" Stirling phase Cahokian practices, objects, and identities as part of a revitalization-like movement.

It appears that the twelfth-century burning events at and around Cahokia initiated processes of *disentanglement* with previous practices and objects, performed within an already existing practice of termination-through-burning, perhaps with further anticipation of renewal (Wilson and Baltus 2014). This renewal may have been enacted through the historical break evident in the American Bottom between the late-twelfth-century late Stirling phase and the thirteenth-century Moorehead phase. This break is materially manifest both at the local level and in large-scale political-religious practices. Cahokia's woodhenge was dismantled and replaced by a series of Moorehead phase households, possibly oriented around a courtyard associated with a newly constructed mound (Mound 44) (Pauketat 1998).

The specialized L-, T-, and circular-shaped structures in which the increasingly politicized religious practices of "Classic" Stirling phase Cahokia took place were no longer built; however, large rectangular "council house" structures continued to be built and used, perhaps indicating an increased concern for inclusivity in religious and/or political matters. One circular structure in the northern American Bottom was terminated via burning during the late twelfth or very early thirteenth century (Jackson and Millhouse 2003), while at the nearby fortified civic-ceremonial Olin site a similar circular structure used during the initial occupation of the site was intentionally excluded during the reconstruction of the palisade (Baltus 2014).

Evidence from Olin and other contemporaneous sites, including Cahokia proper, suggests that the highly iconographic Ramey Incised pottery became less popular, replaced by beakers, plates, and shallow platters decorated with generalized sun symbols (Emerson 1997a, 1997b; Pauketat et al. 2013). At the household level, the so-called Cahokia Cordmarked pottery was suddenly introduced. This utilitarian pottery was globular in shape, with everted rims, cordmarked exteriors, and red-slipped interiors. Cahokia Cordmarked jars from the Olin site include a small sample of vessels with finger-impressed lips. The cordmarking is reminiscent of the Late Woodland period, while the globular shape with increasingly everted rim is similar to a form found in northern Illinois (i.e., Fisher and Huber pottery). Intriguingly, the Fisher phase (AD 1200–1400) of northeastern Illinois is marked by the presence of globular pots with cordmarked exteriors, trailed-line designs, and notched lips on near-vertical rims.

A temporally sensitive change in the twist direction of cordage on the cordmarked jars at the Olin site, trending from z- to s-twist over the course of the Moorehead phase occupation, reinforces the suggestion that fiber production also returned to a local level, an activity believed to be specialized under the "Classic" Cahokian influence (Alt 1999; Baltus 2009; Pauketat 2004).

While the population at Cahokia proper seems to have dwindled by the early thirteenth century and became increasingly restricted to the central area around the Grand Plaza and Monks Mound (Dalan et al. 2003; Kelly 1997), new sites appeared in the surrounding uplands, often reoccupying landscapes that were significant before the twelfth-century "Classic Cahokia." One such region is the Silver Creek Drainage, located nearly due east of Cahokia (Figure 8.2) (Pauketat and Koldehoff 1983). Here the Emerald site was founded early in Cahokia's history, around AD 1050, with a possible occupational hiatus during the late twelfth century (Koldehoff et al. 1993). This large mound center, perhaps a shrine or pilgrimage site (Pauketat 2004, 2013; Skousen, this volume), appears to have been reinvigorated during the thirteenth-century revitalization.

Recent moundtop excavations have revealed artifacts dating to the Moorehead phase (AD 1200–1300) (Koldehoff et al. 1993; Skousen, this volume), suggesting a reoccupation or reintensification of site use. My excavations at the nearby Copper site, a smaller mound center located west of Emerald (see Figure 8.2), have demonstrated that this site was founded during the first half of the thirteenth century. Evidence from the base of one mound suggests a continued practice of platform mound construction over decommissioned buildings, using traditional Cahokian elements of construction (e.g., homogenous "water-washed" silt, "buckshot fill" [an aboriginally engineered mix of light and dark soils], and yellow and dark basket loading) (Pauketat 2008; Pauketat et al. 2010).

The mounds at the Copper site were also not built around a rectangular plaza area, but rather formed a series of parallel lines, possibly adding to and elevating already existing natural knolls. These mounds have an orientation similar to those at the Emerald site. A large rectangular structure, similar in size to "council house" structures excavated at Emerald and elsewhere in the American Bottom, was located near one such mound at Copper, aligned to the orientation of the mounds. This large structure appears to have replaced a small, cardinally oriented square structure with formal hearth, apparently as part of the reorganized thirteenth-century religious politics.

The pottery assemblage from the Copper site demonstrates continuity with the American Bottom (e.g., dark-slipped fineware bowls with bird effigy rims, beakers, trailed plates, and Cahokia Cordmarked jars) while suggesting continued extra-regional connections with the presence of Upper Mississippian–like jars with notched rims, trailed lines, and bifurcated handles (though similar decorative elements are also found on vessels from the central Tennessee area) (Figure 8.3). Seemingly, people are still being drawn to Cahokia to participate in the changed but enduring Mississippian practices perpetuated by the inhabitants of the Copper site during the thirteenth century.

Further Threads to Follow

As in the centuries before, people of the thirteenth-century Midwest were in motion. Various groups making Oneota pottery began to live with and among the Mississippians of the Central Illinois River Valley and, eventually, the American Bottom. These new interactions, though perhaps already based on familiar relationships, continued the processes of intertwining and creating histories, traditions, and identities (Esarey and Conrad 1998). Ceramic and lithic artifacts recovered from the Upper Mississippian Fisher phase Joe Louis site (cal. AD 1065–1225) and the Fisher phase Hoxie Farm site in northern Illinois suggest relationships with western and southern Indiana. Ceramic similarities between Hoxie

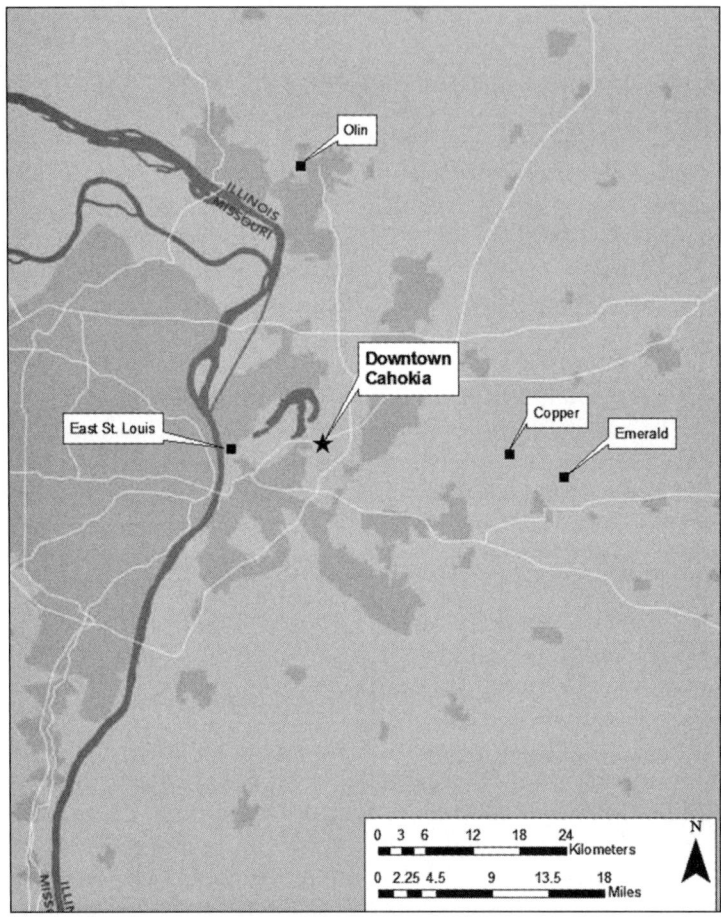

FIGURE 8.2. American Bottom and the upland sites of Olin, Copper, and Emerald.

Farm and the Caborn-Welborn region of southwest Indiana/southeast Illinois indicate continued interactions between people living in these regions into the later part of the fourteenth century (Emerson and Emerson 2014; Jackson and Emerson 2014; Pollack 2004). As Cahokians appear to be disentangling themselves from some of their northern neighbors, from earlier politico-religious traditions, and from the material messages of the early Mississippian Movement itself, southern contacts and connections appear to have become important; by the beginning of the fourteenth century, Cahokia "looks stylistically very much like its southern Mississippian neighbors" (Hall 1991:15).

At the close of the thirteenth century, full-scale Mississippian lifestyles, replete with mound construction and materially rich ceremonialism, appear to come to an end in the northern part of the Midwest, while life itself continued. At the same time, Mississippian ways began to thrive in the greater Southeast, continuing in varying forms until European contact.

Conclusion

Many archaeologists point to the drastic changes marking the twelfth-to-thirteenth-century break as indications of the declining political power of Cahokia. Conversely, I suggest that this period was itself a subsequent social-religious movement—a series of intentional choices made to disentangle previous Cahokian practices and identities. Given the atmosphere of violence in which these changes had their beginning, I suggest that these choices were made to negotiate tensions brought about by certain Cahokian

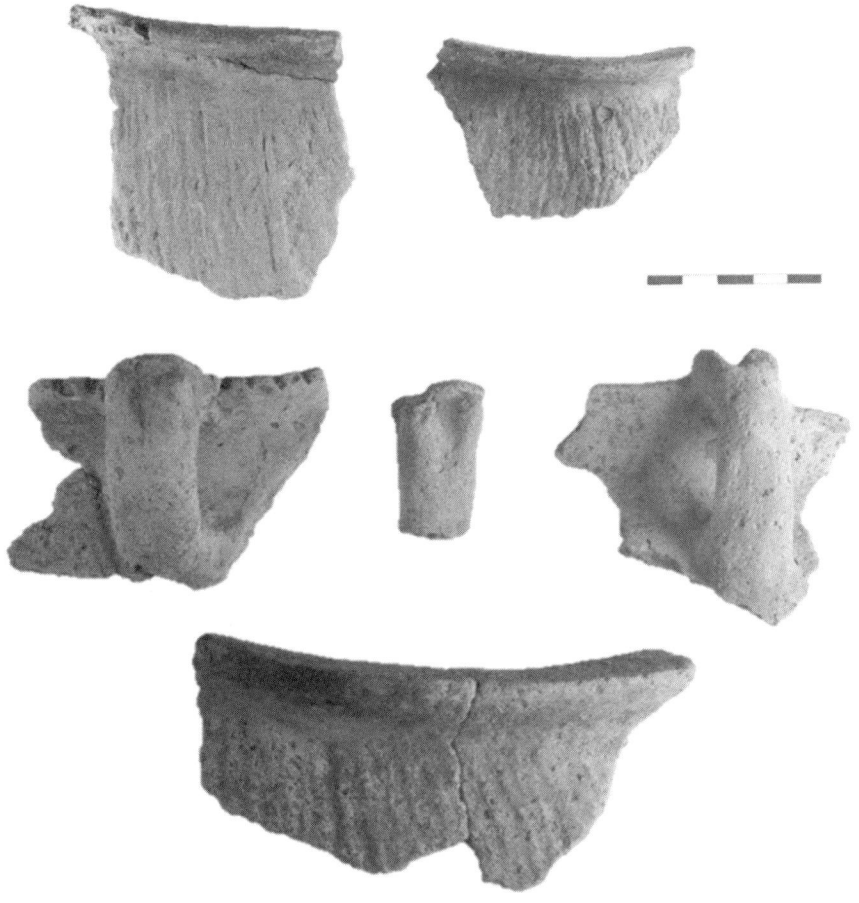

FIGURE 8.3. Jars from the Copper site. *Top row:* Cahokia Cordmarked; *middle row:* possible nonlocal Upper Mississippian styles; *bottom:* possible grooved-paddled jar.

material practices and identities. These material changes represent intentional breaks with certain traditions—most strikingly, with those traditions that appear to have been co-creators of the highly politicized and highly elite aspects of Cahokian Mississippianism.

Rather than represent a political failure of Cahokia, the thirteenth-century political-religious reorganization was a series of choices made to unravel specific relationships between people, places, and objects, simultaneously creating newly entangled relationships. While previous relationships may have been unraveled, the historical ramifications of those interactions remained and reverberated as history and collective memory. People continued to engage in productive movements, community creation, and historical events throughout a midcontinent changed by the Cahokian Movements, in the process continually changing and actively reweaving the landscape.

Acknowledgments

Thank you to Meghan Buchanan and Jacob Skousen for organizing the Society for American Archaeology session from which this volume took root and for their patient editing and fruitful comments in bringing the book to life. Thank you to the Illinois State Archaeological Survey and Thomas Emerson for continued support. I appreciate the thoughtful comments and critiques provided by our anonymous reviewers. Finally, thanks to Timothy Pauketat, Sarah Baires, and Thomas Zych for reading and commenting on drafts of this chapter and for helping me think through some ideas. Culpability for all omissions and errors is, of course, mine.

References Cited

Adair, James
2005 [1775] *The History of the American Indians*. University of Alabama Press, Tuscaloosa.

Alt, Susan M.
1999 Spindle Whorls and Fiber Production at Early Cahokian Settlements. *Southeastern Archaeology* 18:124–134.
2006a The Power of Diversity: The Roles of Migration and Hybridity in Culture Change. In *Leadership and Polity in Mississippian Society*, edited by Brian M. Butler and Paul D. Welch, pp. 289–308. Occasional Paper No. 33. Center for Archaeological Investigations, Southern Illinois University, Carbondale.
2006b Cultural Pluralism and Complexity: Analyzing a Cahokian Ritual Outpost. Unpublished Ph.D. dissertation, Department of Anthropology, University of Illinois, Urbana-Champaign.

Anderson, David G.
1994 *The Savannah River Chiefdoms: Political Change in the Late Pre-historic Southeast*. University of Alabama Press, Tuscaloosa.

Bailey, Garrick A.
1995 *The Osage and the Invisible World from the Works of Francis La Flesche*. University of Oklahoma Press, Norman.

Baires, Sarah E.
2012 Death as Movement: Cahokia's Ridge-Top Mounds as Active Places. Paper presented at the 77th Annual Meeting of the Society for American Archaeology, Memphis, Tennessee.

Baltus, Melissa R.
2007 Retreat in the Uplands: A Preliminary Analysis of the Olin Site (11MS133). Unpublished Master's thesis, Department of Anthropology, University of Illinois, Urbana-Champaign.
2009 Personhood in Production: The Mutual Constitution of Human and Non-human Members of the Cahokian Community. Paper presented at the 66th Annual Southeastern Archaeology Conference, Mobile, Alabama.
2010a Community in Conflict? Warfare and Violence in Cahokian History. Paper presented at the 75th Annual Meeting of the Society for American Archaeology, St. Louis, Missouri.
2010b Making Time: Monumentality and Temporality in Cahokian Mississippian. Paper presented at the 67th Annual Southeastern Archaeology Conference, Lexington, Kentucky.
2014 In-progress dissertation research. Notes on file, Illinois State Archaeological Survey, University of Illinois, Urbana-Champaign.

Baltus, Melissa R., and Sarah E. Baires
2012 Elements of Ancient Power in the Cahokian World. *Journal of Social Archaeology* 12:167–192.

Barrett, Samuel A.
1933 Ancient Aztalan. *Bulletin of the Museum of the City of Milwaukee* 13:1–602.

Beck, Robin A., Jr.
2003 Consolidation and Hierarchy: Chiefdom Variability in the Mississippian Southeast. *American Antiquity* 68:641–661.

Benden, Danielle M., Timothy R. Pauketat, and Robert F. Boszhardt
2010 Early Mississippian Colonists in the Upper Mississippi Valley: 2009 Investigations at the Fisher Mounds Site Complex. *Wisconsin Archeologist* 91:131–132.
2011 The Mississippian Initiative: Year Two at Trempealeau. *Wisconsin Archeologist* 92:73–75.

Birmingham, Robert, and Thomas E. Emerson
2011 A Ceramic "Red Goddess" Figurine from Aztalan. *Wisconsin Archeologist* 92:37–44.

Bluhm, Elaine A., and Allen Liss
1961 The Anker Site. In *Chicago Area Archaeology*, edited by Elaine A. Bluhm, pp. 89–137. Bulletin No. 3. Illinois Archaeological Survey, Urbana.

Boles, Steve, and Erin Benson
2010 Feature 181: A Burnt Stirling Phase Structure at East St. Louis. Paper presented at the 67th Annual Southeastern Archaeological Conference, Lexington, Kentucky.

Brown, James A. (editor)
1961 *The Zimmerman Site: A Report on Excavations at the Grand Village of Kaskaskia, La Salle County, Illinois*. Reports of Investigations No. 9. Illinois State Museum, Springfield.

Brown, James A., and John E. Kelly
2000 Cahokia and the Southeastern Ceremonial Complex. In *Mounds, Modoc, and Mesoamerica: Papers in Honor of Melvin L. Fowler*, edited by Steven R. Ahler, pp. 469–510. Scientific Papers Vol. 28. Illlinois State Museum, Springfield.

Butler, Amanda J.
2011 Playing Detective with Mississippian Period Axe-Heads: Detailing the Results of a Provenance Study Using Portable X-Ray Fluorescence. Paper presented at the Midwest Archaeological Conference, La Crosse, Wisconsin.

Caldwell, Joseph
1964 Interaction Spheres in Prehistory. In *Hopewellian Studies*, edited by Joseph R. Caldwell and Robert L. Hall, pp. 133–143. Scientific Papers No. 12. Illinois State Museum, Springfield.

Collins, James M.
1990 *The Archaeology of the Cahokia Mounds ICT-II: Site Structure*. Illinois Cultural Resources Study No. 10. Illinois Historic Preservation Agency, Springfield.

Cook, Robert A.
2007 *Sunwatch: Fort Ancient Development in the Mississippian World*. University of Alabama Press, Tuscaloosa.

Conrad, Lawrence
1991 The Middle Mississippian Cultures of the Central Illinois River Valley. In *Cahokia and the Hinterlands: Middle Mississippian Cultures of the Midwest*, edited by Thomas E. Emerson and R. B. Lewis, pp. 119–156. University of Illinois Press, Urbana.

Dalan, Rinita A., George R. Holley, William I. Woods, Harold W. Watters Jr., and John A. Koepke
2003 *Envisioning Cahokia: A Landscape Perspective*. Northern Illinois University Press, DeKalb.

Daro, Vinci, Gretchen Fox, and Dorothy Holland
2008 Social Movements and Collective Identity. *Anthropological Quarterly* 81:95–125.

Deuel, Thorne
1935 Basic Cultures of the Mississippi Valley. *American Anthropologist* 37:429–445.

Douglas, John G.
1976 Collins: A Late Woodland Ceremonial Complex in the Woodfordian Northeast. Unpublished Ph.D. dissertation, Department of Anthropology, University of Illinois, Urbana-Champaign.

Emerson, Kjersti
2007 Examining the Place of Ceramics in Mortuary Context: Evidence from the Fisher Site, Will County, Illinois. Master's thesis, Department of Anthropology, University of Illinois, Urbana-Champaign.

Emerson, Thomas E.
1997a *Cahokia and the Archaeology of Power*. University of Alabama Press, Tuscaloosa.
1997b Cahokian Elite Ideology and the Mississippian Cosmos. In *Cahokia: Domination and Ideology in the Mississippian World*, edited by Timothy R. Pauketat and Thomas E. Emerson, pp. 190–228. University of Nebraska Press, Lincoln.
1997c Reflections from the Countryside on Cahokian Hegemony. In *Cahokia: Domination and Ideology in the Mississippian World*, edited by Timothy R. Pauketat and Thomas E. Emerson, pp. 167–189. University of Nebraska Press, Lincoln.
2012 Cahokian Interaction and Ethnogenesis in the Northern Midcontinent. In *The Oxford Handbook of North American Archaeology*, edited by Timothy R. Pauketat, pp. 398–409. Oxford University Press, New York.
2013 Ethnogenesis and Political Formation on Cahokia's Northern Frontier. Paper presented at the 78th Annual Meeting of the Society for American Archaeology, Honolulu, Hawaii.

Emerson, Thomas E., and Kjersti E. Emerson
2014 Late Fisher Phase Ceramics at the Hoxie Farm Fortified Village. In *The Hoxie Farm Site Fortified Village: Late Fisher Phase Occupation and Fortification in South Chicago*, 2nd ed., edited by D. K. Jackson and T. E. Emerson. Research Report No. 27. Illinois State Archaeological Survey, University of Illinois, Urbana-Champaign.

Emerson, Thomas E., and Randall E. Hughes
2000 Figurines, Flint Clay Sourcing, the Ozark Highlands, and Cahokian Acquisition. *American Antiquity* 65:79–101.

Emerson, Thomas E., Randall E. Hughes, Mary R. Haynes, and Sarah U. Wiseman
2003 The Sourcing and Interpretation of Cahokia Style Figurines in the Trans-Mississippi South and Southwest. *American Antiquity* 68:287–313.

Emerson, Thomas E., and Douglas K. Jackson
1984 *The BBB Motor Site*. American Bottom Archaeology FAI-270 Reports, Vol. 6. University of Illinois Press, Urbana.

Esarey, Duane, and Lawrence A. Conrad
1998 The Bold Counselor Phase of the Central Illinois River Valley: Oneota's Middle Mississippian Margin. *Wisconsin Archeologist* 79:38–61.

Faulkner, Charles H.
1972 *The Late Prehistoric Occupation of Northwestern Indiana: A Study of the Upper Mississippi Cultures of the Kankakee Valley*. Prehistory Research Series, Vol. V, No. 1. Indiana Historical Society, Indianapolis.

Fletcher, Alice C., and Francis La Flesche
1992 [1911] *The Omaha Tribe*. 2 vols. University of Nebraska Press, Lincoln.

Fortier, Andrew C.
2007 *The Archaeology of the East St. Louis Mound Center, Part II: The Northside Excavations*. Transportation Archaeological Research Reports No. 22. Illinois Transportation Archaeological Research Program, University of Illinois, Urbana.

Fortier, Andrew C., Richard B. Lacampagne, and Fred A. Finney
1984 *The Fish Lake Site*. American Bottom Archaeology FAI-270 Reports, Vol. 8. University of Illinois Press, Urbana.

Fowler, Melvin L.
1969 The Cahokia Site. In *Explorations into Cahokia*

Archaeology, pp. 1–30. Bulletin No. 7. Illinois Archaeological Survey, University of Illinois, Urbana.

Gibbon, Guy
1991 The Middle Mississippian Presence in Minnesota. In *Cahokia and the Hinterlands: Middle Mississippian Cultures of the Midwest*, edited by Thomas E. Emerson and R. Barry Lewis, pp. 207–220. University of Illinois Press, Urbana.

Goldstein, Lynn G., and John D. Richards
1991 Ancient Aztalan: The Cultural and Ecological Context of a Late Prehistoric Site in the Midwest. In *Cahokia and the Hinterlands: Middle Mississippian Cultures of the Midwest*, edited by Thomas E. Emerson and R. Barry Lewis, pp. 193–206. University of Illinois Press, Urbana.

Green, William
1997 Middle Mississippian Peoples. *Wisconsin Archeologist* 78:202–222.

Griffin, James B.
1943 *The Fort Ancient Aspect: Its Cultural and Chronological Position in Mississippi Valley Archaeology*. University of Michigan Press, Ann Arbor.

Hall, Robert L.
1991 Cahokia Identity and Interaction Models of Cahokia Mississippian. In *Cahokia and the Hinterlands: Middle Mississippian Cultures of the Midwest*, edited by Thomas E. Emerson and R. Barry Lewis, pp. 3–34. University of Illinois Press, Urbana.
1997 *An Archaeology of the Soul: North American Indian Belief and Ritual*. University of Illinois Press, Urbana.

Hallowell, Anthony I.
1975 Ojibwa Ontology, Behavior, and World View. In *Teachings from the American Earth: Indian Religion and Philosophy*, edited by D. Tedlock and B. Tedlock, pp. 141–178. Liveright, New York.

Harkin, Michael E.
2004 Revitalization as History and Theory. In *Reassessing Revitalization Movements: Perspectives from North America and the Pacific Islands*, edited by Michael E. Harkin, pp. xv–xxxvi. University of Nebraska Press, Lincoln.

Hodder, Ian
2012 *Entangled: An Archaeology of the Relationships between Humans and Things*. Wiley-Blackwell, West Sussex, U.K.

Holmes, William H.
1903 *Aboriginal Pottery of the Eastern United States*. Bureau of American Ethnology Twentieth Annual Report, pp. 1–237. Smithsonian Institution, Washington, D.C.

Ingold, Tim
1993 The Temporality of the Landscape. *World Archaeology* 25:152–174.
2006 Rethinking the Animate, Re-animating Thought. *Ethnos* 71:9–20.
2008 Bindings against Boundaries: Entanglements of Life in an Open World. *Environment and Planning A* 40:1796–1810.

Iseminger, William R., Timothy R. Pauketat, Brad Koldehoff, Lucretia S. Kelly, and Leonard Blake
1990 *The Archaeology of the Cahokia Palisade: The East Palisade Investigations, Part I*. Illinois Cultural Resources Study No. 14. Illinois Historic Preservation Agency, Springfield.

Jackson, Douglas K., and Thomas E. Emerson (editors)
2014 *The Hoxie Farm Site Fortified Village: Late Fisher Phase Occupation and Fortification in South Chicago*, 2nd ed. Research Report No. 27. Illinois State Archaeological Survey, University of Illinois, Urbana-Champaign.

Jackson, Douglas K., Andrew C. Fortier, and Joyce A. Williams
1992 *The Sponemann Site 2: The Mississippian and Oneota Occupations*. American Bottom Archaeology FAI-270 Reports, Vol. 24. University of Illinois Press, Urbana.

Jackson, Douglas K., and Philip G. Millhouse
2003 *The Vaughn Branch and Old Edwardsville Road Sites: Late Stirling and Early Moorehead Phase Mississippian Occupations in the Northern American Bottom*. Transportation Archaeological Research Reports No. 16. Illinois Transportation Archaeological Research Program, University of Illinois, Urbana-Champaign.

Kelly, John E.
1990 The Range Site Community Patterns and the Mississippian Emergence. In *The Mississippian Emergence*, edited by B. D. Smith, pp. 67–112. Smithsonian Institution Press, Washington, D.C.
1997 Stirling-Phase Sociopolitical Activity at East St. Louis and Cahokia. In *Cahokia: Domination and Ideology in the Mississippian World*, edited by Timothy R. Pauketat and Thomas E. Emerson, pp. 141–166. University of Nebraska Press, Lincoln.

Kelly, John E., Andrew Fortier, Steven J. Ozuk, and Joyce A. Williams
1987 *The Range Site: Archaic through Late Woodland Occupations*. American Botton Archaeology FAI-270 Reports, Vol. 16. University of Illinois Press, Urbana.

Knight, Vernon J., Jr., and Vincas P. Steponaitis
1998 A New History of Moundville. In *Archaeology of the Moundville Chiefdom*, edited by Vernon

J. Knight Jr. and Vincas P. Steponaitis, pp. 1–25. Smithsonian Institution Press, Washington, D.C.

Koldehoff, Brad, Timothy R. Pauketat, and John E. Kelly
1993 The Emerald Site and the Mississippian Occupation of the Central Silver Creek Valley. In *Highways to the Past: Essays on Illinois Archaeology in Honor of Charles J. Bareis*, edited by Thomas Emerson, Andrew Fortier, and Dale McElrath. *Illinois Archaeology* 5 (1–2): 331–343.

Lopinot, Neal H., and William I. Woods
1993 Wood Overexploitation and the Collapse of Cahokia. In *Foraging and Farming in the Eastern Woodlands*, edited by C. Margaret Scarry, pp. 206–231. University Press of Florida, Gainesville.

McKern, William C.
1939 The Midwestern Taxonomic Method as an Aid to Archaeological Culture Study. *American Antiquity* 4:301–313.

Meinholz, Norman M., Anthony Zalucha, and Jennifer L. Kolb
1997 *The Statz Site (47DA642): A Late Woodland Community and Archaic Lithic Workshop in Dane County, Wisconsin*. Archaeology Research Series Vol. 5. Wisconsin Historical Society, Madison.

Meskell, Lynn
2004 *Object Worlds in Ancient Egypt: Material Biographies Past and Present*. Berg, Oxford.

Meskell, Lynn (editor)
2005 *Archaeologies of Materiality*. Blackwell, Oxford.

Milner, George E.
1998 *The Cahokia Chiefdom: The Archaeology of a Mississippian Society*. Smithsonian Institution Press, Washington, D.C.

Mintz, Sydney
1985 *Sweetness and Power: The Place of Sugar in Modern History*. Viking Penguin, New York.

Muller, Jon
1995 Regional Interaction in the Southeast. In *Native American Interactions: Multiscalar Analyses and Interpretations in the Eastern Woodlands*, edited by Michael Nassaney and Kenneth Sassaman, pp. 317–353. University of Tennessee Press, Knoxville.

Muller, Jon, and Jeanette E. Stephens
1991 Mississippian Sociocultural Adaptation. In *Cahokia and the Hinterlands: Middle Mississippian Cultures of the Midwest*, edited by Thomas E. Emerson and R. Barry Lewis, pp. 297–310. University of Illinois Press, Urbana.

Olsen, Bjornar
2010 *In Defense of Things: Archaeology and the Ontology of Objects*. AltaMira Press, Lanham, Maryland.

Pauketat, Timothy R.
1987 A Burned Domestic Dwelling at Cahokia. *Wisconsin Archeologist* 68:212–237.
1993 *Temples for Cahokia Lords: Preston Holder's 1955–1956 Excavations of Kunnemann Mound*. Museum of Anthropology, University of Michigan, Ann Arbor.
1994 *The Ascent of Chiefs: Cahokia and Mississippian Politics in Native North America*. University of Alabama Press, Tuscaloosa.
1998 *The Archaeology of Downtown Cahokia: The Tract 15A and Dunham Tract Excavations*. Studies in Archaeology. Illinois Transportation Archaeological Research Program, University of Illinois, Urbana.
1997 Cahokian Political Economy. In *Cahokia: Domination and Ideology in the Mississippian World*, edited by Timothy R. Pauketat and Thomas E. Emerson, pp. 30–51. University of Nebraska Press, Lincoln.
2003 Resettled Farmers and the Making of a Mississippian Polity. *American Antiquity* 68:39–66.
2004 *Ancient Cahokia and the Mississippians*. Cambridge University Press, Cambridge.
2005 *The Archaeology of the East St. Louis Mound Center, Part I: The Southside Excavations*. Transportation Archaeological Research Reports No. 21. Illinois Transportation Archaeological Research Program, University of Illinois, Urbana.
2008 Founders' Cults and the Archaeology of Wa-Kan-Da. In *Memory Work: Archaeologies of Material Practices*, edited by B. Mills and W. H. Walker, pp. 61–79. School for Advanced Research Press, Santa Fe, New Mexico.
2010 Comments made in the symposium "Mobility, Temporality, and Social Memory" at the 67th Annual Southeastern Archaeological Conference, Lexington, Kentucky.
2013 *An Archaeology of the Cosmos: Rethinking Agency and Religion in Ancient America*. Routledge, New York.

Pauketat, Timothy R., and Susan M. Alt
2003 Mounds, Memory, and Contested Mississippian History. In *Archaeologies of Memory*, edited by R. M. Van Dyke and S. E. Alcock, pp. 151–179. Blackwell, Oxford.
2004 The Making and Meaning of a Mississippian Axe-Head Cache. *Antiquity* 78:779–797.
2005 Agency in a Post-Mold? Physicality and the Archaeology of Culture-Making. *Journal of Archaeological Method and Theory* 12:213–237.

Pauketat, Timothy R., and Thomas E. Emerson
1991 The Ideology of Authority and the Power of the Pot. *American Anthropologist* 93:919–941.

Pauketat, Timothy R., Andrew C. Fortier, Susan M. Alt, and Thomas E. Emerson
2013 A Mississippian Conflagration at East St. Louis and Its Political-Historical Implications. *Journal of Field Archaeology* 18:57–36.

Pauketat, Timothy R., and Brad Koldehoff
1983 Emerald Mound and the Mississippian Occupation of the Central Silver Creek Valley. Paper presented at the 28th Annual Midwest Archaeological Conference, Iowa City.

Pauketat, Timothy R., and Neal H. Lopinot
1997 Cahokian Population Dynamics. In *Cahokia: Domination and Ideology in the Mississippian World*, edited by Timothy R. Pauketat and Thomas E. Emerson, pp. 103–123. University of Nebraska Press, Lincoln.

Pauketat, Timothy R., Mark A. Rees, Amber M. VanDerwarker, and Kathryn E. Parker
2010 Excavations into Cahokia's Mound 49. *Illinois Archaeology* 22:397–436.

Peebles, Christopher, and Susan Kus
1977 Some Archaeological Correlates of Ranked Society. *American Antiquity* 42:421–448.

Pollack, David
2004 *Caborn-Welborn: Constructing a New Society after the Angel Chiefdom Collapse*. University of Alabama Press, Tuscaloosa.

Porter, James W.
1969 The Mitchell Site and Prehistoric Exchange Systems at Cahokia: AD 1000 ± 300. In *Explorations into Cahokia Archaeology*, edited by Melvin L. Fowler, pp. 137–164. Bulletin No. 7. Illinois Archaeological Survey, Urbana.

Radin, Paul
1970 [1923] *The Winnebago Tribe*. Johnson Reprint Corporation, New York.

Richards, John D.
1992 Ceramics and Culture at Aztalan, A Late Prehistoric Village in Southeast Wisconsin. Unpublished Ph.D. dissertation, Department of Anthropology, University of Wisconsin, Milwaukee.

Schneider, Seth
2013 Oneota Interaction among Three Localities in Eastern Wisconsin: Ceramic Compositional Analyses of Six Oneota Pottery Assemblages. Paper presented at the 78th Annual Meeting of the Society for American Archaeology, Honolulu, Hawaii.

Smith, Bruce D.
1978 Variation in Mississippian Settlement Patterns. In *Mississippian Settlement Patterns*, edited by Bruce D. Smith, pp. 479–503. Academic Press, New York.

Smoak, Gregory E.
2006 *Ghost Dances and Identity: Prophetic Religion and American Indian Ethnogenesis in the Nineteenth Century*. University of California Press, Berkeley.

Spier, Leslie
1935 *The Prophet Dance of the Northwest and Its Derivatives: The Source of the Ghost Dance*. General Series in Anthropology No. 1. George Banta, Menasha, Wisconsin.

Steadman, Dawnie L. W.
2008 Warfare Related Trauma at Orendorf, a Middle Mississippian Site in West-Central Illinois. *American Journal of Physical Anthropology* 136 (1): 51–64.

Stewart, Omer C.
1987 *Peyote Religion: A History*. University of Oklahoma Press, Norman.

Swanton, John R.
2001 [1931] *Source Material for the Social and Ceremonial Life of the Choctaw Indians*. University of Alabama Press, Tuscaloosa.

Trubitt, Mary Beth D.
2000 Mound Building and Prestige Goods Exchange: Changing Strategies in the Cahokia Chiefdom. *American Antiquity* 65:669–690.

Vogel, Joseph O.
1964 A Preliminary Report on the Analysis of Ceramics from the Cahokia Area at the Illinois State Museum. Illinois State Museum, Springfield.
1975 Trends in Cahokia Ceramics: Preliminary Study of the Collections from Tracts 15A and 15B. In *Perspectives in Cahokia Archaeology*, edited by James A. Brown, pp. 32–125. Bulletin No. 10. Illinois Archaeological Survey, Urbana.

Wallace, Anthony F. C.
1956 Revitalization Movements. *American Anthropologist* 58:264–281.

Warren, William W.
2009 [1885] *History of the Ojibway People*. Minnesota Historical Society Press, St. Paul.

Wilson, Gregory D., and Melissa R. Baltus
2014 The Cahokian Crucible: Burning Ritual and the Emergence of Social Inequality in the Mississippian Midwest. Unpublished manuscript.

Zych, Thomas J.
2013 The Construction of a Mound and a New Community: An Analysis of the Ceramic and Feature Assemblages from the Northeast Mound at the Aztalan Site. Unpublished Master's thesis, Department of Anthropology, University of Wisconsin, Milwaukee.

Contributors

Melissa R. Baltus
Department of Sociology and Anthropology
University of Toledo
Toledo, OH

Margaret Brown Vega
Department of Anthropology
Indiana University–Purdue University Fort Wayne
Fort Wayne, IN

Meghan E. Buchanan
Glenn A. Black Laboratory of Archaeology
Indiana University
Bloomington, IN

Eleanor Harrison-Buck
Department of Anthropology
University of New Hampshire
Durham, NH

Stacie M. King
Department of Anthropology
Indiana University
Bloomington, IN

Gerald A. Oetelaar
Department of Archaeology
University of Calgary
Calgary, AB, Canada

William F. Romain
Newark Earthworks Center
The Ohio State University
Newark, OH

B. Jacob Skousen
Department of Anthropology
University of Illinois Urbana-Champaign
Urbana, IL

Index

Acaray, Peru, 105, 106–7
Adena, 55, 67. *See also* Serpent Mound
Adena Mound, OH, 67, 68
agency, 3, 4, 7, 8, 77n14, 87, 123
Ajumawi, 70–71
Andean region: mountain peaks (huacas) in, 103; winds and illness in, 102. *See also* Cerros San Cristóbal, Peru
animic cosmos. *See under* Maya
animism, 4
Apache, 41
archaeological survey: importance of sensory characteristics and experiential information in, 25, 33; incompleteness of, 21; mapmaking in, 23, 24, 25;
archaeology: formation theory in, 8; relational, 2–9; symmetrical, 4
Arias, Arturo, 115
assemblage, 5
astronomical alignments: lunar, at Newark Great Circle, 61, 76–77n6; lunar, at Newark Octagon, 60; lunar standstill, at Emerald site, 42, 45–46; Milky Way and Scorpius, of Serpent Mound, 73, 74; Milky Way, of Great Hopewell Road, 64, 65, 67, 75; summer solstice, at Newark Great Circle, 61, 62
axis mundi, of Ohio Hopewell, 54, 69, 70, 71
Aztalan, WI, 151

Baires, Sarah, 9
balance, as core concept of Mesoamerican cosmology, 27
Bauman site, MO, 89
Bird-David, Nurit, 114
Blackfoot: adoption of gun and horse by, 138; annual movement of, 131–34; effect of missionaries on, 140, 141; effect of smallpox on, 140–41; first interaction with Europeans of, 134–35; fur trade posts established for, 135–38; homeland of, 131–32, 133; modification of places by, 132–33; reservation period of, 141; sacred journeys of, 40–41; Thunder Medicine Pipe Bundle of, 132, 138–39; use of tobacco by, 139–40; worldview of, 131
Bourdieu, Pierre, 2
Brown, Linda A., 23–24
bundling/bundles: connected to travelers, 121–22; as defensive strategy, 93; definitions of, 5–6; as entanglements, 9. *See also* entanglements

Cahokia, IL: burning of structures at and around, 152–53; florescence of, 42, 87–88, 147–49; fortifications and burning at, 88, 151; location map of, 43; Mississippianization of Late Woodland populations by, 150–52; Moorehead phase at, 152–53; movement and, 42, 48–49, 147–48; politicization of, 150; possible revitalization movement at, 149, 152–53; pottery change at, 152–53; preference for nonlocal materials at, 150; reentanglements of, 152–54; sacred journeys crucial to, 42; social-religious meshworks of, 49, 147–51; spread of Mississippian message from, 150; woodhenge at, 152
Cahokia Movement, 149–50
Carlsen, Robert, 115
Cave, Alfred, 40
caves, 27, 28; as permeable places, 91; as portals, 47
Cerros San Cristóbal, Peru: burned offerings in pits on, 106–7; Early Intermediate Period on, 106–7; fortifications of, 103–5; Late Intermediate Period on, 105, 108
Childe, V. Gordon, 7
Choctaw, 38
Ch'uul Xanbal, 122
Common Field, MO: aerial photo of, 90; evidence of violent attacks at, 92–93; human remains at, 92, 93; location of, 86, 89; palisades at, 91–92; use of rocks and minerals for protection at, 85, 91, 93
Cooper site, IL, 153

Copan, Honduras, 119, 120
Crow Creek site, SD, 92

Davis, Edwin H., 61, 63
defensive sites: in Andes, 100–101, 104–5; deposition of sacred material into features at, 91–92; as locales where people seek physical and spiritual defense against harm, 108–9
Descartes, René, 7
Dobkin de Rios, Marlene, 102

Emerald site, IL, 153; ghostly lines at, 45–46; hearths at, 47–48; journeys to, 44, 49; Mound 12 at, 47–48; occupation history of, 42–45; plan of, 44, 45, 46; roadway at, 44; spring near, 46–47
Emerson, Thomas, 151
Emery, Kitty F., 23–24
entanglements: of Cahokia, 49, 147, 148, 150; created by movement, 41, 86, 146, 149; Hodder on, 4; of landscapes, 108; manipulation of material and, 146; of Mississippian war-scape, 89, 94; movement and, 9, 25; past, influence future, 39; potential to cause culture change of, 86; repetitive visits to places as evidence of, 33; sacred journeys and, 40, 41. *See also* bundling; meshwork(s)

Farnell, Brenda, 7
Fidler, Peter, 139
Fort Ancient culture, 77–78n15
Fowles, Severin, 10, 113, 114–15
Friedel, David et al., 116
Furst, Jill Leslie, 114

Ghost Dance, 149
ghostly lines, 39–40, 45–46
Gibson, James, 7
Great Hopewell Road, OH: alignment to Milky Way at summer solstice of, 64, 65, 67, 75; alignment to Sugarloaf Mountain of, 66; description of, 61–64; as metaphor for Milky Way Path, 54; as part of dynamic relational web, 54, 75; as pathway to Realm of the Dead, 69–70
Great Serpent, OH, 71, 73, 75, 78n17
Greenman, Emerson F., 61

Harris, Oliver, 5
Hawkes, Christopher, 9, 12

Hendon, Julia, 115
heurmeneutics, 3
Hodder, Ian, 4–5, 146
Hopewell: axis mundi of, 54, 69, 70, 71; compared with Adena, 55–56; measurement unit, 56. *See also* Great Hopewell Road, OH; Newark Earthworks Complex, OH; Serpent Mound, OH; Sugarloaf Mountain, OH
Houston, Stephen D., 114, 116, 121, 123
Hoxie Farm site, 153–54
Huaura Valley, Peru, 101, 103. *See also* Cerros San Cristóbal, Peru
Hudson's Bay Co. (HBC), 134–36

Ingold, Timothy: on animic cosmos, 116, 120, 121; on entanglements, 146; on ghostly lines, 39–40; idea of meshwork of, 5, 39, 86, 102, 118; knowledge of the world comes from movements within it, 8–9; people live in the land not on it, 24, 25; on places as knots in meshwork, 109
Itzamnaaj: associated with personified beings, 120; avian manifestation of, 121, 122; as earth-sky, 113, 116, 118, 119; personified image of, with serpent body, 118

journeys, sacred: to Emerald site, 44, 49; Native American, 40–42; sacred, and Cahokia's emergence, 49

Katz, Fred, 102
Keane, Webb, 5
Krupp, Edwin, 64, 70–71
k'uh, 116, 117

La Flesche, Francis, 40, 93
landscapes: are alive, 28, 103, 108; as archive, 132, 142; bodily engagements with, 8, 102; entanglement of, 108; sacred, 91, 101; travel across, as spiritual, social, and educational odyssey, 134
Lankford, George, 70, 71, 73
Latour, Bruno, 4
Lepper, Bradley T., 62, 70

Maize God, 121
Marquette, Père, 94
Martin, Simon, 121
materiality, 3, 123
Mauss, Marcel, 6

Maya: animic cosmos of, 113–14, 116, 118, 119, 120–21, 123–24; birds as embodied messengers, 121; ch'ulel, 115, 116; Daykeepers of, 123; itz, 116–17, 118, 119, 120; pantheon, 114; relational ontology of, 113–16, 123; use of "god" is problematic for, 114. *See also* Itzamnaaj

memory work, 3

Merleau-Ponty, Maurice, 7

meshwork(s): of Adena-Hopewell world, 75; of Andean region, 102–3, 109; of Cahokia, 147–51; created by movement, 39, 41, 86–87, 102, 118, 146, 149; Ingold on, 5, 39, 86, 102, 118; lines of, are ever-moving, 8–9, 11; of Mesoamerican animic cosmos, 113–16, 118–22; of midwestern war-scape, 86–87, 89, 94. *See also* entanglements

Milbrath, Susan, 120

Milky Way Path of Souls: Great Hopewell Road as metaphor for, 54, 69–70; leads to Realm of the Dead, 70, 71, 75, 77n9

Miller, Mary, 116

Mishkin, Bernard, 103

Mississippian, 146; violence and conflict in, 87–88, 89. *See also* Cahokia; Common Field; Emerald site; Vacant Quarter

Molesky-Poz, Jean, 114

Mound City, OH, 56, 59, 67, 68

mountains/peaks: agency of, 77n14; as animate forces, 107–8; as an axis mundi, 69; as deities/sacred beings, 103; Early Horizon view of, 107–8; reciprocal relationship with people of, 103; as sacred places, 24, 27, 29, 32–33; St. Francois Mountains, as part of sacred Mississippian landscape, 89–90, 91; winds and, in Andes, 102

movement: Cahokia and, 42, 48–49, 147–48; compels change, 147; as distinctive feature of Mayan animic cosmos, 113–14, 118–19, 120, 121, 122, 123; to and from Emerald site, 44–45; gives meaning to relationships, 25; of Hopewell souls, 64, 57, 69, 71, 73, 75; human bodily, 6–7; is inherent in life, 147; as key component of understanding past realities, 2; knowledge of the world comes from, 8–9, 25; landscape phenomenology and, 7–8, 25; meshwork/entanglements created by, 39, 41, 86–87, 102, 118, 146, 149; of nonhuman entities, 9; remembering associated with, 40–41; traditional Blackfoot, 131–34, 140, 142; two uses of, 146–47

Nanih Waiya, 38

Nejapa region, Oaxaca, Mexico: archaeological survey in, 21, 23, 25, 26, 33; background to, 22–23; place names in, 27; rock paintings in, 28–29, 30, 32; visible evidence of interaction with spiritual forces in, 28–33

Nejapa Viejo, Mexico, stela at, 28, 31

Newark Earthworks Complex, OH, 54; astronomical alignments of, 57–59, 60, 61, 62; causeways of, 64; Eagle Mound of, 60–61; Ellipse of, 57, 59; as focus of mortuary ceremonies, 73; Geller Hill of, 57; Great Circle of, 60–61, 76–77n6; hypothetical spirit path of, 66, 70–71; LiDAR images of, 58; Observatory Circle of, 59; Octagon of, 59; plan of, 55

Nordstrom, Carolyn, 86

Norris Farms #36, IL, 88, 92

Olin site, IL, 152, 153

Orendorf site, IL, 88

Osage, 87, 93

Palenque, Mexico, 119

Parker Pearson, Michael, 8

Pauketat, Timothy, 152; on bundles and bundling, 6, 9, 93, 121; on Cahokia's "Big Bang," 42, 149; on dialectical relationship between agency and structure, 123

Pharo, Lars, 113

Piedra la Boluda, Mexico, 28–29, 31

place names, 27, 34, 35

Polia Meconi, Mario, 103

Popol Vuh, 118

Prechtel, Martin, 115

Prophet Dance, 149

relationality, 1, 2, 3, 4

relational constitution of being, 113, 116, 123

revitalization movements, 149, 152–53

rock paintings, 28–29, 30, 32

Royce, Anya, 27

sacred fires, 47–48

sacred geography: of Oaxaca, 27–33; special qualities that characterize, 32–33

sacred places: in Andes (huacas), 101; Mesoamerican mountains as, 24, 27, 29, 32–33; revisits to, 32, 33; sensory characteristics of, 33

Saline Locality, MO, 89

Salisbury, James and Charles, 57, 59, 62, 66, 76n4

San Bartolo, Guatemala, 121, 122
Schele, Linda, 116
Schellhas, Paul, 123
Serpent Mound, OH, 54, 72; dating of, 77–78n15; observations of Scorpius from, 73, 74; as representation of Great Serpent, 71, 73
Sheets-Johnstone, Maxine, 6
Smoak, Gregory, 149
Smucker, Isaac, 60–61
Snyder, John F., 46–47
Squier, Ephraim G., 61, 63
Stewart, Omer C., 147
Stitt Mound, OH, 67, 68
Strathern, Marilyn, 115
Struever, Stuart, 47
Stuart, David, 114, 115, 116
Sugarloaf Mountain, OH, 54, 66–69; as axis mundi for Ohio Hopewell world, 69
sun dance, 132, 133

Taube, Karl, 116
Thompson, J. Eric S., 114

Trempealeau site, WI, 149
Tuan, Yi-Fu, 69
Turner Earthworks, OH, 59

Vacant Quarter, 85, 88; animated by spirits of the dead, 94, 95; cause of depopulation of, 88–89; map of, 86
Vail, Gabrielle, 123

warfare: abandonment of Vacant Quarter and, 85; as historical process, 85; in the Mississippian Midwest, 87, 89; ritualized, 101. *See also* defensive sites
war-scapes, as way of looking at the meshwork of war-torn regions, 86–87, 89
Watts, Christopher, 1
Williams, Stephen, 88
Winters, Howard D., 47

Zapotec, 27
Zedeño, María Nieves, 6